Glory, Jest and Riddle

Glory, Jest and Riddle

Religious Thought in the Enlightenment

James Byrne

SCM PRESS LTD

0334 02656 3

First published 1996
by SCM Press Ltd
9–17 St Albans Place, London N1 0NX

Typeset at Regent Typesetting
and printed in Great Britain by
Biddles Ltd, Guildford and King's Lynn

Created half to rise and half to fall;
Great lord of all things, yet a prey to all;
Sole judge of truth, in endless error hurl'd;
The glory, jest and riddle of the world!

Alexander Pope, *Essay on Man*, Epistle II

THIS BOOK IS FOR CECILIA

Contents

Preface

Ages of discovery, of great danger or of great opportunity so often give rise to vibrant intellectual ferment; new ideas are explored with a boldness which other times and places would find extravagant and even alarming. Thinkers take risks and change becomes the norm rather than the exception. The Enlightenment was one of those periods of human history when everything appears to be thrown into sharp relief; the leading figures of the period thought they could see through history, nature and the human person with a clarity which previous ages lacked. They thought that they had possession of new knowledge and of a new way of knowing which gave them a privileged position to judge the errors of the past and fashion the achievements of the future.

In the midst of the Enlightenment, forming its most extensive frame of reference, permeating each issue and the temper of the era as a whole, lay the question of religion. It may be difficult for the citizen of a modern Western country to imagine the extent to which religion was then the context in which life was lived from cradle to grave, whose truth it was against which scientific innovations were judged, and which claimed allegiance from King and commoner alike. It was an age in which atheists were relatively rare, in which unorthodox belief could lead to punishment by the law, and in the ups and downs of everyday life the wiles of the devil had to be carefully guarded against. In addition to pervading everyday life, religion was also a powerful political force; in several European countries the wealth of the church almost matched that of the state and – in France for example – leading ecclesiastical figures frequently held direct political power also. The churches dominated education and almost all the intellectual enemies of religion who emerged during the Enlightenment owed their education to religious schools. In the seventeenth and eighteenth centuries a purely secular life was a virtual impossibility; religion impinged on your life whether you wished it to or not.

To talk about religious thought in the Enlightenment is therefore not to talk about something incidental or peripheral to the main business of the day; it is rather to go to the very heart of what the Enlightenment was. 'Enlightenment' has been most famously summarized in Immanuel Kant's dictum that an age of enlightenment is one in which people have the courage to think for themselves, no matter who they are or what their status in life is: philosopher, worker, king or priest. To think for yourself meant to think for yourself *in all things*, including matters of religion. This suggestion would have been, and was, resisted by churchmen, theologians and probably most ordinary people of the time; Christian truth was not something which could be subject to critical investigation as if it were a work of art or simply another part of the world around us. It was eternal, unchanging and authoritative; everything was judged in its light – as Galileo had discovered – and that which was deemed to be in conflict with religious truth was rejected and condemned.

But the tenor of the age was changing and the political and intellectual power of religion was ebbing. The Protestant Reformation had already told people that they did not need a system of intermediaries to discover the truth and to live a good life; it was a short but decisive step from this to the realization that the principle of the inviolability of the individual conscience could be applied to religion as a whole, and not simply to one particular religious system. The freedom to think for oneself is not the sort of freedom which it is easy to revoke.

To study the Enlightenment and to achieve some understanding of its debates and their significance requires an act of imagination. It becomes important not merely to list what happened or to state clearly the central ideas, but to attempt to grasp the motivation, the urgency, the intensity of the time. Such an act of imagination is necessary when we wish to see ideas not as free-floating products of pure reflection but as embedded in a context, reflecting practical concerns and driven by the interests of a mixture of people with a wide variety of motives. To comprehend fully the achievements of the Enlightenment and the ongoing significance of so many of the issues which it raised, one requires some sense of the flavour of the time, of the concerns of the leading figures and the social milieu; one needs to attempt to understand it 'from within'.

Therefore, in this book I have sought to situate ideas in context, to attempt to explain what concerns gave rise to them and, where appropriate, to point out their consequences. This has entailed relating ideas to the social, political and religious framework in which they developed, and in so doing giving some attention to a historical matrix which is wider than the simple appellation 'religious' might suggest. But I am not a historian and this book does not pretend to be a history of the Enlightenment. Where I give a historical description of some aspects of the period (as in Chapters 1 and 2) it is with the express intention of providing a frame of reference in which the reader can perceive that the Enlightenment was not a time of intellectual detachment, when scholars were removed from the general concerns of the day. Enlightenment thought was inevitably tied to practical concerns, such as how to live a good life, how to reconcile traditional religious belief with new scientific discoveries, what to make of the strange new cultures which were being discovered around the world, how to organize society so that people of different religious persuasions could live together in peace.

The spread of ideas was crucial to the Enlightenment period – they often had political and social, as well as religious, repercussions, and both secular and religious authorities kept a close watch on what could be said and what was better kept silent. At the time the number of official censors was a good indication of the presence of new and radical ideas; in France, the most vibrant centre of the Enlightenment, the number of censors increased from about forty in the early part of the eighteenth century to almost four times that by the time of the revolution. Thought was dangerous in the Enlightenment and it was always wise to keep your more unorthodox thoughts to yourself, or to find a less direct way to express them, such as the common practice at the time of publishing under a pseudonym.

For those who shared its values and its central aims, the period was a time of hope and expectation in which taking risks in the name of advancing the cause of humanity was considered a noble and worthwhile endeavour. Knowledge was increasing in virtually all fields of study, education was valued, toleration was defended and new possibilities for travel showed the great cultural richness of humanity. Yet behind the mask of cultural diversity the Enlightenment perceived the one and the same fundamental human nature; it was our common humanity which united human beings and allowed the Enlightenment to attempt the daring task of breaking free of the parameters and limitations of locality – in its cultural, religious and social sense as well as geographical – and dare to think in terms of a science of humanity, of alternatives to traditional religious systems of meaning, and to postulate possibilities for the development of society which had heretofore remained unthought. Despite the differences between the major thinkers and the vast diversity of its expression, it is this unifying vision of humanity and of human potential – a vision not without its own inherent tensions – which allows us to talk of 'the Enlightenment' at all.

The topic of religious thought in the Enlightenment is so enormous that one must take some risks about what to include and how to organize the material. I have chosen to treat some thinkers – e.g. Rousseau and Kant – in more detail by devoting a full chapter to them and leaving the treatment of others – e.g. Voltaire, Locke and Hume – to sections where particular aspects of their thought is relevant. I have also given much more prominence to Diderot than might be expected – in my view he does not receive adequate consideration, by theologians at least. Also, it is not normal practice to deal extensively with Descartes and Pascal in books on the Enlightenment, but in the area of religious ideas I believe that their thinking is crucial to the Enlightenment debates, and that their inclusion and the prominence I have given them is justified. The emphasis and arrangement of the book could therefore have been otherwise and I could have written a very different book on the same topic; the present arrangement reflects simply my current judgment of the relative importance of the different subjects and topics.

To aid fluency of reading I have tried to keep the number of notes within reasonable limits, and have attempted to cite sources which for the most part the student or the general reader should be able to acquire if they so wish. There is, however, an enormous amount of source material available on the Enlightenment – in French and German, as well as in English – and for the serious student no amount of commentary will substitute for engagement with the original material. This, however, should not be a deterrent, for study of the

Enlightenment brings its own rewards and there was not a day during the time I spent working on this book when I did not learn something new and interesting.

My thanks are due to a large number of people, too numerous to mention, who helped me in various ways with sourcing material and by their remarks on different sections. I am especially thankful, however, to Michael Foster and Mary Mills for reading the entire text, to Gordon Hunter for his help with the question of science and religion and to James Clark for the index; their comments were invaluable and any faults are mine alone.

The preliminary work for this book was done in Trinity College, Dublin, while I was the Elrington Research Fellow in the School of Hebrew, Biblical and Theological Studies. I am grateful to Werner Jeanrond, Professor of Systematic Theology at the University of Lund, Sweden, whose tenure as Head of that School enabled me to begin the project. It reached completion in Strawberry Hill in West London, at St Mary's University College (University of Surrey), of which Horace Walpole's eighteenth-century Gothic house forms a central part; a short walk away on the banks of the Thames lie the remains of Alexander Pope's home. It is a fitting environment in which to write on the Enlightenment.

I

Changing Ideals

The term 'Enlightenment' (French *Illumination*, German *Aufklärung*) requires some explanation. In a narrow sense 'Enlightenment' refers to a long period in the middle of the eighteenth century when, particularly in France, there emerged groups of freethinkers intent on grounding knowledge on the exercise of critical reason, as opposed to tradition, established religion, or conventional political and social thinking. The high-point of the French Enlightenment was in Paris during the third quarter of the eighteenth century.

As a concrete symbol of what 'Enlightenment' meant in practice one could point to what was perhaps the single greatest intellectual achievement of the *Illumination*, the publication of Denis Diderot's and Jean d'Alembert's *Encyclopédie: ou Dictionnaire raisonné des sciences, des arts, et des métiers*, an enormous production of some twenty-eight volumes containing often provocative articles by various authors on politics, religion, philosophy, science and other diverse topics. The *Encyclopédie* was designed to give people the most up-to-date knowledge of advances in science, agriculture and engineering; to instruct them on developments in philosophy, theology and political theory; to inform them about the discoveries of new lands, peoples, cultures and foods; to enable them to have access to a source of knowledge independent from the traditional source of learning, namely, the church.

The work of Diderot and other leading French intellectuals of the time – collectively often called the philosophes,[1] although they tended to be well-educated men of letters rather than philosophers in the strict sense – was characterized by vehement attacks on religion and the Christian church in particular. An incident associated with the appearance of volume seven of the *Encyclopédie* shows the turbulent nature of the intellectual climate of the time, and the scandal which could be caused by blatant criticism of religion. The mathematician and philosophe Jean le Rond d'Alembert contributed an entry to the *Encyclopédie* on the city of Geneva in which he praised – with undisguised irony – the clergy of the Calvinist city for their lack of belief in hell, the divinity of Christ and even in revelation itself. The entry was viewed as an attack on all revealed religion and led to the French authorities condemning the *Encyclopédie*. D'Alembert terminated his association with it but Diderot continued illegal publication until the licence to publish was restored in 1765. By the 1770s the scandal had long abated and, in a climate more conducive to the critique of religion, the *Encyclopédie* became a best-seller.

Of the great thinkers of the Enlightenment most are today remembered only by scholars. One leading figure who does still gain considerable popular attention, and whose character and thought are often considered synonymous with the Enlightenment, is François Marie Arouet de Voltaire (1694–1778), who was probably the most infamous critic of Christianity, and whose biting wit and ridicule of the church contributed significantly to the weakening of the power of religion in French cultural and intellectual life. His famous rallying-cry was *Écrasez l'infâme* – 'crush the infamous one' – a cry which he directed first at Christianity but eventually at what he perceived as the simple optimism of the 'natural religion' of the Enlightenment also.

Voltaire and others attacked Christianity for its bloody history and what they saw as its superstitious practices, and in the popular mind they are often associated with the French Revolution and the bitter hatred of the clergy. But the influence which their thinking had on the Revolution is a matter of considerable historical dispute, and as most of the philosophes were reasonably conservative politically, they would most likely have been horrified by events in the 1790s. However, by then most of the leading lights of the French Enlightenment were dead and their influence on political events became a matter for historians to debate. No doubt at the time of the revolution there were still many who placed their faith in the Enlightenment ideals of reason, toleration and education in the hope for something better than the rule of the old regime, but whatever hopes they might have had for a more reasonable and just society came to a definitive close with the outbreak of the post-revolutionary 'terror' in which large numbers of people were put to death. 1789 marks a decisive end to the Enlightenment in France.

But we do not have to restrict the Enlightenment to its high-point in France, for it is possible to adopt a much wider time-span under the concept of 'Enlightenment'. The term may be used to refer to a general intellectual and cultural climate which characterized European thought – particularly in England and Scotland, France, the Netherlands and Germany, but also in several other countries – from the middle of the seventeenth century through to the nineteenth century. The Enlightenment is too diffuse and amorphous a concept to admit of neat definition and delineation, and if one so wished one could argue with reasonable plausibility that 'enlightened' thinking began with Renaissance humanism, with the Reformation, or even with the Greeks. Such historical speculation, however, would be spurious. There is a standing joke among academics about this type of reasoning which in one version runs as follows: a professor teaching a course on Contemporary Philosophy begins by informing his students that to comprehend the contemporary debate they first of all need some background information; by the last lecture of the course the professor is talking about Plato and never deals with the contemporary issues. If there is a moral to this tale it is that one has to begin somewhere and stop somewhere else, and that every delineation of an 'era' is always somewhat arbitrary and could have been different.

If one were to look broadly at the era which we are considering and ask what context was most geared to providing a suitable framework for the first expression of 'Enlightenment' then the political, social and intellectual conditions in England after the political settlement of 1688 – the so-called 'Glorious Revolution' – would be the most obvious place to look. If France was to become the country where the Enlightenment found its most forceful expression, then England was the country where many of the ideas for which French thinkers fought had already been put into place.

In England the established Anglican Church was relatively weak and despite the subjugation of Catholics and Dissenters, in the context of the time they were not treated particularly badly (Ireland, where Catholics were the victims of draconian penal laws, being a clear exception), and the political structure reflected a balance of power between the monarch and the elected representatives in parliament.

Trade was strong and philosophy – chiefly in the form of Locke – had an influence on the political sphere. When Voltaire found himself in England in the late 1720s he saw a society which he thought, rather naively, to be the epitome of reason and tolerance. But much the same case could have been made for the Dutch Republic, which provided the safety and freedom which Descartes, Bayle and Spinoza required, and which like England was to be more of an onlooker than a participant in the type of intense intellectual battles which characterized France in the eighteenth century.

When we employ the term 'Enlightenment' in this broader sense and from the perspective of philosophical or theological thought, the two great intellectual figures which stand at either end of the period are René Descartes (1596–1650) and Immanuel Kant (1724–1804). Descartes is generally considered to be the first great modern European philosopher, and Kant brought many of the philosophical problems of Enlightenment thought into a synthesis which has been the framework for much philosophical and theological thinking in the past two hundred years. Kant's essay *Was ist Aufklärung?* (What is Enlightenment?) summed up the tenor of Enlightenment thinking in the phrase *Sapere aude!* ('dare to think') – i.e. use your own reason and think for yourself. In this book I shall adopt this broader definition, for within this period of about one hundred and fifty years many of the major questions which have dominated subsequent thought emerged and the period is of enormous importance in the history of thinking about religion.

Nevertheless, a warning is in order; this demarcation of the period is not definitive and clear-cut. It is possible to see Enlightenment ideas and ideals in many different times and places; for example, it could be argued that many of the most important Enlightenment ideas can be found in rudimentary form in various philosophical schools of antiquity. Influences closer to the period must also be considered; Descartes' thinking on religion, for example, was indebted to mediaeval scholastic thought. At the other extreme, Enlightenment thinking did not spread uniformly throughout the period under consideration and it influenced many countries (Ireland and Poland, for example) to a much lesser degree than it did Germany or Spain. It is clear that different places and cultures became 'enlightened' at different times. This caveat notwithstanding I shall adopt this wider period of about one hundred and fifty years (1650–1800) as encompassing the mainstream of thought which shall be our subject. Therefore, it is worthwhile outlining briefly some of the characteristic ideas which dominated the period and which have had a bearing on religious thought then and now.

First, and most obviously, there is an emphasis on the power of 'reason' to discover the truth about humanity and the world. However, an exact definition of the notion of reason is elusive. One significant difficulty is that the related term 'rationalism' is sometimes used to refer to the approach which views knowledge as the unfolding of ideas which are inherent or 'innate' in the human mind. This term, however, can appear to restrict reason to the unfolding of 'innate' ideas, whereas a thinker such as John Locke (1632–1704) who was a leading exponent of the power of reason rejected innate ideas in favour of an emphasis on experience. Another major thinker who used reason effectively but who could never be called a rationalist was Jean-Jacques Rousseau (1712–78); his emphasis on the role of feeling and emotion in human life had a significant influence on the development of romantic literature.

In a similar manner the phrase 'Age of Reason', which is sometimes used as synonymous with the Enlightenment, can give the mistaken impression that reason was not used as well before or since. If we wanted a counter-example to the loose application of the term 'Age of Reason' to the period we are considering, we need only recall that this was also the era of the popularity of 'Mesmerism'. The German doctor Franz Mesmer believed, much like modern astrologers, that the movements of the planets had a major influence on our health and state of well-being; he believed that planetary motion effected changes in the human body's 'animal magnetism' (a form of magnetic flow in the body which should be kept moving freely at all times). To ensure the correct flow of 'animal magnetism' Mesmer designed elaborate and bizarre structures which would realign the body's 'animal magnetism'; these he employed at gatherings of patients termed *séances*.

Mesmerism stands as an illustration of how the goal of science to explain natural processes by providing an over-arching explanation which neatly fits the phenomena into the pre-determined theory can go awry. Despite its flaws, which are so obvious to our eyes,

Mesmerism was not an anti-Enlightenment phenomenon, but reflected an Enlightenment project gone wrong. The enthusiasm for explanation – particularly in the field of the medicine where it was so urgently required – resulted in credence being given to a 'scientific' theory which was about as scientific as astrology. This is the reason why, despite being officially censured during the reign of Louis XVI, Mesmer's pseudo-science was widely popular and continued to attract followers well into the nineteenth century and even had an influence upon the founder of the Christian Scientists, Mary Baker Eddy. The pursuit of reason, it is clear, did not always contribute to enlightenment.

The Enlightenment concept of reason, in its broadest sense, is best understood as the use of human thinking in a critical way, which is not hampered by undue deference to authority, custom or religious revelation. Such thinking is not restricted to the period we call 'the Enlightenment' but during that period it achieved a status and success which helped make the period so important in intellectual history. Reason in this sense is not so much the possession of knowledge, but rather a dynamic 'force'[2] which dismantles established thinking in order to build knowledge up anew.

At times this model of reason gave rise to vehement anti-religious sentiment and action; the culmination of this process at its most aggressive was seen in the enthronement during the French Revolution of the Goddess of Reason in the cathedral of *Nôtre Dame de Paris*. This was an act of conscious intellectual rebellion against Christianity, but the very fact that this rebellion was itself expressed in a religious form is indicative of the fact that religion was the framework within which the new secular consciousness existed: the rejection of Christianity did not necessarily mean the rejection of all forms of religion. As the incident of the enthronement of the Goddess of Reason indicates, even the most fervent of new thinking used religion as a point of reference within which ideas were expressed. Thus a modern commentator can say that 'the coherence, as well as the confidence of the Enlightenment, rested on religious foundations'.[3] By this is meant that many Enlightenment ideas which were ostensibly anti-religious, actually rested on a profound religious and even Christian basis: the idea that there is a universal morality that all can follow, that nature is 'designed' in a way which enables it to be studied with coherence, that humanity is a unity with the light of reason given to all – these and many other ideas which were crucial to the period are indebted to a religious world-view.

A second characteristic of the Enlightenment is the scepticism with which it approached the venerable institutions and traditions of the past. The church was, of course, one of the main targets but by no means the only one; in France there was a fierce quarrel between those who looked back to the glories of the classical past of Greece and Rome (the 'ancients') and those who supported the view that the contemporary era was superior to all that had gone before (the 'moderns'). The humanism of the Renaissance had greatly admired the political, scientific, cultural and artistic achievements of ancient Greece and Rome; even the Christian, as Aquinas and others made clear, could look to the pagan virtues as useful guides to live the life that would lead to heaven. However, the discovery of new lands and scientific advances, such as those in astronomy, began to suggest to enquiring minds that perhaps the European Christian was neither at the centre of the universe nor the only part of the great divine plan of things. The feeling which cultured Europeans of the Renaissance had that the world was a beautifully balanced and harmonious place and that they themselves were the fulcrum around which all of reality turned, began to give way to a realization that rather than being the epitome of everything, they were themselves simply a part of something greater.

In the seventeenth century, as many scientists and scholars began to think of the human being in this way, the human person became an object of investigation alongside other phenomena in the world. But to investigate anything requires the assumption that the present understanding of it does not offer definitive answers; in the case of the human being itself this meant an admission that human nature was not something about which everything was already known but rather something about which knowledge remained to be gained. This fundamental shift in consciousness – epitomized in the quarrel between the ancients and the moderns – distinguishes the Enlightenment from the era of Christian humanism which marked the mediaeval world. The Enlightenment was not afraid to ask whether the past had anything more to offer than the present; does the present age have something new to add to our understanding of ourselves, or should we continue to look to the glorious accomplishments of the past as a model for our own age? Scientific advances and historical studies which showed the past to be not so rosy as some assumed, meant that the views of those with 'modern' sympathies eventually won out and the eighteenth century was characterized by an assumption that the era and its achievements, institutions and culture were in the main superior to those of the past.

This optimism about the contemporary age sometimes expressed itself (especially in the latter part of the century) in the view that society was improving under the guidance of reason or of Divine Providence. Among the former the most prominent champion of the notion of progress was the Marquis de Condorcet (1743–94), active in the French Revolution (see Chapter 7). Condorcet believed that human potential was virtually limitless and that the era of Enlightenment had given human beings the vision and potential to eradicate the horrors of the past and create a shining new future.

Others placed more hope in Providence than in merely human achievements; the English scientist and philosopher Joseph Priestley (1733–1804) combined a form of materialist philosophy with his own robust if somewhat idiosyncratic form of Christianity. Priestley's confident faith, however naive it appears to us now, has left us with one of the better anecdotes from the Enlightenment period. At dinner on a visit to Paris a fellow guest points out to Priestley the Bishop of Aix and the Archbishop of Toulouse, remarking that neither of them is any more a believer than Priestley or himself. When Priestley protests that he is indeed a Christian, his incredulous interlocutor refuses to believe that anyone so apparently sensible could also be a believer.

Priestley was confident that the modern era, as much as any past age, bore the mark of the hand of the creator. In his *Lectures on History* (1788) he defends his view that the progress the modern world has made over the ancient world in religion, science, government, law, commerce, manners and even happiness is due to the benign Providence of God. Priestley *assumes* that the historian is going to find numerous instances of improvement in the state of the world; for him what remains to be done is to persuade the reader that this improvement bears the mark of proceeding from the *intention* of the Divine Being and not from human ingenuity or mere chance. There can be, for Priestley, no other adequate explanation to account for the manner in which the present age has so clearly advanced on ages past, and if the historian cannot agree that this is indeed due to Providence then let him suspend judgment.

Despite their differing explanations for the characteristics of their time, Condorcet and Priestly shared with many of their contemporaries the view that the age in which they lived was a significant improvement on any previous age and that it had unlocked the key to continued social, scientific and political progress.

Not everyone, however, had such confidence in progress, be it of secular or divine origin. In his *La Scienza Nuova* (*The New Science*, 1725) Giambattisto Vico (1668–1744) presented an understanding of history which broke away from the Enlightenment assumption that human nature and culture was designed to increase in knowledge and wisdom. Vico inverted the common Enlightenment priority of privileging the 'natural' sciences over the 'human' sciences. He rejected the view that the natural sciences can give us certain knowledge, for as nature is not our own creation we can only ever reach a partial understanding of it; human society, however, because it comes from us, is capable of clear explanation. But an analysis of human societies shows that unlimited progress is a dream and societies can regress as quickly as they have progressed. Our cities, said Vico, could return to forests and men become beasts again. After Vico some of the more sceptical among the philosophes – most notably Voltaire – began, from the more prosaic premise of simply observing the course of events, to reject a simple confidence in reason and ridicule the naivety of the idea of 'progress'.

Such scepticism about the value of inherited institutions and ways of thinking was paralleled by a more thoroughgoing scepticism about the very basis of knowledge. Although the amount of knowledge available about the world was increasing all the time, many thinkers struggled with the problem of how something as apparently immaterial and elusive as a mind could 'know' anything about the way things really were outside itself. Such speculation made the basis of our knowledge of even everyday objects such as trees and dogs problematic, and had important consequences for the question of the existence of God and the value of religious experience. When the theory of knowledge tends towards pessimism about knowledge of everyday objects then a secure knowledge of less tangible entities such as a divine being begins to appear less than likely. In the scepticism of major thinkers such as David Hume (1711–76) about ordinary knowledge and about religious truth we see a nascent agnosticism which in the century would develop into a systematic articulation of atheistic philosophy.

A third notable aspect of Enlightenment thought is the emergence of a scientific way of thinking which offered intellectuals a viable alternative approach to knowledge from that which had dominated mediaeval thought. The remark of the philosopher and scientist Francis Bacon (1561–1626) that science could not advance by 'engrafting new things upon old' but must begin from new foundations, is a clear précis of the Enlightenment attitude to the possibilities opened up by the scientific discoveries of the age. In his *Novum Organum* (1620) Bacon set out an inductive scientific method which was to be a major influence on the development of modern science. Science in the Baconian vision proceeded through experiment and observation of the phenomena; the scientist observed the conditions under which certain phenomena pertained and the conditions under which they did not. This methodology allows the formulation of tentative laws which would form the basis for a new set of experiments, these experiments give rise to the formulation of new laws and so a step by step increase in scientific knowledge is attained. Bacon was insistent that scientific investigation be independent of what he called 'idols', by which he meant philosophical, personal, cultural or other presuppositions which could determine the results of experimentation on the basis of factors other than the observed phenomena and well established laws. Bacon's scientific method marked a distinctive break from the mediaeval understanding of the foundational unity of all knowledge, and laid the basis for the independence of science from pre-determined philosophical or religious interpretations of nature.

In the view of many theologians of the Middle Ages, proper knowledge was the contemplation of the beauty of God's creation, a foretaste of the absolute beauty of the beatific vision in heaven. Investigating nature in a scientific way was often seen as probing too deeply into God's mysteries, and denounced as mere 'curiosity'. When Galileo Galilei was condemned by the Pope in 1633 for holding the view of Copernicus that the earth revolved around the sun, a gap was opened between religion and science which was to be exacerbated in the Enlightenment (see Chapter 7). While many of the key figures of the Enlightenment (e.g. Descartes and the scientist Isaac Newton) attempted to harmonize religion and scientific investigation, the reality is that each scientific advance was more often than not viewed as a negative moment for religious belief. The mediaeval view that true knowledge was indivisible, and that therefore religious truth and scientific truth were merely two aspects of the same reality, came under severe pressure as the new methods of science came into conflict with established beliefs.

One area where this is most clearly seen is in biblical scholarship. In a situation where interpretation of the Bible was overwhelmingly in the hands of representatives of the mainstream religious denominations, the key to understanding scripture was that above all it was divine revelation; therefore, any uncomfortable discrepancies between different parts of the Bible, factual claims which conflicted with mounting evidence or sections which appeared to be myth or fable could be explained away by pointing to the divine origin of the whole of scripture, or by reference to the authoritative views of the church fathers and leading theologians. This meant that any 'scientific' facts defended by religious authorities often owed more to a pre-established metaphysical and theological framework (e.g. the omnipotence and omniscience of God which would preclude any error in his revelation) or a simple literal reading of scripture (e.g. using genealogies to establish the age of the earth) than to science in the modern sense.

For example, the historical veracity of the biblical account of creation – held equally by Catholics and Protestants – was gradually dismantled by the steady rise of the new sciences of geology and biology. As early as 1655 Isaac de la Peyrère's work *The Pre-Adamites* argued on scientific grounds that Adam could not be literally considered the first man; its author suffered much the same fate as Galileo. In 1678 the French Catholic cleric Richard Simon (1638–1712) published his *Histoire critique de Vieux Testament* (*Critical History of the Old Testament*), one of the first works of modern biblical criticism.

Owing much to Spinoza, Simon's *History* was significant in that it was prepared to treat the Old Testament as a document with a history, put together over time by a variety of authors with a variety of motives and interests, rather than a divinely-revealed unity. Simon's

work was condemned by all shades of Christian denomination, but
once an important move such as this happens it cannot be undone. In
the eighteenth century biblical scholars such as Johann Salomo
Semler (1725–91), who was greatly influenced by Simon, began to
interpret the scriptures historically and rejected the use of the biblical
texts as simply a mine for quotations applied to the defence of particular doctrines. Semler was aware of the gulf which separated the contemporary interpreter from the world of the Bible and consequently
appreciated the complexities involved in any interpretation. Semler's
adoption of a historical-critical method of reading the Bible led him to
reject the traditional Christian reading of the Hebrew scriptures which
saw in them typological prophecies of Jesus Christ and the Christian
movement. During the Enlightenment era he and other Protestant
theologians contributed to the demystifying of the scriptures through
their willingness to read them on many levels – historical, textual,
cultural and linguistic – other than the strictly theological.[4]

After Christian scholars had themselves begun to question the
standard interpretations of scripture and its use as doctrinal
justification, the way was now open for other scholars to make ever
bolder inroads into the churches' control of the interpretation of
scripture as writers such as Voltaire began to treat the Bible as simply
another product of human history and culture. Thus the limitations of
the Bible as the source of historical accuracy and scientific knowledge
were increasingly evident, and it was inevitable that as knowledge of
the natural world grew it became ever more difficult for the religious
authorities to hold together the particular synthesis of science and
religion which had been so characteristic of mediaeval thought.

Within the confines of the religious denominations themselves, the
Reformation had created the possibility that doctrinal dissent and
schism might take place in the name of the gospel and had uncovered
theological problems which had been suppressed for centuries. In the
seventeenth and eighteenth centuries the main Christian denominations attempted to clarify doctrine and stamp out dissent, but the
depth of the issues which presented themselves meant that the period
was one of intense theological debate. Within Calvinism, for example,
the seventeenth century saw the bitter Arminian conflict over grace; in
1618–19 the Synod of Dort condemned what it perceived as the
Roman/Pelagian view of Jakob Arminius that divine grace could be

resisted and that humans played some role in their own salvation. In England this theological conflict over grace came to have important political overtones. In 1646 the English Parliament, through the Westminster Confession, adopted the ruling of the Synod of Dort and thus turned the Church of England in a more orthodox Calvinist direction; monarchists, however, tended in the main to be Arminians and the theological difference came to be one of the marks which distinguished the monarchist from the Calvinist republican.

If Arminianism could be described as Calvinists leaning back somewhat towards Roman Catholicism, then Jansenism, with its strict doctrine of grace, could be described as Roman Catholics leaning towards Calvinism (see Chapter 4). The Jansenist dispute lasted for over a hundred years and resulted in crisis after crisis for the papacy. In addition to these major doctrinal disputes there were many others, especially about the nature of Christ. Arianism (the belief that Christ was less than the Father), or something close to it, became a tempting alternative for those who were reluctant to take the doctrine of the incarnation too literally; Locke and Newton were probably Arians of a sort.

Socianism, the doctrine that Christ was not divine but rather a creature with a special mission from God to show us the path of righteousness, was especially appealing in an age which was suspicious of the more metaphysical doctrines and which valued the efforts of people to forge and follow fundamental human values. In England the tempering of awkward doctrines by some divines earned them the name 'latitudinarians', meaning that they were prepared to countenance a great flexibility in matters of doctrine. In fact, the term was something of a misnomer because what the 'latitudinarians', like the seventeenth-century Archbishop of Canterbury John Tillotson, tended to preach was the simplicity of Christianity and in particular its moral message. Such preaching was popular because it minimized doctrinal difference – which gave rise to endless dispute and to more serious conflict – and offered instead a relatively benign religion which merely requested that people live decent and honest lives.

The significance of these disputes is that they continued down to the Enlightenment one of the major intellectual results of the Reformation, namely that Christian belief was not a fixed body of doctrine, clear and unambivalent for all to see and believe. It was rather something about which one could have views and argue, for which the evidence was not at all clear and in which widely different beliefs could exist under the banner 'Christian'. When the eighteenth century saw more direct attacks on the fundamental structure of Christianity itself this took place in a context in which, to put it crudely, the nature of Christianity was up for grabs. Was Christianity primarily a personal faith in Jesus Christ, loyalty to the Pope, membership of a particular church, a commitment to the moral values of the gospel, an over-complicated version of a simple message, or just a very big mistake? All of these views and many others can be found in the Enlightenment.

This all too brief and simple outline of three key concepts which characterize the period – a dynamic concept of reason, scepticism, and the emergence of scientific methodology – could give rise to the misleading impression that there was a coherent movement, project or school of thought which developed these ideas explicitly as the Enlightenment progressed. Such an impression would be far from the truth; the reality was that the Enlightenment period was one of intellectual exploration and even thinkers who are sometimes brought under the same label actually held widely divergent views. For example, we shall see in Chapter 5 that while deism is commonly held to be characteristic of the Enlightenment, it is quite difficult to find two thinkers who held precisely the same views. In addition, some of the major thinkers – e.g. Voltaire – changed their views or oscillated between apparently contradictory positions. In an age of discovery ideas seldom stand still. If one was to venture a generalization, however, one could say that above all diversity the Enlightenment period was concerned with the study of humanity in conjunction with the natural world in all its aspects; to paraphrase the Scottish historian and philosopher Adam Ferguson (1723–1816), human nature was the trade of the Enlightenment thinker. From the question of religion to the structure of society; from a love of education and discovery to the study of the mind itself; from the study of the laws of nature governing all life to the universal morality governing all humanity, there was intense investigation, argument, disagreement and, undoubtedly, there was progress also.

One significant stimulus to this questioning attitude to the world and our place in it was the increase in knowledge about other cultures and civilizations which the voyages of discovery had begun to provide; from Columbus and Vasco da Gama in the fifteenth century to Cook and Bougainville in the eighteenth, wondrous tales poured back to Europe (along with the plentiful gold, silver, silks and spices) about the manifold societies dotted around the globe. These discoveries evoked enormous curiosity in the population. It had been the custom of the Christian Middle Ages to view the newly-found non-Christian as either heathen (the Jews and Muslims who must be resisted on religious grounds) or pagan (savages who are interesting as curiosities and useful as slaves); in either case they could be explained away as either having rejected the true faith or being otherwise undeserving of the Christian dispensation. But as accurate knowledge of the sheer number and variety of other civilizations grew and as more sophisticated historical and cultural comparisons became possible, such simplistic categories were impossible to sustain and Europeans were forced to come to terms with the complexity of human diversity and the fact that civilizations had existed (as in Egypt) or continued to exist (as in China) which were older than European society and in many respects more advanced (such, for example, was the admiration for the idealization of the achievements of the Chinese that Leibniz wondered whether or not they should send missionaries to Europe).

This knowledge of other cultures could not be repressed and it had a profound effect on how Europeans understood themselves. No longer could they look out at the world and judge it from their own absolute perspective; they had to acknowledge that they too were being looked at and judged. A favourite literary device became the visit of outsiders to Europe, where they commented on the peculiar habits and customs of the natives, a genre exemplified by Montesquieu's *Lettres persanes* (*Persian Letters*, 1721) in which some Persians visit Paris and give their observations on French social and political habits. As well as being a conveniently oblique method of engaging in criticism of one's own place, this genre rested on an awareness of the value of the perspective of the other person or society and thereby made it possible for Europeans to ask about the value of their own society compared to that of others and made cross-cultural criticism possible. However, few Europeans either would or could shake off their inherent assumption of European superiority (they, after all, were the voyagers and scientists discovering and studying the new lands and peoples) and even fewer were ready to take the more drastic step of becoming cultural anthropologists by evaluating each society in terms of its own rules and customs.

European thinkers were thus faced with a wide range of questions to consider; the nature of human beings in general, the differences between various political and economic systems, family structures and the customs governing the expression of sexuality (Bougainville was the first to bring back news of the joys of Tahiti which was to capture the French imagination down to the twentieth-century artist Paul Gaugin and beyond), religious beliefs and practices, even different types of food and dress, all provided a rich source of speculation and debate for European intellectuals to challenge the dominant assumptions of their own culture.

This awareness of the customs and beliefs of other cultures raised crucial issues for Christian theology and the dominant role of the Christian church. If civilizations had existed for thousands of years without hearing of Christ then was revelation insufficient? Had God condemned all the members of these 'primitive' societies to hell and if so why? Could one be saved without Christ and if so why should one be a Christian at all? How were their exotic beliefs and deities to be understood in relation to the Christian God? These were profound and deeply challenging questions, and the responses to them of Christian theology over the past three hundred years is in itself a fascinating story. It is a story, however, which is beyond the bounds of the present work; what is significant from the perspective of the Enlightenment is that these questions made it possible for thinkers from a Christian culture to begin to think of their own religion as one among many and not as the one, single true religion given by the one and only God. This awareness marks a seismic change in the history of Christianity for it effectively marks the end of the possibility of maintaining 'Christendom' as a totalizing concept embracing and unifying all aspects of known society (even though the reality was that 'Christendom' had already been decisively fractured by the Reformation).

During the Enlightenment the dominant role which religion had played in European society, regulating everything from the appointment of kings and emperors to the rhythm of life which reflected the liturgical year, came under sustained pressure (for example in many

Catholic countries the late seventeenth and eighteenth centuries saw a steady diminution in the number of religious feast days, which had for centuries provided much needed leisure time for peasants, serfs and other manual workers). While the move away from religious belief and practice in the eighteenth century was to a great extent confined to intellectuals (among ordinary believers almost everyone believed in the existence of angels and hardly anyone in the existence of atheists), in the nineteenth century larger numbers of the general population ceased to participate in conventional religious practice. The reasons why the grip of religion on life was so diminished are complex. One could point to the decline in the power of the papacy, the loss of a united religious front after the Reformation and the further fragmentation within Protestantism, the growth of a merchant class independent of the clergy, the emergence of alternative forms of knowledge (e.g. advances in biology and medicine), the inherent inability of an inflexible theology to cope with changed circumstances, and several other factors. However, the intellectual ancestor of the de-Christianizing of Europe was the Enlightenment attack on Christianity which sowed the seeds of the predominantly secular society in which we live today.

In the eighteenth century there developed a secular and public sphere of discourse which, given the importance of religion in culture and society, could not be divorced from engagement with religious questions but which gradually gained autonomy from both religious authority and the intellectual framework within which all questions were considered in some way or another to have a religious dimension. One important factor in the emergence of such a secular discourse, in particular in the sciences, was a marked decline in a magical understanding of nature and of religion. Quite simply the world gradually became, to use the later phrase of the sociologist Max Weber, a much less 'bewitched' place.

One intriguing phenomenon, which gauges this shift in the way in which large numbers of people encountered the world and the parts of it which they could not comprehend, was the decline and virtual disappearance of the belief in 'witches' which marked the century from about 1650 onwards. Of course belief in 'witches' and in the use of dark powers is as old as the human race, but as Keith Thomas points out in his magisterial study, *Religion and The Decline of Magic*, in the late Middle Ages there developed the notion that the power of the witch was due to her having made a pact with the Devil.[5] This interpretation of the witch's powers had the important effect of making the witch akin to a heretic and thus instigating the persecution of those who in previous centuries would have been treated with a mixture of respect and fear.

It is perhaps difficult for the modern person to comprehend the depth of this belief in the malevolent power of witches and the trepidation which it induced in large segments of the population of Europe in the sixteenth and seventeenth centuries. The persecution of witches in the sixteenth and seventeenth centuries reflects the fear of a largely unknown and often hostile world; it had its roots deep in mediaeval Europe's abhorrence of heresy and the propaganda of the heresy-hunters, and it was fed by the disruption of the religious wars which followed the Reformation (it is no coincidence that 'witches' tended to be found more among minority communities – Huguenots in France and Catholics in England, for example – than among those considered to be orthodox believers of whatever persuasion).

Sometimes – as in northern Germany in the 1580s and 1590s and in southern Germany in the 1620s – the attack on witchcraft was nothing more than institutional and social hysteria which resulted in the persecution of anyone who was suspected of dissidence or simply odd behaviour. Catholics, Calvinists and Lutherans alike persecuted witches, thinking that they were thereby preventing the devil's work; that they were hardly at the same time doing the work of the Christian God seems only to have occurred to a few. Their enthusiasm for the truth resulted in the deaths of tens of thousands of innocent people (between 1623–33, six hundred 'witches' were killed in the Germany city of Bamberg alone).

The decline in the belief in witches and the accompanying cessation of persecution has no simple explanation.[6] The ending of the religious wars and the social disruption which they brought, horror at the sheer scale and barbarity of the executions, the emergence of more benign expressions of religious belief (e.g. German Pietism) and, no doubt, the prudent observation that today's accuser might be tomorrow's victim all played a role. But to these must be added the crucial factor, namely the emergence of ways of looking at the world which no longer viewed it as the sphere of the finely-balanced battle between the Lord and the Devil, the forces of light and darkness, but rather as the place in which systematic and rational investigation brings the truth into the light and banishes the darkness of ignorance. It is only possible to think of the disappearance of the belief in witchcraft in a context which offers a convincing alternative and that alternative was given in the work of seminal Enlightenment thinkers such as Bacon, Descartes, Locke, Newton and others. The natural world could be viewed at last as a place which was to some extent within our control and within the limits of our comprehension. The beginnings of the Enlightenment were not the only cause of the disappearance of this cruel phenomenon, but they were the crucial blow in its eventual downfall.

When the sophisticated eighteenth-century critics thought of religion, what came to mind more often than not was the barbarity of the persecutions and the official theological rationale which had guided them. The kindly local pastor or the art-loving bishop were to many Enlightenment intellectuals merely the pleasant mask which covered something far deeper and more sinister. Voltaire's pithy remark in his *Philosophical Dictionary* is representative of the views of the philosophes: 'In a word, less superstition, less fanaticism; and less fanaticism, less misery.' There was an almost physical revulsion among people like Voltaire at the thought of the horror of people dying for beliefs which the more enlightened considered products of a distorted imagination. But if they needed reminding of what was possible they did not have far to look; there were occasional outbreaks of the persecution of witches in Europe in the eighteenth century – particularly in isolated areas – and the last judicial execution of a witch occurred as late as 1782, in Switzerland. Even in the Enlightenment the past was not very far behind.

It would, however, be both simplistic and inaccurate to attribute the decline in witchcraft solely to the effect of the Enlightenment, for it was a phenomenon which was already well in decline before then. This assumption was common among the leading lights of the Enlightenment; they were generally quite quick to point to the darker side of religion and to assume all too easily that all progress of the time was due to the influence of reason and the progress of the age. While many Christian assumptions and practices were in need of critique and while much progress was indeed made in many areas, we can nevertheless turn the question of progress back on to the

Enlightenment and ask about the effect of Enlightenment ideals in areas where they might have been expected to have made a significant impact. This is, of course, an enormous question and not one to which we can give a full answer here; however, as an illustration of the issue and its significance we can look briefly at the situation of two important groups whom we might expect to have benefited from the new thinking, namely women and Jews.

Women, of course, being the major victims of the witchcraft craze, had most to gain from its decline and eventual disappearance. Given this improved climate it might therefore be thought that the Enlightenment's stress on a common human nature – either in its empiricist version of the human mind as a blank page *(tabula rasa)* or in its rationalist version of the universality of reason – would have made a significant difference to the understanding of women and led to a change for the better in their status and role in society. However, deeply ingrained cultural attitudes about gender are very difficult to change and the Enlightenment was no exception in this regard. During the eighteenth century it was all too easy for the ideal of reason as objective, unemotional, productive, and resolute to be equated with the qualities of the male, while the female was regarded as subjective, emotional, receptive, and susceptible to whimsical change. The ease with which reason was identified as masculine led to a situation in which, as one commentator puts it, 'for many intellectuals, the categories of gender became almost polarized during the Enlightenment'.[7] This polarization was simply the intellectual rationalization of the actual condition of women in European society where roles were clearly differentiated and the full political, social and educational emancipation of women an almost undreamed of possibility.

But if the rational male was considered to be the closest approximation to the Enlightenment ideal, women were far from being absent from intellectual life. While it is easy to point to those sophisticated Parisian women whose *salons* provided the meeting-ground for the predominantly male intellectuals of the French Enlightenment as the epitome of female influence, there were many women intellectuals active in diverse fields. Among the pioneering women writers of the age were educationalists such as Mary Astell (1668–1731) and Catherine Macaulay (1731–91), novelists such as Fanny Burney

(1752–1840) whose *Evelina, or the History of a Young Lady's Entrance into the World* (1778) and other works make her an important figure in the history of the novel, scholars such as the Marquise du Châtelet (1706–49) who translated Newton's *Principia* into French, and women of letters such Lady Mary Wortley Montagu, whose *Turkish Letters* (1717) telling of her travels in the orient was one of the most popular works in English at the time. These and numerous other women, sometimes with great difficulty, broke into an intellectual world which was commonly regarded as the exclusive domain of men.

Where women did succeed it was an enormous achievement given the generally poor opportunities for women to gain an education and profound philosophical and cultural prejudices which equated women with forces of disorder, while at the same time sentementalizing them as objects of male adulation. Rousseau epitomizes the view that women were destructive of the male order in his comment to d'Alembert that the disorder induced by women is more destructive to a people than an excess of wine.[8] Like the confusion induced by too much alcohol, too much femininity, thinks Rousseau, will destroy the rational order constructed by the clear male mind.

Among the female writers and activists of the Enlightenment, one of the most significant was Mary Wollstonecraft (1759–97) whose *A Vindication of the Rights of Woman* (1792) is a landmark in the history of feminism. Wollstonecraft argued that the subjugation of women had more to do with the enforced cultivation of certain 'feminine' traits and sensibilities and with lack of adequate education than with any inherent inferiority, that reason is as much proper to women as to men, and that marriage would be more successfully based on the friendship of two rational people than on the dominance of one over the other. She perceived clearly that women in the eighteenth century, in attempting to please men first of all and to succeed in the world through advantageous marriages and the vicarious achievements of their male offspring, were actually acting contrary to their real interests. Wollstonecraft's work stands as an act of consciousness-raising in the name of Enlightenment, but it also stands as an indictment of both the Christian rhetoric of human equality and the Enlightenment ideal of universal rationality, neither of which achieved the realization of the high principles they so easily espoused.

Jews too might have expected more from the ideals of both

Christianity and the Enlightenment. European Jews suffered a long list of oppressive measures in most places where they lived: they had to live in designated areas; they could not hold public office or own land; they were barred from most of the professions; they were subject to special taxes; and, of course, the Jews of the ghettos lived in fear of the mob violence of the pogrom. But, on the other hand, many Jews – such as the relatively well-educated Sephardic Jews who had been expelled from Spain in 1492 and had ended up in the major cities of the north – became successful in the financial and trading centres of Europe such as Amsterdam, London and Frankfurt. In the United States with the adoption of the First Amendment to the Constitution in 1789 (guaranteeing freedom of speech and worship) Jews found themselves with complete civil and political rights. In France after the revolution Jews were given citizenship but this was not put into effect until Napoleon, and even this limited progress was tempered by the fact that the old, deeper, cultural and religious prejudices remained.

That toleration might only mean the absence of direct persecution rather than acceptance is evident even among the ostensibly more Enlightened philosophes; here too a deep-rooted anti-Semitism was very difficult to eradicate. Voltaire – the self-styled champion of tolerance – considered the Jews more fanatical than the Christians and also responsible for giving Christianity to the world, a great crime in his eyes. In his entry on the Jews in the *Encyclopédie* Diderot castigated their lack of reason and philosophy, accusing them of confusion, obscurity, fanaticism and a blind obedience to authority. It seems that in the case of the Jews the philosophes were prepared to make an exception of their belief in the universality of reason and the benefits of education; to the majority of the philosophes the Jews were entirely ignorant and superstitious. This had the unfortunate effect of stigmatizing the Jews with something other than the death of Jesus Christ, namely incorrigible ignorance and stupidity, so that even atheists could have a reason to hate them. If the philosophes had any positive influence on the situation of the Jews it was indirectly through their general rhetoric on toleration and their ongoing attacks on Christianity and its claims to universal truth.

Where there were attempts by the authorities to lessen the burden on Jews they were often met with public outcry. Joseph II of Austria discovered to his cost that his subjects did not favour equal treatment for the Jews; even in relatively tolerant Britain public hostility forced the abandonment in 1753 of an attempt at legislation to extend civil rights to them, and similar attempts in Prussia met with no more success. While in very general terms Jews in western Europe lived under slightly better conditions than those in the east – Russia, Poland and Lithuania – nowhere were their overall conditions in any way comparable with the rights of the majority of the population (only in Holland did they enjoy the protection of the law); this was the case even for those relatively wealthy bankers or tradesmen whose rights to hold their wealth was always at the discretion of the local political rulers.

Although this demographic distribution of the Jewish population meant that most Jews did not encounter Enlightenment ideas directly, two Jewish thinkers stand out in the Enlightenment period: in the seventeenth century there was the philosopher Spinoza (who as we shall see in Chapter 5 was ostracized from his own community for his unorthodox views) and in the mainstream of the eighteenth-century Enlightenment the German Jew Moses Mendelssohn (1729–86).

Mendelssohn was a brilliant philosopher and linguist in his own right (his entry defeated Kant's in the famous Berlin newspaper competition of 1764) who instigated the Jewish Enlightenment *(Haskalah)*. He translated the Pentateuch into German and stimulated dialogue between Jewish thinkers and Enlightenment ideas, the result of this encounter being the emergence of Reformed Judaism. Mendelssohn's view of religion comprised a form of Jewish deism influenced by Spinoza, optimism about human nature, belief in immortality and a profound mistrust of coercion in religion. Mendelssohn was widely admired – although his defence of Judaism earned him vitriolic criticism from some Christian quarters – and was the inspiration for his friend Lessing's play *Nathan the Wise* (1779).

From the difficulties encountered by women and by minorities such as the Jews we can see that the Enlightenment was not, to use Kant's apt description, an enlightened age but rather an age of enlightenment. It was an age struggling to realize itself, but which very often failed to live up to the high ideals which it preached. As Roy Porter comments on English philanthropy in the eighteenth century: 'Tears for the exploited, the unfortunate and the afflicted flowed freely, but sympathy cost little, and was only occasionally translated into action."[9] Much the same could be said about the situation of women and Jews.

This serves to remind us that most of the thinkers who formed the driving force behind the Enlightenment belonged to the fringes of the aristocracy or to the urban middle classes. It is not surprising therefore that they were tempted to see themselves as set above the common masses of humanity by their learning and sophistication. Even among the most enlightened of the philosophes their class superiority often overcame their profession of the universality of reason; in an age in which education and knowledge were highly valued the educated often forgot their Lockean principle that everyone was born with the capacity to reason and to learn, and the uneducated were frequently despised as unworthy of learning.

It was easy for the sophisticated to point disparagingly at the beliefs of the people, their superstitions and their naive faith in religion, saints, amulets, relics and miracles. In a time before universal education it was easy to despair of the masses ever reaching the enlightened stage to which reason could bring them. As the social sciences were in their infancy it was a challenge to the intelligentsia to perceive that the ignorance of the ordinary people was due to the lack of an adequate educational system more than to any innate disposition towards superstitious beliefs. Kant's father, for example, was a poor harness-maker but his son's early education made him despise the morality and pastimes of the common man until, later in life, his philosophy led him to respect the capacity of everyone to obey the moral law.

The Enlightenment, therefore, was primarily the privilege of a relatively few educated people. The philosophes were not reluctant to point out what they thought was good for others, but fortunately for the mass of the population in the countries most affected by the Enlightenment this paternalism was in the main beneficial. Whether it was Rousseau's rather vague idea that somehow power should emanate from the 'general will' of the people or the new American ideal of everybody's right to the pursuit of happiness, it is to the Enlightenment that we owe the Western political principle that everyone in society should have a share in society's benefits and opportunities (although this in turn has roots in the Christian belief in the equality of all in the sight of God).

The ideals of the Enlightenment, even where they owed their

origins to Christian values, emerged in their own right as ideals which could be pursued by each and every person. And if these ideals were often slow to be realized (as in the case of women and the Jews) this failure did not proceed from any inherent flaw in those ideas themselves. Few among the educated in the eighteenth century could disagree with the principle that tolerance was better than bigotry, that education was preferable to ignorance and that science gave us power over elements of life which had hitherto been beyond our comprehension. The Enlightenment placed an unlimited value on the principle that knowledge was worth pursuing at almost any cost, and in the context of this new methodology of investigation many of the assumptions of what was assumed to be the Christian world view came under sustained pressure.

If one wished to state a simple thesis about the changes which marked the Enlightenment off from all previous eras and which was inevitably to lead to a conflict of ideals with the religious world view, one could simply repeat the claim that in the Enlightenment the world became 'rational' (and even those thinkers who so opposed 'rationalist' philosophy – such as Hume – operated within the 'rational' assumption that there was one, final clear and definitive explanation to the problems with which they grappled). However, one must immediately point out that this does not mean for one moment that everyone behaved rationally or that everything was explained in a rational manner; rather, what 'rational' means here is that enough was achieved politically, scientifically and intellectually for the *assumption* that the world was rational and therefore capable of a naturalistic explanation to become fixed as a basic and foundational assumption of modern European culture. This assumption could not but cut across the previously dominant explanation, that of Christian theology and its attendant anthropology and cosmology. The result of this shift in consciousness was that much of the religious conflict of the Enlightenment is simply the realignment of ideals towards the dominance of reason over faith, the authority of the scientist over that of the bishop and the methodology of investigation over the explication of doctrine.

That the Enlightenment was in the main critical of religion is beyond dispute; that it also depended upon religion, and that it took many of the central ideals of Christianity and gave them a secular rationale is also beyond dispute. What is perhaps the tragedy for Christianity is that in its attempts to respond to many of the – often shallow – attacks it endured, its intellectuals too often resorted to condemnation. The Enlightenment's avowal of the freedom to investigate all subjects, to bracket authority in the name of inquiry, and its insistence on secular thinkers' independence from religious interference all came across to religious leaders and many theologians, otherwise well-disposed towards innovative thinking, as simply an attack on the foundations of religion as such. Of course in some cases this is precisely what it was, but the inability of so many theologians, bishops and elders to see the potential for theological development in the new ideas of the time meant that Christian thinking often stood still while the modern world was formed about it. It is not without significance that the 'father' of modern philosophy, René Descartes, died in 1650 and the 'father' of modern theology, Friedrich Schleiermacher, died in 1831. Between them lay the Enlightenment and almost two hundred years of changing ideals and, from the viewpoint of Christian thought, many lost opportunities.

2

Enlightenment, Power and Context

Ideas do not spring into being free of all contact with the variable and difficult world in which we live; they are always formed in a context and the major ideas of any period will reflect the concerns of the age from which they come. This is as true of the religious thought of the Enlightenment era as it is of the ideas of any other time. The writers, philosophers, theologians, statesmen and scientists of the seventeenth and eighteenth centuries were for the most part aware of this fact. They were therefore not interested in religion simply as metaphysical speculation or personal experience, the abstruse speculations of the scholastics were not for them. With their practical cast of mind they were interested in what religion had to say about human nature and the physical world, in how it functioned in society, how it influenced the lives of the people and the apparatus of state. In many countries, particularly those of western Europe, this issue was of much more importance two to three hundred years ago than it is today, for three reasons. First, at that time religious belief was virtually universal among the people; secondly, religious leaders frequently had significant political power and influence (especially in France); and, thirdly, the context in which much intellectual debate took place was that of the supremacy of theology among the academic disciplines and the fact that any alternative views – from the question of the age of the earth to the existence of the soul – had to come to terms with the Christian teaching on that particular subject.

It was impossible in these circumstances for major political events and developments to be devoid of religious overtones, and for religious debate to be without public, if not directly political relevance. In this important regard the Enlightenment period differs from our situation today where in Western countries (with some exceptions such as the United States, Poland and Ireland) the arguments and debates of the state and the church overlap to a less significant degree than they did centuries or even decades ago and where religion plays a much reduced role in public life. For us fully to appreciate the public nature and importance of the debates on religion in the Enlightenment it is fruitful to look at some of those factors and places where relevant ideas and events overlapped, especially when it came to have a bearing on the interaction of church and state. This will also enable us to look at the Enlightenment in some of the more significant countries, an exercise which shows that there was no single form of 'enlightenment', but only the attempt in each particular context to formulate ideas and advance the understanding of human society and of the natural world. In this chapter, therefore, we shall examine some factors influencing the interaction of politics, religion and the Enlightenment, focussing on some of the major nations, namely Britain, France, Austria and the United States.

In appraising the factors which influenced the attitude to religion of the Enlightenment's leading thinkers, one contextual factor which deserves particular attention, but whose precise impact is difficult to gauge, is the destruction caused to Europe's social and economic infrastructure by the bitter wars which laid so much of the continent to waste in the first half of the seventeenth century. The Thirty Years War (1618–48) – which was really a series of wars – was the last great European conflict in which religion was a vital element. As with many conflicts in which religion is a factor, the substantial issues which concerned the protagonists were not directly religious, but had to do with power, wealth, land and political domination. In the Thirty Years War all of these factors were fundamental to the conflict, but, in the context of the time, religious differences were perceived as crucial also. In such a situation religion can act as a pretext for aggression, as a way of forming alliances or as a focal-point for propaganda. For the critics of the Enlightenment the wars of the first half of the seventeenth century were religious wars, even if that view was a somewhat misleading interpretation of the real issues involved.

The Thirty Years War began with the attempts of the Habsburgs to return the Protestant principalities to the Catholic Church and ended with Catholic France in alliance with Protestant Sweden against Spain and Austria. In the meantime huge areas of Europe had been laid to waste, cities destroyed, whole peoples displaced and the population reduced, in places by as much as forty per cent. The wars ended with the Peace of Westphalia in 1648, a crucial event not just for European political history but for the status and future of religion in European society.

After the Thirty Years War European leaders realized that religious differences could no longer be allowed to dictate the policies of states and the relations between them. The Reformation principle of *cuius regio, eius religio* (as the ruler is, so too is the religion), which allowed a prince to dictate the religion of his subjects, was modified so that if the prince changed his religion he could not force his subjects to follow suit. This more or less halted the political progress of the Catholic Counter-Reformation – which had been very effective in forcing many Protestant areas to revert to Catholicism – and the refusal of even the Catholic leaders to heed the Pope's protest against the treaty marked a clear demarcation of the interest of the state from that of the church. The Reformation age of astonishing religious development and upheaval, but also of religious darkness, was coming to a close. An era was approaching in which not only the political but also the intellectual power of religion was to lose much of the sovereignty which it had exerted on European society for centuries.

There is little doubt but that the divisions within Christianity – with the resultant wars – contributed significantly to the disillusionment of many with the Christian churches and with Christian belief. In the eighteenth century such fractiousness among the children of God was contrasted sharply with the agreement brought about by a universal science which laid bare the laws which governed the universe. As Voltaire put it with characteristic wit: 'there are no sects in geometry'. The apparent simple beauty of the laws of the universe was contrasted with the obscurantism of theology. Surely, if the laws of the universe can be made so clear and intelligible, then there must also be a simple and direct way to understand religion. This desire for clarity and order in all things led, as we shall see throughout this study, to the strong propensity in the eighteenth century for many leading intellectuals to search for the theological equivalent of the new physics and to attempt to simplify religion. They endeavoured to reduce it to a few core factors (e.g. the existence of a deity, the immortality of the soul) which could be established by rational means and would be acceptable to all Christian denominations and even to all religions. The rational religion which resulted was often very far from traditional Christianity and often not much removed from atheism.

All of this does not mean that the majority of people ceased to believe, but it does mean that it became possible for more and more people not to believe. The divisions in Christianity engendered by the Reformation and the religious wars helped bring to an end the comparatively homogeneous society which had characterized previous centuries. Historians sometimes use the term 'compulsory society' to delineate societies in which more fixed and stringent forms of social, political and religious relations predominate. In such societies, the power of the individual person to choose what to believe, who should rule them, where they could live, etc. was severely limited compared with the freedoms which the leading thinkers of the Enlightenment championed so strongly and which most citizens of democracies enjoy today. This was particularly true in the realm of religion, where orthodox belief was a routine and expected part of the individual's life, and where deviation from the norm could often result in persecution. Not that such persecution had been universal in Christian history, but in the eighteenth century the memory of the religious inquisitions, post-Reformation wars and the burning of witches was still fresh in the memory of the scholar and the wider community alike. The Enlightenment greatly expanded the possibilities for freedom of belief, even if in practice this luxury was in the main confined to those intellectuals with enough money and influence to feel secure in their views.

For the average person even the religious reforms of the sixteenth century – aimed as they were at the abuses in the dominant religious system – did not end the compulsory society; for the ordinary person there was often little difference in life under a Protestant prince than under the previous Catholic ruler. It was only with the end of overt religious strife and the flourishing of ideas in the Enlightenment period that toleration of freedom of belief was gradually extended to the individual citizen. In England, for example, the first half of the eighteenth century saw the repeal of many minor laws designed to make life difficult for Catholics and Dissenters (Presbyterians, Baptists, Congregationalists and Quakers), and while Anglicanism remained *de jure* the state religion, people were *de facto* free to belong to whichever Christian denomination they wished. In France, by contrast, the revocation in 1685 of the Edict of Nantes (which had guaranteed toleration of Protestants) gave rise to a context of religious oppression from which the philosophes gained much ammunition for their attacks on the French church.

Due to the well-established fact that the Enlightenment period saw an increased and sustained critique of religion, it is tempting to look back two hundred and fifty years and conclude that the period saw a sharp decline in interest in religion. In fact, the contrary is the case: the attacks by intellectuals on revealed religion and the search for a more rational form of belief, the presence of a fashionable atheism in the *salons* of Paris, the exciting advancement of science offering the possibility of an alternative world view, and a general willingness of leading thinkers to engage with religious issues, all point to the con-clusion that the Enlightenment took religion with the utmost serious-ness. One leading commentator goes so far as to make what might appear a surprising claim: 'It would be false to tax the Enlightenment with indifference to religion. It would be more discerning to say that it was obsessed with it.'[1]

Also, it is worth emphasizing that beyond the bounds of the arguments and doubts of a limited number of influential thinkers, the eighteenth century remained, on the whole, a period of widespread religious practice and even revival. The century saw Protestant Pietism take a strong hold in Germany (where it influenced Kant and other thinkers of the German *Aufklärung*) and the revivalism of the Methodists in England under the leadership of John Wesley. These important movements ran parallel to the Enlightenment and were largely untouched by it; they were particularly important in articulat-ing the need for people, in particular those without access to learning, to have a religion with which they could engage personally at the level of prayer and worship and which depended more on the subjective commitment of the individual than on the judgment of the mind about its inherent truth or falsity.

The eighteenth century therefore did not see any widespread exodus of the general population away from Christian belief, but what the militant freethinkers of the Enlightenment provided was the intellectual weaponry which opened up the possibility of widespread disbelief. Believers and unbelievers gradually lost touch with the total-izing aspects of mediaeval Christianity; institutions developed which did not need the support or patronage of the churches, and learning which was once the sole preserve of the monk came within the reach of anyone with enough money and leisure.

The emergence of the secular world was gradual; as one commentator puts it: 'religious institutions and religious explanations of events were slowly being displaced from the centre of life to its periphery.'[2] This was hardly surprising, for some form of decline in religion was probably inevitable in the face of what was the first major intellectual movement to develop outside the borders of the Christian church since Christianity had become the official religion of the Empire almost a millennium and a half earlier. Furthermore, as John McManners puts it in his study of death in eighteenth-century France, changes in the practice of religion – e.g. a decline in the number of vocations to the religious life, a falling off in the number of religious publications, or a decrease in church attendance – can be indicative of modification and change in the way people practise their religion more than it is indicative of a clear decline. It was only with the post-revolutionary 'terror' that France was effectively 'de-Christianized'; during the *ancien régime* 'tendencies towards deism, scepticism, irreligion and anticlericalism' do not amount to evidence that religion was experiencing any dramatic slump in its fortunes.[3]

There was, therefore, no great gulf between religion and either ordinary or intellectual life. The changes in the way in which human beings understood themselves, their place in the world and their relation to the divine, which occurred in the period we are studying cannot be considered in isolation from the wider social and political context in which they took place, for they are in many respects inseparable from it. At a time during which many central aspects of life, which today operate in distinctively independent spheres, were considered inseparable – e.g. science and religion, politics and religion – it is impossible to consider religious thought in isolation from the broader context within which it developed.

In Britain, for instance, the world-view associated with the philosophy of Locke and the physics of Newton – which had a major impact on the way in which God's relationship to the world was understood – was quickly assimilated into the wider world of commerce, literature and the popular culture of the literate classes. British military and commercial power in the eighteenth century combined with a relatively tolerant political climate (which tempered the worst excesses of monarchy with the parliamentary system of checks and balances) meant that both the economic and cultural life of the country flourished.

While throughout the eighteenth century England produced relatively few great thinkers, it hardly needed to. Both the state and the church were relatively weak and the intellectual climate did not call for grand gestures of resistance against intellectual or political oppression as they did in France. England had no Voltaire, for the object of his biting ridicule was much more fluid and elusive in England than it was it France; it had no Kant, for the great speculative system which he developed to overcome the scepticism of Hume was considered less than necessary in a pragmatic society where getting on with the business of the day was solution enough to the sceptic's dilemma. As Roy Porter puts it, in England the 'real intelligentsia was not chairbound but worked in the marketplace' and in this marketplace 'ideas were a trade, produced for a wide popular readership'.[4]

Nor, in England do we find the bitter anti-clericalism of France. There was no papal influence and there were no powerful religious orders with control over education; above all there was no Anglican equivalent of the Jesuits. In this relatively relaxed religious climate the minority denominations were able to continue without undue fear: Nonconformists were treated lightly after the Toleration Act of 1689, and while Catholics continued to suffer under the rule of law, in practice their numbers increased and with it their freedom of worship (with occasional setbacks – due more to 'no popery' mob violence than systematic oppression – such as the Gordon riots of 1780). Among the educated and uneducated alike there was a certain indifference to religion which manifested itself in a marked reluctance to bother with the formal business of actually attending church and not with any vehement or violent reaction against the institution of religion which, like poverty, was probably always going to be with them.[5]

In Scotland (where Presbyterianism ruled) there was, despite the Toleration Act, somewhat less scope for religious dissent. Yet the rational religion of the early eighteenth century in England made its presence felt in Scotland too, and the General Assembly of the Church of Scotland was forced to issue periodic warnings against the dangers of reason in religion and reminding its ministers that revelation was the true foundation of belief. Later, the Scottish Enlightenment of David Hume, Adam Ferguson, Thomas Reid and Adam Smith benefited from this ground-breaking flirtation with rational religion and from the well-established links between Scotland and the Continent which had persisted since the Reformation.[6]

Among the educated at least, the tenor of British social, political, economic and also religious life in the Enlightenment period was that of a pragmatic and phlegmatic approach to all things. If Voltaire, in the sixth of his *Letters Concerning the English Nation*, could admire the tolerance shown between Muslim, Jew and all forms of Christian on the floor of the Royal Exchange it was because there they 'give the name of infidel to none but bankrupts'. The practice of commerce came before the exchange of *anathemas* and the pursuit of prosperity before the pursuit of the hereafter. When later in the century Jeremy Bentham (1748–1832) elevated the pursuit of pleasure into the doctrine of utilitarianism, he was only expressing for the philosopher what his more prosaic countrymen had been practising for some time, namely the principle that the greatest happiness for the greatest number was a goal to be achieved through the business of the day.

While the English took the Enlightenment down to earth and assimilated it to the needs of the nation, the situation in other parts of Europe was more taut. In France, in particular, the political situation had very great consequences for the way in which leading Enlightenment thinkers approached religion, and religious thought – in particular the dominant orthodoxy of the upper clergy – was itself influential in political decision making. Between 1643 and the establishment of a republic in 1792 France was ruled by three kings, Louis XIV (reigned 1643–1715), Louis XV (reigned 1715–74) and Louis XVI (reigned 1774–92). The relative stability of France during the reigns of Louis XIV and Louis XV was founded on the balance of relations achieved between the monarchy and other powerful forces in society, usually termed the 'Three Estates', the nobility, the clergy and the remainder of the populace, of which the increasingly influential bourgeoisie was the most important element.

The church was at or close to the centre of power and Catholicism was integral to France's political and cultural identity during this period; the revocation in 1685 of the Edict of Nantes signalled the fact that France was to remain Catholic and that dissent was not to be tolerated. The close bond between the church and the monarchy was forged out of fear of the danger of Protestantism but also out of rejection of papal interference in French ecclesiastical policies. The Gallican controversy of the late seventeenth century (in which Louis XIV demanded control over certain aspects of the French church) cemented a bond between church and state; in 1682 the General Assembly of French clergy adopted four principles which rejected papal authority over princes, affirmed that councils of the church are superior to popes, demanded power for local churches and required universal assent to papal decrees. These principles were taught in all French seminaries and, with the exception of religious orders such as the Jesuits who were loyal to Rome, they helped create in the majority of the French clergy an attitude of religious patriotism. The church – in the form of its higher clergy – was thus accepted in France as an integral part of the ruling elite, and in its control of education and through its power to raise its own sources of revenue it exerted an independent source of social control and influence. The theology faculty at the Sorbonne was a permanent source of orthodox vigilance against theological deviancy and had considerable influence on the decisions of the state censor, a factor which was to make it one of the most implacable opponents of the philosophes in the eighteenth century.

Senior church figures were seldom far from the centre of power. For example two of the most important figures in the political history of France in the period we are considering were the theologian Fénelon (1651–1715) who exercised considerable influence at the court of Louis XIV and was greatly instrumental in the suppression of Protestantism in France, and Cardinal Fleury (1653–1743), who was Regent for part of the reign of Louis XV before the boy-king came of age. These men and the many others like them who formed part of the court of the old regime ensured that the Catholic Church in France was never a spiritual body solely, but was an integral part of the political fabric.

In the eighteenth century the church controlled about ten per cent of the land of France, from which it received large tax revenues, usually as a percentage of the agricultural produce; in addition, the church had the rights to a small proportion of all taxes raised which, when taken together, made it a powerful source of independent wealth. But despite the fact that the vast majority of people were believers and Catholicism dominated French religious life, there was considerable resentment among the people against this wealth and power. This resentment was due in part to the very fact that taxes were levied at all, but more importantly to the fact that when collected the taxes were used primarily for the benefit of the wealthier clergy. The hierarchical structure of the French clergy – as in other European countries – reflected the structure of society in general. Almost all of the bishops, abbots and upper clergy came from the nobility and were well educated, whereas the lower clergy (parish priests and curates) were from the lower bourgeoisie or, sometimes, peasant stock. The taxes raised in the parishes of these lower clergy went directly into the coffers of the upper clergy, from which the local priests and curates were paid a meagre salary.

As many of the key positions in the church were dispensed by royal patronage, the church became, for the noble families, simply another way to progress in the world; the acquisition of clerical benefices for personal or family gain meant that many bishops had little interest in residing in their diocese – especially if it was a provincial backwater. This was in direct contravention of the disciplinary decrees of the sixteenth-century Council of Trent, which had stipulated among its reforms that clergy were to be resident in the diocese or parish to which they were officially attached and from which they drew their income; this rule was applied quite strictly to the local clergy but was interpreted more liberally in the case of their noble colleagues.

Thus the church's income was distributed upwards from the laity and the lower clergy to the upper-class clergy. Such a patently unjust arrangement was a recipe for the growth of anti-clericalism both at the level of the church-going masses and at the level of the educated commentator – the most vociferous of which was the indefatigable Voltaire. Therefore in the eighteenth century it was quite possible for a deep piety among the people to exist alongside an equally deep scepticism about the motivation and behaviour of the upper clergy, who could be distinguished from the rest of the nobility more easily by their fine mode of dress and their lifestyle than by their piety and evangelical poverty.

By the time of the revolution in 1789 the church in France had become so identified with the court of Louis XVI that it was virtually impossible in the climate of the time to be opposed to the one without being equally opposed to the other. Thus, when the cataclysmic collapse of the *ancien régime* occurred the church suffered violent persecution and its wealth became a target for the new government and the looter alike. But the moves of the revolution against the power of the church were not without the support of some clergy, the most significant of whom was probably Bishop Henri Grégoire (1750–1831). A priest at the time of the revolution, Grégoire supported the insurrection and was made a bishop in the 'constitutional' church established in 1790. Grégoire advocated the establishment of a republic and wanted the clergy to identify fully with the Third Estate; as a member of the national Assembly he used his position to oppose slavery. However, the predominant mood of the revolution, especially from 1792 onwards, was strongly anti-church and Grégoire and others like him could do little to prevent the enormous persecution of clergy which followed. Nevertheless, despite the attempts of the leaders of the post-revolutionary 'terror' to extirpate Christianity from French life, the depth of piety ensured that such attempts were not to be successful; when freedom of religion was again allowed in 1795 the Catholic Church began to restructure itself and it has been remarked, and not without a grain of truth, that Napoleon Bonaparte owed much of his popularity in France to the fact that he reopened the churches after their closure during the revolution.

A different but no less intriguing scenario of church-state relations can be seen in the case of Austria, which provided possibly the most fascinating clash of religion with Enlightenment ideals. The Austro-Hungarian Empire was ruled by the Habsburg dynasty, descended from Charles V, the Holy Roman Emperor during most of the Reformation. For forty years between 1740 and 1780 Austria was ruled by the indomitable figure of the Empress Maria Theresa, who succeeded to the throne when her father Charles VI died of mushroom poisoning, allowing Voltaire to make the immortal comment that a pot of mushrooms had changed the history of Europe.

Maria Theresa was a conservative Catholic with no inclination to indulge the new ideas of the philosophes, and little interest in the reforming impulses of the Enlightenment. During her reign

Catholicism was the only Christian denomination officially permitted and the Empress explicitly rejected any possibility of religious toleration. She regarded Protestants and Jews as dangerous both to the church and the state and moved actively to suppress them, even though many of the state's civil servants had been educated in Protestant universities in Germany and some had been sufficiently influenced by that experience to convert.

The Empress was as innately conservative in matters of state as in those of religion, but for reasons of expediency – namely the requirement to strengthen Austrian bureaucratic and military efficiency in the face of the continued threat from the Prussia of Frederick II, who had marked her accession to the throne by marching his armies into Silesia and seizing it without opposition – she did implement some reforms. She introduced the provision of universal primary education, permitted non-Catholics to attend university, and made an attempt to tax clergy and nobles which was only partly successful. The devoutly Catholic Empress even allowed the introduction into the universities of secular subjects such as law which helped in the decline of theology as the central plank of university education. The universities had been under the almost exclusive control of the Jesuits until 1759, when control was removed from them. The Jesuits in Austria (and elsewhere as we shall see) were implacable opponents of the Enlightenment, but by the middle of the eighteenth century their counter-Reformation successes were waning and they were finding it difficult to adapt to the challenges of the new era.

So, despite some faltering steps towards reform which roused the anger of the church, such as the 1751 reduction in religious feast-days, Maria Theresa was essentially a defender of the church's power and influence and a staunch opponent of the Enlightenment. In this her views were in stark contrast to those of her co-regent from 1765 and eventual heir, Joseph II, the second of her sixteen children. As a young man Joseph read widely, including the works of the philosophes which his mother despised and which were banned in the Empire through both state censorship and the church's *Index* of books forbidden to Catholics. But despite his familiarity with the works of the leading thinkers and his sympathies with many Enlightenment ideals, Joseph's eagerness to implement reform was to be frustrated during the fifteen years he spent as co-regent. Although he held the title of

Holy Roman Emperor from 1765, while his mother reigned he was never allowed to make independent decisions and real power remained in the hands of the Empress. Joseph was resentful of this lack of influence, and when he eventually succeeded to the throne on Maria Theresa's death in 1780 he undertook reform with a zeal that was to prove his undoing.

One of the first and prime targets of Joseph's reform was the church, whose enormous power and influence he considered to be the prime barrier to social and educational reform. As co-regent he had succeeded, with the aid of the State Chancellor Kaunitz, in persuading his mother to increase state control over the church, but the action which he took on becoming sole ruler was far in excess of these earlier steps and proved to have enormous consequences.

Joseph's first moves were to abolish serfdom (somewhat unsuccessfully as many nobles refused to co-operate) and issue Edicts of Toleration which allowed Protestants, Eastern Orthodox Christians and even Jews to have their own schools and places of worship, an action which brought upon him the wrath of the Roman Catholic Church. This was undoubtedly a reform based on genuine conviction, but Joseph was not prepared to extend it to all religious expression: when some Bohemians declared themselves to be deists, he decreed that they be flogged. Toleration did not mean that people could believe anything they wished.

But toleration for Joseph did mean the easing of censorship, and Vienna quickly became a vibrant centre of free thinking. Scandalously for the church authorities the *Index* was no longer the unofficial guide for the state censor, as it had been in the reign of Maria Theresa, and the works of freethinkers and Protestants circulated with impunity. Satire was permitted, even against the Emperor, and the usual flood of ribald commentary on the supposed illicit activities of monks and nuns materialized in a very short space of time.

Motivated by the pragmatism of his century that both individuals and institutions should exist for some useful purpose or not at all, Joseph set about curbing the size and influence of the church. In Austria at the time between thirty-five and forty per cent of the land was under church control and there were over 2,000 religious houses. Many of these ran schools, hospitals, orphanages or other charitable institutions, but many others were simply contemplative monasteries,

dedicated in principle at least to the pure monastic ideal. It was to
these latter that Joseph turned his attention.

In November 1781 Joseph – using an incident in one monastery as
a pretext – instructed that all monasteries which did not engage in
what he considered to be useful work were to be dissolved, on the
grounds that 'those orders which are entirely useless cannot be pleasing to God'.[7] Like many Enlightenment thinkers the Emperor
despised that which was viewed as unproductive, and the most obvious candidates were the contemplative monastic orders; these monks
and nuns were widely regarded as lazy and grasping, giving nothing in
return for what was commonly perceived (whatever the reality) as
their indolent and luxurious lifestyle. Under Joseph's orders almost
one third of the monasteries in the Empire were closed and their
property confiscated by the state, although the erstwhile monks and
nuns were provided with a pension or re-trained and employed as
teachers. Even those monasteries which were allowed to remain open
were forced to reduce the number of monks and nuns; the state took
over effective control of the monasteries' wealth and none of their
property could be sold without the permission of the authorities.
Throughout the 1780s the government continued a highly successful
appraisal and confiscation of church property, using as a rationale the
claim that it was in reality the property of the people as a whole.

The Emperor employed the confiscated wealth to good effect,
establishing a fund for building hospitals and schools, and turning
over many of the buildings to be used for housing and industry. New
laws were passed which prevented the monasteries from receiving
inheritances, thus robbing them of one of their most effective means
of building up wealth. The Piarist order – the leading teaching order
after the Jesuits – was given the backing of the state and other 'useful'
orders were encouraged to view education not as a luxury to be
indulged in for its own sake but as a means to an end of improving the
state as a whole.

In addition to his reform of the monasteries, Joseph was influential
in improving the seminaries. He reduced their number to five and
added secular knowledge to the curriculum, insisting that future
priests should study agriculture and other practical subjects which
would make them of pragmatic and not simply of spiritual benefit to
their communities. He combined this with the abolition of the tithe

which was paid by the peasants to the local priest, and placed the clergy on state salaries, which effectively turned them into civil servants; the government also began a huge church-building programme to provide parishes for the new clergy. Thus Joseph's reforms were in no manner designed to extirpate Christianity; they were designed rather to simplify it and make it a useful and productive part of the lives of his subjects. The new Catholicism of the Austrian Empire was to be a religion in the image of its chief architect: rational, functional and moral, based on firm Enlightenment principles of utility and practicality.

To achieve his end Joseph decided on some drastic measures which were relatively minor in their own right, but which were eventually to be the greatest stumbling block to all his reforms. He wanted a simple religion, so he attempted to ban candles and church decorations, allowed only one religious procession per year, and decided that kneeling before the sacrament as the procession went by was no longer permitted (a simple doffing of the hat being now homage enough). The paraphernalia which surrounded the people's worship – relics, lamps, clothing on statues, etc. – were severely curtailed; the state even exercised control over the type of hymns sung in the liturgy and, amazingly, about how long candles could be. Discussion of religion in beerhouses and other places of relaxation was banned, a surely futile move as the Emperor's endless and increasingly bizarre decrees provided all the subject-matter for conversation his subjects could ask for.

If all of this were not sufficient to explain the anger of ordinary people at the pettiness of the reforms and call into question the Emperor's judgment, then the most ludicrous of his decrees surely provides evidence enough. In 1784, having previously issued a decree on the size of coffins and the material allowed for their use, he passed a law banning them completely; henceforth each deceased Austrian was to be buried in a linen sheet or bag. The rational Emperor considered this a hygienic and inexpensive way to dispose of what was to him nothing more than a piece of rotting meat, and was bemused and annoyed by the reaction which the law engendered in the population. Such was the anger caused by the coffin law that it was repealed within months.

While it is notoriously difficult to measure the extent to which Joseph's reforms were inspired by Enlightenment ideals as such or by more pragmatic considerations, there is no doubt but that he must be seen as representative of the spirit of the age; many of Joseph's religious reforms were necessary and effective means of improving the role of the church in the Austrian Empire and whether through design or chance they reflected the desires of many of the philosophes that the power of the church should be curbed. But his singular failure to perceive the crucial distinction between abuses and the largely innocent religious practices of the masses caused his reforms to meet with strong opposition from the very people he was attempting to help.

He also, as might be expected, ran into strong opposition from the church hierarchy and from the Pope. The Emperor's attack on the church's wealth and prestige led to one of the most astonishing events of the Enlightenment era, the visit of Pope Pius VI (1717–99, Pope from 1775–99) to Vienna to attempt to persuade Joseph to change his mind about his policy on the church. It was highly unusual for popes of the time to leave Rome and the news that Pope Pius was to cross the Alps into German territory to meet with Joseph II was met with incredulity; emperors might visit popes, but popes did not visit emperors.

Everywhere the Pope went in the Austrian capital he was met by large and enthusiastic crowds, but the enthusiasm of the populace for the pontiff was not shared by their rulers. Joseph received the Pope in a polite enough fashion but made it clear that in matters of reform he was not for turning. The incapacity of Pius VI to influence matters of state in even this most Catholic of countries was graphically symbolized in a most comic way by his visit to the palace of the State Chancellor Kaunitz, a cynical and resolute foe of the church. Kaunitz did not go do the door to meet the Pope but awaited him in his room wearing a dressing-gown and hat, and on the arrival of his guest neither stooped to kiss the Pope's ring nor doffed his hat as a mark of respect. The Pope, used to more deferential treatment, eventually removed his hat whereupon the Chancellor did the same; the pontiff then replaced his hat and Kaunitz, making his views on papal status perfectly clear, promptly replaced his. This eighteenth-century chaplinesque routine over, Kaunitz treated the stunned Pius to a tour of his art collection.

This moment of humiliation in Vienna was perhaps the low-point of the papacy in the eighteenth century; how far it all was from the symbolic high point of mediaeval papal power, when in 1077 Pope Gregory VII (the monk Hildebrand) had forced the young Holy Roman Emperor Henry IV to kneel penitently in the snow at Canossa and beg his forgiveness. But the power of the mediaeval papacy was by now long gone and the Pope had no longer any effective diplomatic or military weight with which to enforce his views. Throughout the eighteenth century several European states followed the example of France under Louis XIV and curbed the power of the Pope over the local church, thus further reducing the Pope's status from ruler of all kings to the lowly level of an Italian prince.

These blows to papal prestige came to a head with the dissolution of the Jesuits in 1773. The order, founded as a bastion of the Catholic Reformation, had gained increasing influence in the seventeenth century through the rigorous training and commitment of its members, its emphasis on education, and its strategy of targeting the centres of power (Jesuits were the leading confessors to Europe's kings and queens). But this influence brought with it the capacity to make enemies and the Jesuits' international organization and vow of loyalty to the Pope meant that they were never quite free of the suspicion that their loyalties were divided between Rome and the various states in which they operated.

The popular view which sometimes prevailed – and remains even in the twentieth century – that the Jesuits were the outright enemies of progress and learning is, however, far from the truth and owes more to the successful propaganda of their enemies (both Catholic and Protestant) than to reality. The students at Jesuit schools and colleges received an excellent education, there was a broad curriculum based on the traditional disciplines of philosophy and theology but emphasizing also mathematics and the natural sciences. Many of the philosophes were Jesuit educated and, while they often found themselves in conflict with their former masters, the discipline of mind and thirst for knowledge which drove the Enlightenment ideal in Catholic countries owed a great deal to their initial schooling.

In the colonies of the Catholic states the Jesuits were in the main a source of enlightened humanitarianism compared to the soldiers, adventurers and fortune-hunters who so exploited the native peoples. In South America they attempted to protect the natives from the worst excesses of the colonizers by the establishment of 'reductions', akin to reservations where traditional customs and ways of life could continue unharmed. In the East – India, China and Japan – their pragmatism led them to adapt Roman liturgical and sacramental rites to local customs. This innovation, particularly in the case of the adoption of a Chinese rite by the Jesuit Matteo Ricci at the turn of the eighteenth century, led to condemnation from Rome and the cessation of the experiment; it is tempting to speculate that had the curial officials in Rome been more enlightened much of China might have become Christian.

In Europe, however, the Jesuits came under increasing pressure for their political scheming and were caricatured by the philosophes and others as enemies of progress. When the opportunity arose various governments took the opportunity of expelling them; the Portuguese dictator Pombal took the lead in 1759 and the Jesuits were subsequently expelled from France in 1765, Spain in 1766 and the Kingdoms of Naples and Parma in 1767. Finally, in 1773, Pope Clement XIV bowed to international pressure from the Catholic rulers and suppressed the order. There is no doubt that this was a huge blow to the papacy and to the power of the Catholic Church in general; not only did the church lose its most potent force for direct political influence, but it also lost the most effective intellectual weapon it possessed, namely the Jesuit dominance of education. The suppression of the order caused a vacuum in education in Catholic countries – a vacuum which the philosophes and others were quite willing to fill with their own Lockean view that the mind was a blank page ready to receive information more useful than that provided by the Jesuits.

But if the Jesuits were far from being the friends of the philosophes, they were not alone in their opposition to much of the new thinking. There were of course thinkers who did not share the central tenets of Enlightenment thought. For example Vico's emphasis on the historical and cultural characteristics of societies highlighted the difference between them, in contrast to the more usual Enlightenment tendency to seek universal laws which could be applied to all people, places and times. Vico was not very influential during his lifetime, but the views he held were shared by others to a greater or lesser degree; for example David Hume's empirical critique of the pretensions of rationalism and the development in Germany in the later part of the eighteenth century of a more individualistic, emotive and particularist view of society and the human person, led by writers and thinkers such as Goethe, Herder, Hamann and Schiller show that there was not one simple and uniform concept of 'Enlightenment' which ran unchallenged throughout the whole period.

Then, after the French Revolution and the mayhem which followed, there was no shortage of minor commentators who were prepared to associate the Enlightenment and the philosophes as individuals with the catastrophic events in France in the 1790s, often choosing to portray the revolution as a plot organized by the philosophes and their masonic friends. Of more serious note were the conservative political commentators such as Edmund Burke (1729–97) and Joseph de Maistre (1753–1821) who, rightly or wrongly and in their different ways, saw an unquestionable connection between the revolution and Enlightenment ideas such as universal reason, individual rights, liberty of thought and political innovation.

In his prescient and influential *Reflections on the Revolution in France* (1790), which owes much of its fame to its correctly forecasting the 'terror' and eventual dictatorial rule for France, Burke defended the compromises of the British form of government against the revolutionary destruction perpetrated on the old regime. He spoke eloquently in favour of what he called 'prejudices', that is beliefs, customs and practices which have worked relatively well up to this point and therefore should not be discarded overnight. In his pragmatic conservatism he saw religion as one of the foundations of a stable society; in England, said Burke, 'We are not the converts of Rousseau; we are not the disciples of Voltaire; Helvetius has made no progress among us. Atheists are not our preachers; madmen are not our lawgivers.'[8] While this was a conservative vision it was never a reactionary one. Burke was in favour of progress, but not at the expense of what was valuable in the past; he was in favour of political change (he backed self-determination for Ireland, India and the American colonies) but only through careful and considerate policy; and he was in favour of reason, but only if it was devoid of ideology and not destructive of that which experience has shown to be of value.

De Maistre was an even more vociferous critic of Enlightenment thought. In his view the French Revolution was precipitated by the abandonment of the Christian foundations of social harmony and the idealization of an impossibly optimistic concept of reason. Human beings are far from rational and talk of reason only serves to attribute to them qualities which they do not possess. In this less than optimistic vision a state of war is what is closest to the reality of human relations and therefore a strong hand is needed to keep our destructive natures in check. The foundation of such control in de Maistre's view is religion in the form of papal absolutism which rests on its own claims to authority and not on the spurious claims of reason, which only encourages critique, thereby undermining the very thing which it purports to uphold. The best form of government to complement papal spiritual power is monarchism, which unlike republicanism does not seek to justify itself before the court of reason nor submit itself to the judgment of the masses.

If theorists such as Burke and de Maistre saw in the Enlightenment the seeds of revolutionary destruction, they tended to overestimate the direct impact of the new thinking on political reality, for the Enlightenment thinkers themselves had no easy passage to influence and power. In France in particular there was strict censorship which attempted to control anything which could prove inimical to the interests of the state or the church. The state was not liable to invite criticism and the church was protective of its traditional role in the control of thought; between the official censors (of whom there were over two hundred) and the theology faculty at the Sorbonne the monarchy and the church ensured that there was little proliferation of dangerous ideas. This was especially true in the later part of the seventeenth century and the early part of the eighteenth century during the reign of Louis XIV.

After the exodus of thousands of Huguenot refugees to England and especially to the Dutch Republic the more liberal laws of these countries on freedom of speech saw a flood of anti-French and anti-Catholic writings surface clandestinely in France. French authors with something provocative to say soon took advantage of the proximity of a nearby source of uncensored publishing houses and it became common practice to have potentially dangerous books published in Holland; this also served their vanity in that it avoided, albeit at the price of anonymity, the stigma that any book which had the censor's *imprimatur* was merely the mouthpiece of officialdom. Some enterprising French publishers, keen both to preserve their trade and avoid closure by the authorities, took the clever and prudent step of indicating on the fly-leaf of some titles not 'Paris' but 'Amsterdam' or 'The Hague' as the place of publication.

These broadsides found a ready audience, particularly among the increasingly prosperous and literate bourgeoisie – the traders, lawyers, merchants, and intelligentsia of the towns, who were eager for new sources of knowledge and ideas. The eighteenth century saw a considerable growth in literacy and this required a corresponding increase in publications. The breadth of publications was impressive: religious works ranging from theology to devotional prayers, practical handbooks, travel literature telling of the wonders of far-off places, romances, scientific treatises, pornography, books on magic and on agriculture fed the curiosity of the century for ideas old and new. As the eighteenth century progressed the numbers of scientific and literary books increased as the numbers of religious works decreased. While much of this was of no direct harm to the authorities the censors found it increasingly difficult to keep up with the proliferation of books, newspapers, almanacs and pamphlets which were being churned out. Eventually, censorship became as much impractical as it was undesirable.

It was also common practice to circulate dangerous material privately; among the middle- and upper-classes this material often took the form of atheistic philosophy or political treatises (the works of Spinoza, for example, being a favourite); among the lower classes it was often in the form of personalized attacks on some local notable such as the bishop or tax-farmer (the government tax-collector). Many leading authors – including Diderot, d'Holbach and Voltaire – made use of this underground method to vent ideas which they did not dare express in public and much energy was expended in speculating on the true authorship of this or that tract. Sometimes lenient censors combined the occasional clampdown to show their serious intent with an otherwise quite lenient regime; in France the most influential censor in this regard was Malesherbes (censor from 1750–63) whose tolerance greatly aided the publication of Diderot's *Encyclopédie* (see Chapter 6).

The rise in numbers of publications helped to create a sphere of public discourse which neither state nor church was able to control. There was an increase in public libraries and reading clubs which facilitated access to books for those who previously could not afford them; even the eighteenth century's favourite beverage, coffee, played its part through the provision of reading material in cafés. The new, if not yet quite reputable, profession of journalism emerged and the public at large became much better informed about the wider world beyond their own locality.

It was therefore inevitable in this situation that the role of the church as the main locus of intellectual authority would diminish, especially among those who were thirsty for new ideas. In the eighteenth century it became possible for the ordinary person who was literate to have a personal view on subjects that were previously considered fixed for all time. Is this age better than all previous ages? Does God really exist? Can an atheist be a moral person? What is the best form of government? Are human beings naturally evil or naturally good? These and myriad other questions became matters for discussion and were no longer considered to be topics fit only for the learned theologians to solve in their own time and manner.

The country where those with Enlightenment sympathies achieved greatest political success with the least violence was the United States. Many of the major figures of the American Revolution and its aftermath – most prominently Benjamin Franklin (1706–90), Thomas Paine (1737–1809) and Thomas Jefferson (1743–1826), all three of whom spent considerable time in France – were men deeply involved in the spirit and thinking of the age. To take Franklin as an example: the politician, inventor, writer, publisher, and many other things besides was for eleven years before the French Revolution the American ambassador to Paris. In religion he quickly moved away from the Calvinism in which he was raised, thinking (like many of his contemporaries) that its rejection of good works was inimical to morality. Franklin was for a while a deist, but eventually he settled for a sort of benign and sceptical indifference in religious matters. Despite his friendship with many of the leading French thinkers of the time, he never developed the warlike attitude to religion which was the characteristic stance of the philosophes. Franklin's generosity of spirit is demonstrated by an incident recounted by J. R. Pole which occurred during the American War of Independence and when Franklin was the American envoy in Paris. At the time France had joined the war on the American side; when news came that the great explorer Captain James Cook's ship was returning from the Pacific, Franklin agreed with his French counterpart that she would not be attacked due to the benefits her discoveries would bring for all civilized nations, including those currently at war. Even the spoils of battle could sometimes come second to the growth of knowledge.[9]

There is no doubt that Franklin's relaxed attitude to religion was due mostly to his own character, but we must also take into account the fact that the American situation was quite different from that of France. As Pole points out, in America the leading Enlightenment thinkers were themselves part of the establishment and therefore, unlike in France, the achievements of the American Enlightenment 'never resulted from serious conflict with political or ecclesiastical authority'.[10] This meant that rather than opposing power like so many of their European counterparts, the leading figures of the American Enlightenment sought to gain it: one only has to recall, for example, that Thomas Jefferson became both President of the American Philosophical Society and President of the Union. Pole further highlights the fact that American desires for freedom and independence in politics and religion have very deep roots and cannot be viewed simply as products of Enlightenment thinking, and European thinking at that.

As in the case of France, the relationship between Enlightenment thought and American political revolution is not at all one of cause and effect: the American desire for independence from British colonial rule found a supporting rationale in many Enlightenment ideals but was also inspired by the example of England's own political settlement of the seventeenth century and by that particular American search for freedom which had sent the colonists westward in the first place. And for those Europeans who too quickly assume that the French Revolution was the fulfilment of Enlightenment ideals, it is sobering to recall that the American Revolution took place thirteen years earlier and owed comparatively little to those ideals.

In his book, *The Enlightenment in America*, Henry F. May argues that the American Enlightenment cannot be understood apart from the dominant religious context in which it took place and which framed its development, namely, Protestant Christianity. The American Enlightenment, says May, is so closely bound up with Protestantism that in the American context one cannot write about the

Enlightenment *and* religion but only about the Enlightenment *as* religion. Considered from this perspective as religion May offers a simple and straightforward definition of Enlightenment, contained in two propositions: 'first, that the present age is more enlightened than the past; and second, that we understand nature and man best through the use of our natural faculties.'[1] His intention with this sparse definition is to exclude from the definition of Enlightenment those who would look beyond our 'natural faculties' for guidance (to tradition, revelation or some other source).

May sees four phases in the American Enlightenment: (1) The Moderate Enlightenment (1688–1787) which mirrored the reasonableness of early eighteenth century England, (2) The Sceptical Enlightenment (1750–89) which was influenced by Voltaire and Hume but which had much less impact in America than in Europe, (3) The Revolutionary Enlightenment (1776–1800) influenced by Montesquieu, Rousseau, Paine and other radical critics of monarchy and oligarchy, and (4) The Didactic Enlightenment (1800–15), which saw the consolidation of Enlightenment ideas and their influence on the nineteenth century. Although such divisions are always somewhat arbitrary, they can be useful in helping to clarify the development of ideas and the origins of political and religious thought through the different reactions which Enlightenment thought gave rise to in the course of the eighteenth century. It hardly needs to be pointed out that these phases did not follow in a neat linear progression, nor that there were often tensions between them. For example, the natural political caution of the Moderate Enlightenment came into play in the period following the French Revolution as fear of radical Enlightenment ideas grew. Space does not allow me to treat the different phases of the American Enlightenment in depth, so I shall restrict treatment to some general points.

The foundation of American Enlightenment thought was the Moderate Enlightenment, which was imbued with the spirit of Newton, Locke and Samuel Clarke. English-speaking Americans were in the main as widely read as their counterparts in England and their reactions to the achievements of Newton and Locke were much the same: they believed in a rational universe, in the value of reason and the benefits of education; they mistrusted extremes, particularly enthusiasm in religion, and looked to the rational theology of Clarke and others for a religion which could co-exist with the new learning. The crowning achievement of the Moderate Enlightenment was the American Constitution which enshrined the principle that there must be complete separation between church and state. Many of the framers of the constitution – among them the third and fourth presidents, Thomas Jefferson and James Madison (1751–1836) – saw the separation of church and state not as a tactic to negate the influence of religion on American life but as essential to the true possibility of religious freedom, the alternative being a limited form of toleration which would vary from state to state depending on which denomination was in the majority.

But, as May points out, the Constitution did not push the Enlightenment ideal as far as it could and it reflects one of the failures of this phase of the Enlightenment in America, namely the belief that all issues could be settled by compromise between reasonable people. The major issue which the Constitution sidestepped was slavery. It was evident to many that there was a conflict between slavery and the professed ideal of liberty and freedom for all, for one person's liberty to produce cotton at the lowest possible price might mean another person's slavery. If the Constitution proclaimed that life, liberty and the pursuit of happiness were 'self-evident' truths – pointedly avoiding any recourse to grounding these truths in a detailed biblical or theological argument – it remained to be determined precisely *who* was considered worthy of such freedom. But because so many of the founders and first leaders of the new nation were both Enlightenment sympathizers *and* slave owners, it was not them but radical and dissenting Christians (Quakers, Methodists and others) who continued to fight the battle for total emancipation in the period from the Revolution to the Civil War.

As in the case of Europe it needs to be emphasized that Enlightenment thought in America had to co-exist with strains of thought which someone like Benjamin Franklin would have considered far from enlightened. While the Sceptical Enlightenment had its adherents among the intelligentsia, and orthodox divines railed in their sermons and theological papers against backsliders such as deists and Arminians, there were those who felt that Christianity itself was in need of less cold rationality and more spiritual commitment. In the first half of the eighteenth century the revivalism of Jonathan Edwards

(1703–58), beginning in the mid-1730s, led to the Great Awakening, an eruption of Protestant enthusiasm which flourished mainly among the rural poor.

Edwards, George Whitfield, Gilbert Tennent and others deemed the complacency of the Episcopal (Anglican) establishment as nothing less than religious indifferentism and they bemoaned what they saw as the weakness of the faith of their own flocks. Their emphasis on personal commitment and inward faith demonstrated through vibrant outward expression was one of the aspects of religion which the cool detachment of the Enlightenment ideal found most repugnant; here, if more evidence was needed, was another clear incidence of Hume's contention that human beings are governed by their passions much more than by their reason. The drama between fundamental American Enlightenment ideals and revivalist Christianity continues to be played out in American public life to this day, in such conflicts as the question of prayer in schools (separation of church and state) and the teaching of evolution (priority of science over revealed truth).

The examples of Britain, France, Austria and the United States show clearly that there was no simple unified 'Enlightenment' which was developed by philosophers and then applied as a form of medicine to cure the ills inflicted on state, society or religion by the delusions of the past. The Enlightenment could only emerge in context and as the context varied from nation to nation and from culture to culture it was inevitable that different concerns would come to the fore in different places and that the Enlightenment would emerge in manifold form. This fact which we can assert with so much confidence points to a tension inherent in the origins of the Enlightenment, for the thinker who stands at the gateway to enlightenment, the first modern 'man of reason', was deeply and earnestly suspicious of context, diversity of culture and the changes wrought by the passing of history. For René Descartes our path to error begins in our inability to perceive that there is only one map of reason and only one way to read it.

3

God and the Clarity of Reason:
René Descartes

René Descartes, often referred to as 'the father of modern philosophy', was born near Poitiers in France on 31 March 1596 in a small village which now bears his name. His family were well-off without being wealthy, and when Descartes' father died René sold his inheritance and funded his scientific and philosophical work from the proceeds. Although French and Catholic, Descartes spent most of his working life in the more liberal surroundings of Protestant Holland, one of the few places in seventeenth-century Europe where adequate intellectual freedom was allowed. Perhaps only in Holland could a thinker such as Descartes steer a narrow course through the Scylla of Catholic scholastics on the one hand and the Charybdis of Calvinist theologians on the other, each of whom embroiled the peace-loving Descartes in controversy on the grounds of deviation from their own particular theological and philosophical orthodoxies.

The importance of Descartes for the development of modern religious thinking is twofold. First, as we shall see, his own philosophical ideas had direct bearing on subsequent Christian theology, its foundations, its content and its relation to other forms of thought. Secondly, Descartes was the originator not only of the philosophical procedure known as *rationalism*, but also of a broader mode of intellectual investigation which went well beyond anything he himself had envisaged and contributed significantly to the development of modern, critical means of thinking. These consequences of Descartes' thought are not without a certain irony, for Descartes himself was a conventional religious believer who went to great lengths not to offend against religious orthodoxy or enter into controversy with theologians.

Descartes' intellectual achievement and his influence on subsequent thought can only be understood by reference to the dominant philosophy and theology of the time, namely scholasticism, a philosophical and theological system which developed from the 'schools' of scholars formed in association with the developing European universities in the twelfth and thirteenth centuries. Scholastic thought in philosophy, theology and the natural sciences owed a great deal to the use of the thought of Aristotle in the context of Christian theology; it had dominated European intellectual life – particularly in Catholic countries – since the thirteenth and fourteenth centuries. Scholastic thinking relied heavily on the quotation of authorities and at its best, as in the enormous achievements of Thomas Aquinas and Bonaventure in the thirteenth century, it had contributed greatly to the resurgence of intellectual life in Europe and to the growth of the universities. While its dominance had been weakened since the fifteenth century and the rise of Renaissance humanism, the Roman Catholic Church continued to value scholastic theology as its 'in house' style, so to speak, and in the post-Reformation climate of entrenchement it was not open to new developments and the official endorsement of Aristotle remained in place. By the beginning of the seventeenth century therefore, scholasticism had degenerated into a stagnant orthodoxy which was ill-equipped to cope with the revolution in thought which was about to take place.

The young Descartes was educated from the age of ten by the Jesuits at their recently-founded college at La Flèche. In his final years there he was taught philosophy, physics and mathematics (the latter broadly interpreted to include not only geometry and arithmetic but also music and astronomy), with a curriculum which depended heavily on the works of Aristotle. Descartes was later to show an ambivalent attitude towards this education, rejecting the scholastic method but acknowledging the grounding in many fields (particularly mathematics) which he had received. Despite his rejection of most of Aristotelian thought and the genuinely revolutionary character of his philosophical programme, Descartes' thinking and terminology remained indebted to the scholastics. Thus he stands as a bridge between two intellectual eras; it was his attempt to do away with the prevailing methods of scientific and philosophical analysis and start afresh from new foundations which gave him his distinctive place in the history of thought.

On leaving La Flèche, Descartes studied law at the University of Poitiers, graduating in 1616. He then abandoned formal academic life for most of his twenties, joining the Dutch and Bavarian armies as a means of, as he put it, reading 'the great book of the world'. There is no evidence to suggest that his military career was anything other than that of a gentleman accompanying the army, particularly in the light of his habit (ostensibly for health reasons) of lying in bed reading until midday.

During a winter lull in fighting in 1619, near the town of Ulm in southern Germany, Descartes had an insight which was to change not only his own life but the future course of Western thought (although Descartes presented this insight as having the character of a sudden revelation, it was actually the product of many years' reflection). In his *Discourse on the Method* (his first published work) Descartes describes how he was resting in a small heated room with no 'cares or passions' to trouble him so that he was completely free to occupy himself with his own thoughts. Reasoning from some (dubious) historical examples Descartes concluded that it is permissible for an individual to sweep away completely all the opinions he had held up to that time in order to direct his life better than if he had relied on the opinions given to him in his youth, opinions whose truth he had not fully investigated.

The radical nature of this view in the context of the authority-based thinking of the time cannot be underestimated. Descartes wished to wipe the slate clean and write everything anew. In a world riddled with error, change and conflict it must be possible to say that something is certain; despite the vicissitudes of history, the tensions between cultures and the differences of opinion between individuals and schools of thought there must be one truth and one path to that truth. Descartes is bewitched by the Platonic dream: to cut through the world of change and discover behind it some absolute point of reference, some Archimedean point by which the whole world can be moved. In the *Discourse* Descartes warns that he is not advocating a method for everyone to follow, but this modesty should be understood as part of his natural reticence to engage in public debate; he wanted to discover a method by which all knowledge could be established and the clean, bright room of reason swept clear of the cobwebs of culture, authority and history. His diffidence also indicates that he was already aware that his method of philosophizing constituted a radical departure from established norms and would most likely be the object of much criticism.

Part of Descartes' desire to place his own thoughts about the world on a more sure foundation than the opinions he had been given appears to have its origin in the experiences of his travels. In the *Discourse* he engages in a rudimentary form of cultural comparison when he observes that those of a different culture are not necessarily barbarians and that the same individual could become quite different if raised in another culture; and he casts a cold eye on the passing vagaries of fashion which makes something that was acceptable in the past and will be again in the future appear ridiculous to contemporary taste. He does not allow philosophers to escape, saying that even as a young student he was aware that there was no idea so strange or incredible that it was not held by some thinker or other. Descartes is here raising a very modern issue, which has been in dispute among philosophers and theologians since: if what is regarded as true varies over time and between cultures then how can we be certain that there is any truth at all which could transcend the cultural and temporal limitations of our own time, place and language? It is this question which raises the issue of relativism and has so many consequences in any branch of scientific investigation – such as philosophy, theology, ethics, political science, etc. – which seeks answers to the most important questions of human life

Descartes' proposed solution in the *Discourse* to what he regards as the problem of uncertainty begins with the establishment of four rules of procedure which he thinks can be followed in any pursuit of know-ledge. These are: (1) 'never to accept anything as true if I did not have evident knowledge of its truth ... and to include nothing more in my judgments than what presented itself to my mind so clearly and so dis-tinctly that I had no occasion to call it into doubt'; (2) 'to divide each of the difficulties I examined into as many parts as possible'; (3) 'to direct my thoughts in an orderly manner, by beginning with the simplest and most easily known objects in order to ascend little by little, step by step, to knowledge of the most complex'; and, (4) 'to make enumerations so complete, and reviews so comprehensive, that I could be sure of leaving nothing out.'[1] While Descartes' aim was to achieve for philosophy the clarity of geometry, which he saw as a model for all scientific investigation, these rules in themselves indicate no unique methodological principles; indeed they appear to be the epitome of commonsense.

The heart of the Cartesian (from *Cartesius*, the Latin form of Descartes) method is contained in the injunction in the first rule to accept as true only that which is so clear and distinct that it cannot be doubted. That this activity of doubting and the search for a clear and distinct foundation for knowledge is carried on by the lone individual, independent of all authority or coercion, is one of the most innovative things in Descartes' thought; it influenced not only the major philosophers after Descartes but also the popular assumption in the West that each of us must search out and determine the truth for ourselves. In recognizing the centrality of the method of doubt in Descartes' thought, however, it is important to note that he was not a sceptic; his method of doubting was a heuristic device by means of which he could lay down the foundations which would overcome scepticism. Indeed Descartes came in for intense criticism from many for not taking the challenge of scepticism seriously enough, for example, in not realizing that deciding to doubt everything is itself a form of belief (to be really radical one would have to doubt the method of doubt).

But Descartes was not unduly concerned with scepticism because he thought that there was somewhere where scepticism was ineffective, namely mathematics. It was in the clarity of mathematical formulation that Descartes sought the model for the 'clear and distinct' ideas which he required. In Descartes' view, the disputes, arcane terminology, obfuscations and confusions of scholasticism were due to lack of clarity in the language and concepts used. In mathematics, on the other hand, conclusions followed from premises which could be universally agreed, and as the premises were certain the correct procedure from them would ensure that the conclusions too were completely reliable. But what if the certainties of mathematics could be achieved in other areas as well? What if one could devise a method which would prove effective in all rational investigation? Then all the commentaries on commentaries which served as authoritative sources, all the products of fancy and imagination, all useless hypotheses and unproven guesses would be swept away and nothing would remain except pure, clear knowledge. In Descartes' brave new world the problem of the grounds of all knowledge can be solved by following a model of mathematical reasoning.

Descartes' desire, then, is not simply to find the solution to this or that problem, but to find a method which would, in theory at least, allow us to solve all problems. Later in the *Discourse* (Part IV), he asserts the principle indicated by the first rule, namely that it is necessary to doubt everything in order to establish knowledge. But if everything is in doubt how then can we be sure of anything? Descartes' path back from the edge of this epistemological precipice entails his most famous philosophical principle. He contends that while he was trying to think of everything as false, he realized that it was necessary that the 'I' who was doubting was something (on the basis that the doubting of everything cannot be done by nothing). Thus he concludes that the foundation of all philosophy is the principle 'I am thinking, therefore I exist' (*Je pense, donc je suis*).

This principle is best known in its Latin form, *Cogito ergo sum* (or simply as the *Cogito*). Descartes was not the first to suggest a form of argument for one's existence based on some indubitable principle of reason. St Augustine had put forward a similar view in *The City of God*, on the principle *fallor ergo sum* ('I err, therefore I am'). What makes Descartes' project unique is that his principle grounds a scientific project which moves outward from one epistemological principle to engage all knowledge under the umbrella of a method. The Cartesian *Cogito* is not simply an existential perspective on one's own being but also a statement about how scientific investigation should be carried on.

The clearest exposition of the principle is to be found in Descartes' most important work, the *Meditations on First Philosophy* (although it does not use the Latin formulation *Cogito ergo sum* directly). There he addresses in six 'meditations' (i.e. thought experiments) the nature of the foundations of knowledge, the existence of God, the idea of an external world and other questions. In the First Meditation, proceeding with the method of doubt outlined in the *Discourse*, Descartes describes in vivid detail the prospect that everything that he thinks he knows to be true is in fact illusion. He says that he believed many things in childhood which turned out to be false; now, sitting by the fire in his dressing-gown he recalls that he has sometimes dreamt about sitting by the fire in his dressing-gown, so how does he know that this is the reality and not the dream? Assuming that he is dreaming – and everything around him is an illusion – he nevertheless asserts that there are some things of which he can be certain, and these exist in the realm of geometry and mathematics (e.g. the mathematical principles that two and three make five and that a square always has four sides are true whether or not he is awake or asleep). But can he confirm the certainty of geometry and mathematics? Pushing the method of doubt even further, he wonders whether God, who is all-powerful, has so arranged things that he is mistaken even about these apparently certain things. Descartes states that God's goodness precludes such deception, but there may be a 'malicious demon' as powerful as God, but less good, who has deceived him about everything – sky, air, earth, colours, shapes, sounds, etc. may all be illusions created by this demon.

We should not be misled here by the mythological, devil-like qualities of Descartes' 'deceiver', for the salient point is not the nature of the deceiver but the fact that doubt can be pushed to such an extreme that the very existence of the most basic characteristics of reality can be made problematic. Descartes finishes the First Meditation with the poignant thought that if he is dreaming a world in which things seem real, it is more bearable than the 'real' world in which he knows that all is illusion. He fears waking up to a nightmare.

At the start of the Second Meditation Descartes feels as if he is drowning in doubt. Changing the metaphor, he longs for a single point of certainty akin to the fixed and immovable point of Archimedes which would enable him to move the world. Where is this point to be found? – of course in the very fact that there is something (René Descartes) which is being deceived by this demon. If a demon is deceiving him then he must exist, for if he did not exist he could not be deceived. Therefore, concludes Descartes, the proposition 'I am, I exist' must be true at any time when he puts it forward or conceives it in his mind. There is an immediately apparent difficulty with this assertion – namely the question of how the assertion that 'I am, I exist' follows reasonably from the assertion that I am thinking – as it is by no means apparent how Descartes makes thinking a clear and distinct certainty in the first place.[2]

But this difficulty notwithstanding, if at this point we stay with Descartes' thought experiment, we can see that to establish the certainty of an 'I' that thinks is by no means to establish the certainty of the other factors we normally associate with a person (e.g. a body,

interaction with a world, knowledge of others). Descartes acknow-
ledges this and restricts his certainty to the fact that he thinks. In a
famous passage in the Second Meditation he explains what he means
by thinking: 'But what then am I? A thing that thinks. What is that? A
thing that doubts, understands, affirms, denies, is willing, is unwilling,
and also imagines and has sensory perceptions.'[3] So thinking is more
than raw rationality; it involves a number of activities such as imagin-
ing and willing, and the reference to 'sensory perceptions' would
seems to indicate the union of mind and body. (A little earlier in the
Second Meditation Descartes had said that he is 'only' a thing that
thinks. The *non-sequitur* involved in moving from the claim that I am
a thing that thinks to the claim that I am 'only' a thinking thing did
not appear to worry Descartes unduly, although he was aware of the
objection.)

Despite this relatively broad definition of what it means to think, it
is important to note that Descartes still maintained that certainty
could only be established by finding something *a priori* in the mind.
He rejected totally the scholastic dictum that 'there is nothing in the
mind which was not first in the senses'. Descartes thinks that if this
were the case then we could never be sure of anything, given how
unreliable the senses are and given the great multiplicity of interpretations which people place on the data which they receive through the
senses. This was the problem which was so to worry Hume when,
following Locke, he rejected innate ideas but realized with Descartes
that sensory perception offers us no certainty, and it was the problem
to which Kant was to offer such a brilliant solution (see Chapter 9).
For Hume and the other empiricists of the eighteenth century the
scholastics were correct in their emphasis on knowledge coming
through the senses, but for them this was precisely the problem, for
how then could the 'I' be anything other than in Hume's words, 'a
bundle of perceptions'? So, when Descartes says that thinking
includes sensory perception, he is admitting that the senses play an
important role in what this 'I' is, but they can never give us any
certainty about the way things are. Such certainty only comes through
the *Cogito*, that is through establishing that the core of the thinking 'I'
is independent of all sensory perception.

Having gone some considerable way towards ascertaining what constitutes this 'I', in order to make further progress in his search for

knowledge Descartes is now faced with what has become one of the fundamental questions of modern epistemology: how does one move from the certain knowledge of one's own existence to the certain knowledge that the world which I perceive is really the world as it is? We could put this another way: I am certain that I experience something, but this only means that I am certain of myself as experiencing. I have no guarantee that what I am experiencing is a true reflection of reality outside myself. It is the search for certain knowledge of things other than the thinking 'I' which turns Descartes' attention to God.

Descartes is now in a position where, to obtain certainty of anything outside himself, he must proceed solely from the contents of his own consciousness. The way he chooses to do this is to get rid of the hypothetical demon and to establish the existence of a non-deceiving God who can ground the reality of the world outside the mind of the individual. At first this appears a simple and profitable manoeuvre. However, as we shall see, it raises some of the most serious difficulties for Cartesian epistemology and for theological thinking.

In his Third Meditation Descartes re-affirms his certainty of his own existence: let the demon deceive him about the reality of the world outside his mind, but of the reality of his own thinking self he is unshaken. However, the doubt about the nature and reality of things outside the mind remains. This can only be removed totally by enquiring whether there is a God; and if there is a God, knowing whether or not God is a deceiver. Descartes offers two arguments for the existence of God, one in the Third Meditation and one in the Fifth.[4] In between these arguments, in the Fourth Meditation, he establishes that God cannot be a deceiver.

The argument for the existence of God in the Third Meditation rests on a much disputed argument from causality. In its form and content the argument draws upon scholastic modes of thought. In a nutshell the argument rests on the claim that God's existence is necessary to explain the presence within us of the idea of God. The premise of the argument is that the content of each idea within the mind must have a cause, otherwise it would come from nothing, and this is impossible. Some ideas are innate (e.g. thought itself), some come from outside me (e.g. sounds) and some are the product of my imagination (e.g. mythological creatures). But the idea of God belongs in a special category of its own. Descartes reasons that when he considers all the perfections of God he cannot conceive that these per fections come solely from his own, imperfect, mind. Nevertheless he does have within him an idea of God. Employing the double principle that something cannot come from nothing and that the more perfect (God) cannot come from the less perfect (the human mind), Descartes concludes that the idea of God within us must have as its cause a truly existing God who possesses all the perfections which we consider God to have. As Descartes puts it graphically, the idea of God within us is like the mark of a craftsman stamped on the work. The weaknesses in this argument, as was pointed out by contemporaries of Descartes, are that things may have causes which are not necessarily more perfect than themselves and that the notion of causality may be applicable to events in the physical world but cannot be transferred directly into the world of thoughts.

In the Fifth Meditation Descartes presents his second argument for the existence of God. It takes a form which, since Kant, has been called 'the ontological argument'. The argument is so-called because it proceeds from the definition of the being of God and what is proper to the essence of that being; hence the ontological argument is an *a priori* argument, resting as it does on concepts and not on our experience. The ontological argument follows the rationale that the essence of God, by definition, includes all perfections and attributes. Among these attributes is the attribute of existence; therefore, it is impossible to think of God without thinking of God existing. As Descartes puts it, one can no more think of God without existence than one can think of a triangle without three angles which make up two right angles.

The type of 'ontological' argument for God's existence did not originate with Descartes. It had been developed in its most famous form by St Anselm in the eleventh century. Anselm had argued that God, a being than which nothing greater can be thought (*aliquid quo nihil maius cogitari possit*), must exist in reality as well as in thought, otherwise the definition implies a contradiction in that if such a being lacked existence it could not satisfy the terms of its own definition. The argument in this form was rejected by Thomas Aquinas, principally on the grounds that the argument simply establishes a logical connection between the concept of a supreme being and the concept of existence; it says nothing about the real existence of such a being. Although Descartes' form of the ontological argument is not identical to that of Anselm, the Thomistic objection to Anselm was put forward by Descartes' scholastic opponents and he never responded to it in a satisfactory way.

We shall return to the ontological argument in connection with its most effective opponent, Kant. With Descartes, however, what is of most importance is not the specifics of his arguments for God's existence, but rather the way in which he uses God in his epistemology. We recall that Descartes requires a bridge to enable him to proceed from certainty of his own mind to certainty about the external world. For Descartes God is this bridge; he wishes to proceed from certainty of himself to certainty of God to certainty of the external world. The fulcrum of this movement is that the existence of God can be established, and once God's existence is certain we can see that God is perfect. Therefore we are not being deceived by God about the external world when we perceive that world 'clearly and distinctly'. This is argued by Descartes in the Fourth Meditation: if we make mistakes in knowledge it is because we have misused our own free will and not followed adequately the four rules; we must restrain ourselves and accept as true only that which is really clear and distinct.

So what is it in the world that we can perceive most 'clearly and distinctly'? The most fundamental truths about the external world are those expressed by geometry and mathematics (on the grounds that the essence of matter is extension and this is expressed by geometry). Whereas in the First Meditation Descartes had posited the existence of a demon who might deceive him even in simple addition, he has now established the existence of a non-deceiving God who guarantees these 'clear and distinct perceptions'.

On these grounds Descartes now makes a remarkable and consequential claim for God: all knowledge which is true depends on prior knowledge of God. This claim is entailed logically by Descartes' method of procedure, but it raises the arcane question as to how much then can an atheist really know? Is an atheist who does not know the true God incapable of addition and subtraction? Descartes' reply to this objection seemed to take the form of a distinction between those who had knowledge but no guarantee of its validity (e.g. an atheist scientist) and those who had a certain validation of knowledge (the believer who knew that epistemology depended on the existence of

God). With the benefit of three and a half centuries of hindsight it is difficult for us not to smile at Descartes' scientific naivety. To do so, however, would be to miss the point: the way in which Descartes used God in his epistemology was one of the origins of an issue which had important consequences for Western thought and society. The question of how much an atheist can know is only incidental to the wider question of the relation of religion to science.

Descartes has now used God to establish those things which are outside the mind but which can be known clearly and distinctly. There now appears an immediate and difficult problem, one which was apparent to Descartes' contemporaries. This is the problem of the so-called 'Cartesian circle' and while it is one of the most difficult problems in Cartesian epistemology it can be stated quite simply: if the existence of a non-deceiving God is necessary for us to be certain that our clear and distinct perceptions of an external world are true, how can we be sure of either the existence of God or the certainty of our perceptions since the proofs for God's existence depend on clear and distinct perceptions which have not yet been established? Descartes himself never answered this charge convincingly, but the consequences of the conundrum were important. When God is used this way in the quest for knowledge, two consequences present themselves: (1) the circularity of reasoning is broken and true knowledge is gained without recourse to God; hence science becomes an activity autonomous from God and religion (this is what has actually come to pass); (2) the circularity of all attempts to ground knowledge in a metaphysics of rationality are abandoned and the result is scepticism. Both possibilities came to influence Western thought since Descartes. The sceptical consequence of Descartes' method is well expressed in the entry on Descartes in *The Encyclopedia of Philosophy*: 'The historical significance of this [Descartes' epistemology] is that while Descartes' epistemological problem of "working out" from the data of consciousness remained central, his transcendental solution to it rapidly ceased to carry conviction. This is a primary way in which the Cartesian system, which is in itself a religious and dualistic metaphysics, containing many scholastic elements, was the true ancestor of many later sceptical, subjectivist and idealist developments.'[5]

We could put this another way: after Descartes many thinkers accepted his method of doubt, his individualism and his rationalism;

fewer accepted his arguments for the existence of God or his meta-physical/theological solution to the problem of radical doubt. In terms of his use of God to solve the fundamental problems of epistemology, Descartes' heritage was not his solution but the difficulties which he raised and, perhaps most importantly, the way in which he raised them. His grandiose attempt to ground all knowledge on God was not successful, but in posing the issue as he did he boosted the possibilities for science to exist as an activity autonomous from all theological and ecclesiastical interference. Also, while it is important not to blame Descartes for all that followed after him, it must be acknowledged that in his use of God to ground knowledge he contributed to the alienation of religion from science down to the present day. More optimistically, however, it must also be said that his method of doubt shows us that it is not adequate in any form of scientific investigation (including theology) to rely solely on tradition, enforced authority or mere opinion.

Let us now look at some other aspects of Descartes' thought which are of importance for theological thinking. The most significant of these is the distinction – or, one could say, separation – made by Descartes between mind and body. This is often referred to as the 'real distinction'. We have seen how Descartes reached the conclusion that he exists by recourse to the faculty of thinking. But this 'thing that thinks' (Second Meditation) is quite distinct from the body of René Descartes, for the body is composed of matter and in Cartesian physics the basic characteristic of matter is extension – the mind for Descartes is not something which is extended physically and therefore he concludes that there is a real distinction between mind and body. As Descartes writes in a famous passage in the Sixth Meditation: 'On the one hand I have a clear and distinct idea of myself, in so far as I am a thinking non-extended thing; and on the other hand I have a distinct idea of my body, in so far as this is simply an extended non-thinking thing. And accordingly, it is certain that I am really distinct from my body and can exist without it.'[6] This is as succinct a description of mind-body dualism as one is likely to find; and when present-day commentators refer to dualism they often mean it in this Cartesian sense of the existence of the mind independently of the body.[7]

Descartes' dualism involved a mechanistic view of the living body. He rejected all obscurantist theories which accounted for the movement of matter by means of some 'spirit' or 'force'. Animals were mere machines; only in the case of humans was it necessary to make allowance for a 'soul', but this was to aid explanation of our faculty of reason and not to elucidate the movements of the body. Such reductionism may seem simplistic to us but it can be understood by considering two factors. First, in an age in which physiology and medical science were in their infancy it was a considerable advance to view the functions of the living body as governed by laws and not by some mysterious and ethereal principle (in a similar fashion it was a major medical advance that disease – at one time often viewed as divine punishment for moral laxity – came to be seen as caused by natural processes). Secondly, as the seventeenth century progressed, mechanical inventions became more commonplace and mechanical metaphors were used more widely (for example, only seven years after the death of Descartes, Huygens applied the principle of the pendulum to the clock, thus increasing accuracy and making minute and second hands possible; from now on events could run 'as smoothly as clockwork').

Nevertheless, Descartes' 'real distinction' between mind and body sounds strange to modern ears, knowing what we do of the dependence of consciousness of neural impulses between brain cells. However, even allowing for his understandable ignorance of neurology, Descartes' arguments for the real distinction are not convincing. There is the obvious problem that if I am a thing that thinks, it by no means follows of necessity that I am *only* a thing that thinks. In addition, as one of Descartes' most astute critics, Antoine Arnauld (1612–94), pointed out, the fact that I can truly perceive one thing as distinct from another does not mean that they are in reality independent of each other. Descartes appears to make the error of thinking that because God underwrites our perceptions, a distinction so clearly perceived must, under divine guarantee, be given an absolute status.

The real distinction holds strongly in relation to the cognitive areas of intellect and will, but Descartes allows a closer unity between body and mind when it comes to the senses (pain, hunger, etc.). For example the mind *experiences* pain and does not simply note it in an abstract way. This observation leads Descartes to say that we are not merely *inside* our bodies like a pilot is inside a ship but that we are 'intermingled' with our bodies (Sixth Meditation). Yet it is not clear how the mind can be independent of the body and simultaneously 'intermingled' with it. Here we see a tension in Descartes which was to be reflected in the subsequent course of Enlightenment philosophy – it is the tension between rationalism which gives prominence to that which can be determined by the faculty of reason, and empiricism which gives priority to experience. Descartes is routinely described as a rationalist, but we see here that a project of pure rationalism is very difficult to attain and it is doubtful whether Descartes himself can be counted as a pure rationalist.

Despite these difficulties the ontological distinction between mind and body had a large impact on subsequent thought, in particular the philosophical tradition of German Idealism. The major effect of mind-body dualism was a privileging of the rational, intellectual and abstract over the physical, sensuous and practical. This in turn reinforced the trend in Western thought – a trend which had roots in a particular Christian anthropology – to view the body as the locus of error, weakness and sin. One of the more pernicious consequences of this re-enforcement of mind-body dualism was what Genevive Lloyd has called 'the sexual division of mental labour'.[8] The world of reality is the world of the mind and entry into this world requires education, money and leisure – the prerogatives of the male in a traditional patriarchal society. The male must transcend the realm of the body if he is to know reality; woman, meanwhile, preserves the sensuous world to which the rational male returns for comfort after the hard day's work of thinking. Mind-body dualism is one of the pillars of patriarchy. Once again we must be careful not to lay the blame for this development at the feet of Descartes. In a world in which women were seldom educated or taught Latin (the language of the academy) he himself saw his method as a way of cutting through the intricacies of scholasticism and opening the door to knowledge for everyone; his long correspondence with Princess Elizabeth of Bohemia on philo-sophical matters gives the lie to any anachronistic reading of his thought which would place him among male supremacists. For Descartes reason is universal – it is a faculty of rational woman as much as of rational man.

When Descartes says that he can exist without his body he is of course echoing a doctrine which entered Christian thought through the influence of Greek philosophy, namely the idea of the immortality of the soul – if the real 'I' can exist independently of the body there is no reason to doubt that it can survive the death of the body. There are good reasons to believe that Descartes had in part a theological motivation for holding the mind/soul (he made no distinction between them) to be independent of the body. The first edition of the *Meditations* carried the subtitle, 'in which ... the immortality of the soul is demonstrated'; this was dropped in the second edition, possibly because Descartes was loath to make too many philosophical claims for something which was also a matter of faith. However he dedicated the *Meditations* to the members of the Theology Faculty at the Sorbonne and in his dedicatory letter makes no separation between his attempt to prove the immortality of the soul and his argument that there is a 'real and true distinction between the human soul and the body'.

It is perhaps unimportant whether Descartes' theological or methodological/metaphysical reasons for believing the mind to be independent of the body came first, but is worth noting that the theological and philosophical beliefs appear to support each other – if that which makes my existence certain (mind) is identified with that which is immortal (soul) then there is little reason to doubt that the mind is independent of the body not only after death but before it also. (In his *Synopsis* of the *Meditations* Descartes offered a metaphysical argument for the immortality of the mind/soul based on the scholastic distinction between pure substance and accidents or incidental features. The mind is pure substance – i.e. unchanging – and is therefore immortal.) As Descartes says in the *Discourse* (Part V), he cannot contemplate the possibility that we have as little to fear or hope for after death as do flies and ants.

This question of the theological elements in Descartes' theory of the real distinction between mind and body raises the broader issue of his attitude to theology and the problem of faith and reason. We have already noted that Descartes shunned theological controversy. This can be explained partly but not wholly by his quiet disposition. However, one event early in his intellectual career appears to have had a marked influence on his subsequent attitude to theological controversy. About 1630 he began a work entitled *The World* on the subject of astronomy; in it he agreed substantially with the Copernican theory that the earth revolves around the sun. In 1633 Galileo was condemned by the Pope for teaching the same principle and Descartes immediately dropped plans to publish *The World*. Later, in the *Discourse* (Part V), Descartes refers obliquely to 'certain considerations' which prevented him from publishing *The World*. With tortuous caution he refuses to say that he agrees with the Copernican theory, only that he could find nothing in it – before its condemnation – which was offensive to church or state (Part VI). This fear of official censure from the authorities of the Roman Catholic Church helps account for the clear distinction which, despite his proofs for the existence of God and the immortality of the soul, Descartes maintained between faith and reason. In the third of his *Rules for the Direction of the Mind*, having outlined the rational path to sure knowledge, he then goes on to say that anything not known by the rational method should be considered erroneous and dangerous, *except* matters which have been divinely revealed. The explanation he gives for this disjunction is that matters of faith have to do not with our intelligence (i.e. our reason) but with our will, that is, we can decide to give our assent to something which we do not fully understand.

We have already seen the difficulties Descartes encountered in dealing with the immortality of the soul. Another example shows the difficulty which a seventeenth-century thinker could face in dealing with theological matters from a philosophical perspective. The example in question is that of the Roman Catholic doctrine of the Eucharist. In the dispute with the Reformers over the Eucharist, Catholic doctrine had reaffirmed the mediaeval doctrine of transubstantiation, which defined the belief that Christ was truly present in the consecrated bread and wine, even though the outward appearance of the bread and wine remained unchanged. In the Aristotelian parlance of scholastic thought, the act of consecration changed the 'substance' (i.e. the essence) of the bread and wine while the 'accidents' (i.e. the appearance) remained unchanged.

Now for Descartes the fundamental characteristic of matter is extension (length, breadth, depth); other factors such as weight, texture and colour are not essential to the nature of matter in general. It was pointed out to Descartes by his correspondent and critic Arnauld that such a definition of matter conflicted with the doctrine of transubstantiation. The objection was made on the grounds that if the essence ('substance') of matter is extension, then the bread and wine *after* the Eucharistic consecration still maintain their essential nature (i.e. they undergo no change in extension). But the doctrine is that the essence of the bread and wine *do* change (into the body and blood of Christ); hence Descartes' definition of matter appeared to contradict the doctrine.

Although Descartes thought he could actually defend the doctrine – a concern which brought on him the scorn of the English philosopher Thomas Hobbes, who like Spinoza thought that Descartes only wished to appease the Jesuits – the exact nature of his reply to the objection need not concern us. What is most interesting is why the issue, which appears arcane to many modern ears, was important in the first place. It shows us how closely philosophy was subject to theology and through theology to the Aristotelian philosophy which was then dominant. Discussion of an apparently strictly scientific question such as the properties of matter could be hampered by theological beliefs which relied on a particular philosophical premise. It is characteristic of Descartes' philosophical acumen that he managed, for the most part, to maintain theological orthodoxy while at the same time undermining the Aristotelian/scholastic concepts and categories on which that orthodoxy was based.

Had he been more forthcoming about theological matters and drawn some clearer conclusions from his own philosophical premises his life may not have been as peaceful. In the entrenchment of theology which followed the Reformation and the Catholic reforms made at the Council of Trent, one of the fundamental tests of Catholic loyalty was belief in the Real Presence in the Eucharist – to be seen to undermine this belief philosophically was tantamount to heresy. Such a charge could have had serious negative consequences for Descartes' reputation and career – the shadow of the condemnation of Galileo hung over him. It is therefore not surprising to hear Descartes say that 'it is more satisfactory to have a theology as simple as that of the country folk than one which is plagued with countless controversies, and thus corrupted, opening the way for disputes, quarrels, wars'.[9] Nevertheless, Descartes' works were placed on the *Index* of forbidden books in 1663 and the controversy over the Eucharist continued well after his death, as many of his followers were suspected of holding views contrary to the official doctrine.

Therefore, given the intricate links between philosophy and theology and the ecclesiastical atmosphere of the time, it is not surprising that Descartes maintained a clear demarcation between reason and faith. He often refused to engage in discussion on theological topics which he considered to be beyond the limits of philosophical debate. In the Preface to the French translation of *The Principles of Philosophy* (1644) Descartes outlines five means of acquiring wisdom (four common means and the philosophical path of seeking first principles), but he places divine revelation in a category of its own by saying that it does not lead us step by step (as a philosophical method should) but raises us right away to knowledge of the infallible truth. Not only is there undoubted irony in this theological courtesy, but there is the astute distinction between faith and reason made by a man who knew that his ideas were potentially in conflict with orthodox teaching. In the same Preface Descartes attacks the philosophical principles of Aristotelianism on the grounds that little progress has been achieved in the centuries in which they have been followed. This is a very modern criticism; progress is seen as positive and truth can develop. Such a view could have been interpreted by the scholastic theologians as denying the eternal nature of religious truth; it is again a remarkable achievement of Descartes' that he managed to attack and ultimately undermine the dominance of Aristotelian philosophy without being condemned for heresy during his lifetime.

All of this serves to show the historical importance of Descartes' philosophical project. He presented philosophy, theology and the natural sciences with a new starting-point for knowledge, a new method for attaining knowledge and a whole new set of questions. While his own solutions to his questions were frequently less than convincing, the questions themselves very often endured. Even his opponents were constrained within the boundaries of the issues he raised.

In 1649 Descartes was prevailed upon – against his better instincts – to go to Sweden to give instruction in philosophy to Queen Christina. The Queen set her lessons for 5 a.m., an hour which was still the middle of the night in Descartes' normal routine. Forced to go outdoors in the harsh winter to reach the Royal Palace, Descartes caught what would appear to have been pneumonia. On 11 February 1650 he died, his life's work only partially complete.

Descartes' pioneering work broke apart the scholastic synthesis and created a series of questions in philosophy, theology, physics, geometry and even medicine which were to stimulate many advances made by others. But much of Descartes' own thought did not survive these advances. While in the decades immediately after his death his influence was immense, by the turn of the eighteenth century several central aspects of his thinking were quickly becoming obsolete as others took up the issues he raised and went beyond his solutions. Locke's empirical philosophy dealt a severe blow to rationalism and the theory of innate ideas, and in physics the discoveries of Newton made Descartes appear outdated. In the face of the increasing influence in mainland Europe of English empiricism, some of Descartes' former opponents even adopted him to their own cause.

However, in the intervening period before being claimed by the forces of theological orthodoxy Descartes did have more noteworthy followers (especially in France and Holland) who refined and developed significant aspects of the rationalist project. The most prominent of these was Nicholas Malebranche (1638–1715) who gave his own particular interpretation to the issues raised by Descartes and is also an important thinker in his own right.

Malebranche is best known for the theory of 'occasionalism' which stemmed from the mind-body problem in Descartes' philosophy, but which also has deeper theological connotations. If mind and body are distinct entities – as the Cartesians thought – then how can the mind act on the body at all, or, how can the immaterial mind cause the material body to move? Further, as Arnold Geulincx (1624–69) asked, how can the material body place in an immaterial mind an image or idea of any physical action which occurs? To resolve this problem Malebranche suggested that everything in the world which appears to cause some effect is not the true cause; the true cause of everything is the will of God. So, on occasions when I want to comb my hair or on occasions when the wind blows an apple to the ground, neither my mind nor the wind are the true causes of the effect, neat hair and wind-fall apples. Rather, God is the ultimate cause of everything and in his wisdom he sees to it that on each occasion when I intend to comb my hair this is what happens, and when the wind blows with a certain force we will get apples lying on the ground. Each such event is the occasion of the divine will at work; hence the name of the theory, *occasionalism*.

Malebranche is not asserting – as he is sometimes mistakenly taken to be – that God simply decides on a whim whether or not a particular apple will stay on the tree or fall to the ground, or whether my comb will tidy my hair or jab me in the eye. God shows us his power through general laws which he has prescribed to govern the world and which prevent a chaos in which the mind could understand nothing. But as these laws are put there by God they have no inherent power in themselves. Malebranche's intention here is to give everything which happens in the world a divine foundation; the whole physical world moves according to the divine will. Although it is not theologically heterodox this theory did cause controversy among theologians and further damage Descartes' standing with the Roman Catholic Church (in so far as Malebranche was considered to be his follower), for it clearly contradicts the Aristotelian view, adopted by Aquinas, that each thing holds within it its own particular causality which then produces certain effects proper to that thing's distinctive nature.

By the early part of the eighteenth century, therefore, Descartes – though still revered by many for his victory over scholasticism – was considered to have been mistaken on most of the major points of importance. Voltaire, in his *Letters Concerning the English Nation* (1733), compares Descartes unfavourably with Locke and Newton, maintains that few people in England read him, and that his 'Works indeed are now useless.'[10] Voltaire lists the areas where (he thinks) Descartes was in error; among other things he points to the nature of soul, the proofs for God's existence, the question of matter, the laws of motion, innate ideas and, in general, the nature of man. But, magnanimously for him, Voltaire recognizes that even if Descartes was frequently wrong his mistakes were useful and, in an apt comment on his predecessors, he gave 'sight to the blind'.

Others, even though they were undoubtedly influenced by Descartes, considered him something of a charlatan; Leibniz's view of Descartes could be summarized by saying that he thought him both profound and original, but what was profound was not original and what was original was not profound. In this he was only echoing the many voices who said that most of Descartes' key ideas were borrowed from others, the Greek sceptics, Augustine, Anselm, etc. There is no doubt but that by the middle part of the eighteenth century Descartes' grandiose project was defeated; in natural philosophy by Newton and in his theory of the mind by Locke. What is deeply ironic is that at the time when his thought was being superseded, many of his former enemies (such as the Jesuits at the Sorbonne) found refuge in him as the influence of Locke's empiricism grew and some French philosophers began to toy with theories of materialism.

But while philosophers sought for non-theological explanations of the mind and the basis of knowledge, and theologians looked for ever more subtle ways of defending the rationality of religion, the very premises on which this debate was conducted – namely, the primacy of reason in discussing the matter of religion – found a new and powerful adversary.

4

Burning Faith: Blaise Pascal

By the end of the seventeenth century Descartes' rationalism was challenged in philosophy by the empiricism of Locke, and the advances achieved in physics by Newton and others made much of his speculation redundant. The Enlightenment was carried forward not as the project of pure reason but as a practical project involving an understanding of reason as a tool to aid in the investigation of nature. Hypotheses were now to be judged not primarily by their internal and logical harmony but by their coherence with the observed phenomena. The priority of rational deduction gave way to the priority of investigative technique. Voltaire and other advocates of the new model of reason came to view Descartes as part of the old world of speculation; innate ideas were as dubious as the presence of angels or the existence of the devil. Locke's empiricism turned attention away from the deductive processes of the mind to the human subject as the location of experience and to an emphasis on knowledge of the things of this world.

Empiricism fitted well with the requirements of the new sciences that knowledge was gained through investigation and analysis and in that respect it remained firmly within the 'rational' Enlightenment project. However, from the middle of the eighteenth century a reaction had begun to set in against the way in which both deductive rationalism and inductive empiricism appeared detached from the living concerns, fears and joys of the individual person. Were not love and death as important as discovery and progress; were not impulse and spontaneity as much a part of the human being as detachment and judgment; did not reason often lead up a blind alley? As the Enlightenment was reaching its high-point Jean-Jacques Rousseau, Goethe and others began, in the name of the living, breathing, whole human being, to call into question many of the dominant cultural premises of the age and laid the basis for the later flourishing of romanticism.

In religious thinking, however, there had already occurred a vigorous response against the rational Cartesian project in the years following Descartes' death, a protest which was to endure throughout the Enlightenment as a critique of many of its most cherished assumptions. While Descartes had always had his critics among the scholastic establishment, the most enduring critique of the religious dimensions of his thought came from a troubled young French polymath, Blaise Pascal. Pascal's critique of Descartes and his own anguished formulation of the religious impulse left an abiding legacy to the theological problem of faith and reason, and foreshadowed the existential subjectivism of another tortured religious thinker, Søren Kierkegaard.

On 23 September 1647 the eminent scholar Descartes met the young Pascal in Paris. The occasion of their meeting was a dispute over experiments Pascal had conducted in attempting to prove the existence of the vacuum, a theory which conflicted with aspects of Descartes' metaphysics (Descartes thought that all of the natural world was composed of matter, and that therefore a vacuum was an impossibility). A large number of Parisian scientists and intellectuals attended the meeting but, due to the numbers present and Pascal's already ill-health, little was achieved. The two met again on the following day, but little is known about their conversation. No one could then envisage that the greatest gulf that was eventually to separate them would be found not in the realm of science but rather in Pascal's vigorous reaction to what he saw as the entirely negative consequences for religious faith of Descartes' philosophical method.

At the time of his meeting with Descartes, Pascal was immersed in his scientific work, for which he had shown outstanding aptitude from an early age. Educated by his father, he is reported to have discovered independently (at the age of twelve) many of the propositions of Euclidean geometry. As a teenager he wrote an influential essay on acoustics and in 1642 he invented a calculating machine. He made discoveries in hydraulics, probability theory (possibly an offshoot of his interest in gambling) and physics, eventually establishing the existence of the vacuum. This latter discovery was in conflict not only with the established scientific theory of the time but was also contradictory of the scholastic maxim that 'nature abhors a vacuum'. Pascal's success helped in the development of modern science and in his defence of experimental method he aided the disappearance of the dependence of scientists on the increasingly archaic theories of Aristotle and others. As we shall see, Pascal did not extend this justification of innovation to questions of religion, which he regarded as essentially different from scientific investigation or speculative philosophy. This distinction contributed greatly to his rejection of the Cartesian project.

In studying Pascal it is impossible to isolate his ideas on religion from the events of his own life. Pascal's involvement in what he did was total, and his writings on religion emanated from a total commitment to Christianity born of an intense religious experience. As a young man, however, Pascal showed some ambivalence towards religious matters. When his sister Jacqueline decided to become a nun in the convent at Port-Royal, Blaise objected strongly; this was somewhat surprising given that it was his study of the theological teachings of the Abbé de Saint-Cyran – a follower of the Bishop of Ypres, Cornelius Jansen (1585–1638) – which had first stirred his sister's interest in the convent at Port-Royal. Following his sister's entrance into the convent Pascal joined fully in the vibrant social life of Paris. There he enjoyed not only the pleasures of the good life, showing a particular fondness for gambling, but also came into contact with anti-clericals and freethinkers. Their disregard for conventional religion was influential in his later insistence that people cannot be rationally convinced of the truth of religion, but that they must be shown that it is actually within their interest to believe.

Despite the attractions of his social life, Pascal was never quite at ease with the world of the *salons*, and he yearned for something more profound. His indulgent lifestyle began gradually to disillusion him to the point of disgust and he spent more and more time visiting his sister at Port-Royal. He felt that the world offered nothing of substance yet he was unable to commit himself to God in the way his sister had done.

This situation of spiritual limbo was to change suddenly and dramatically on the night of 23 November 1654. Pascal was caught in a storm in Paris and the experience seems to have given rise to an intense religious experience, the exact nature of which remains a mystery but which lasted about two hours and had the effect of changing him so completely that the remainder of his life was dedicated to the defence of Christianity. Later, alone in his room in the late evening, the intensity of the experience appeared to continue and Pascal wrote down an enigmatic description of his spiritual experience. Our knowledge of the events of that night comes from the tiny piece of parchment on which Pascal recorded his prayerful reaction and which was found sewn into the hem of his coat after his death. Known as the *Mémorial*, it captures some of the intensity of what Pascal experienced: 'From about half past ten at night until a half hour after midnight. FIRE. God of Abraham, God of Isaac, God of Jacob, not of the philosophers and of the learned. Certitude, certitude, feeling, joy, peace. (*God of Jesus Christ*.) God of Jesus Christ ... I am separated from Him, I have fled him, renounced him, crucified Him. Let me never be separated from Him.'[1]

The *Mémorial* is written with an almost hysterical intensity, the words rushing out on to the page to attempt to grasp the depth of the experience. How much further could we be from the rubrics of conventional religious practice or the deliberations of Cartesian philosophy? Pascal's contrast of his own experience with the God 'of the philosophers and of the learned' indicates his own future course of religious writing; his repeated cry of 'certitude' is in sharp contrast to Descartes' methodical search for a certain foundation to knowledge. In the *Mémorial* we see not simply the disjointed account of one man's experience which is ultimately inaccessible to us, but also the presentation of a way of knowing which is not based on the intellect. Pascal's 'certitude' is an existentialist commitment born not of his own strivings but of an encounter which would appear to have come to him from outside himself. Even if one were to consider such 'mystical' experience as illusion or even madness, its reality for Pascal and its impact on his life cannot be denied.

Between his 'conversion' in 1654 and his death in 1662 Pascal became an ardent defender of Christianity, and in particular of the teachings of the Bishop of Ypres, Cornelius Jansen. In 1640 Jansen's work *Augustinus* was published posthumously; it was a Catholic interpretation of Augustine's theology of grace along lines which made it appear as a Catholic form of Calvinism, emphasizing the depravity of the human condition and the overwhelming sovereignty of God's grace. The Jansenists became the bitter enemies of the Jesuits, whose more tolerant stance on moral issues they perceived as laxity and as a form of Pelagianism (the doctrine, opposed and defeated by Augustine, that allows for some human co-operation with God's saving grace). By the time of Pascal's definitive religious experience in November 1654 the convent at Port-Royal had become the centre of Jansen's teaching. Through his sister's influence Pascal became increasingly involved in the growing controversy, as the Jesuits and the theologians at the Sorbonne attempted to have the teachings of Jansen condemned and the convent closed.

In 1653 Pope Innocent X had condemned five theological propositions, stating that they were to be found in the *Augustinus* of Jansen. The leading defender of the Jansenist position, Antoine Arnauld – singularly isolated in the Sorbonne faculty – argued that the propositions were indeed heretical but that they were not to be found in the writings of Jansen. Arnauld was finally condemned by the professors at the Sorbonne in early 1656, and it was at this point that Pascal was approached by his Jansenist allies to respond to the dilemma in which they now found themselves. There followed in quick succession during the winter of 1656–57 the publication of eighteen brilliant polemical letters (written anonymously under the title *Letters written to a friend in the provinces* and now commonly titled *The Provincial Letters*) which ridiculed the Jesuits and the theology professors for their moral laxity and casuistry, while staunchly defending the Jansenist position.

Pascal and the Jansenists despised the Jesuits for the manner in which they appeared to accommodate the harsh requirements of Christianity – as the Jansenists saw it – to the decadent lifestyle of the royal courtiers of Europe. Indeed the Jesuits' closeness to European royalty – a strategy which had been developed in the attempt to keep the princes and kings of Europe within the Roman Catholic fold – had led to a certain amount of moral laxity, in particular through tortuous casuistry which gave the impression of having one moral law for the aristocrats and another for the rest.

Pascal's *Letters* are written with biting wit and irony and their style is a landmark in the development of French prose writing. A brief extract from the fourth letter shows both Pascal's comic brilliance and the ridicule which he poured on Jesuit casuistry. The author of the

Letters is discussing theology with a Jesuit who introduces him to the thoughts of the Jesuit Father Antonio Escobar on the subject of fasting:

> 'But tell me pray', continued the monk, 'do you take much wine?'
> 'No, my dear father,' I answered, 'I cannot endure it.'
> 'I merely put the question', returned he, 'to apprise you that you might, without breaking the fast, take a glass or so in the morning, or whenever you felt inclined for a drop; and that is always something in the way of supporting nature. Here is the decision at the same place, no. 57: "May one, without breaking the fast, drink wine at any hour he pleases, and even in a large quantity? Yes, he may: and a dram of hippocrass [spiced wine] too." I had no recollection of the hippocrass,' said the monk, 'I must make a note of that in my memorandum-book.'
> 'He must be a nice man, this Escobar', observed I.
> 'Oh! everybody likes him', rejoined the father ...[2]

The *Letters* sold approximately 10,000 copies each and caused acute embarrassment to the theological and political establishment; it was an extraordinary public success for a man who believed that the problem with human beings was that they did not know how to stay quietly in their rooms. In writing the *Provincial Letters* Pascal not only ran great personal risks – the printers were imprisoned, the police frantically sought the author and the *Letters* were placed on the *Index* of condemned books in 1657 – but also established the theological positions which were to mark the collection of ideas for which his fame mostly endures, the *Pensées*.

In the years following the publication of the *Letters*, Pascal continued his scientific work while remaining engaged in the theological debate under his own name. During this period he began to compile notes for a major work of Christian apologetics. When he died these notes were found tied together in bundles on his desk; they were published posthumously under the title *Pensées (Thoughts)*.[3] The *Pensées* constitute a remarkable legacy of Christian apologetics, highly original in style and tenor and quite different from either the prevailing scholastic theology or the emerging rationalist theology. Although the work was unfinished, and it is sometimes difficult to know which are the views of Pascal and which are the views he was noting in order to refute, they are consistent enough for us to extract the dominant themes and identify a coherent and unified argument.

Pascal's thought in the *Pensées* is marked by a rejection of the rationalist approach to the question of God which characterized both the classical arguments for the existence of God and the philosophy of Descartes; natural theology – the attempt to develop a rationally persuasive argument in favour of the basic truths of religion, such as the existence of God – was considered futile by Pascal. In his philosophical position Pascal was influenced primarily by two philosophers, the Stoic slave-philosopher Epictetus (*c*.55 – *c*.135? AD) and the French philosopher Michel Eyquem de Montaigne (1533–92). His views on these thinkers are expressed in a conversation he had in 1655 with a Jansenist priest, M. de Saci, at the convent of Port-Royal-des-Champs.[4] As a young man Pascal had been introduced to the sceptical thought of Montaigne through reading his *Apology for Raymond Sebond* (1580) in which Montaigne elucidates the scepticism of Sextus Empiricus (*c*.200 AD); although he was later to reject Montaigne for his lack of belief and what Pascal saw as the absence in his thought of any resolution of the human predicament, this sceptical influence stayed with him and he never held the confidence of Descartes in the power of reason to discover the foundations of knowledge.

From Montaigne Pascal received the critical weaponry he needed to attack those who were prepared to have too much pride in the abilities of human reason, those who look to science for ultimate truth, and those who think that the power of reason can be used to deny the mysteries of religion. Such philosophical scepticism dovetailed perfectly with the Jansenist belief in the corruption of the human powers of reasoning, and the conversation with M. de Saci shows this: Pascal and he are in agreement on this point even though Saci's rationale comes from Augustine and Pascal's from philosophy. What Pascal rejected in Montaigne was what he perceived to be the outcome of his scepticism, namely a pessimism about our ability to achieve any goodness or knowledge at all, a pessimism which he perceived as eventually giving rise to intellectual laziness and indolence.

Pascal was also influenced by the thought of Epictetus, who emphasized the dignity and power of human effort in the face of the pain and difficulty of life. Pascal admired Epictetus' stoical indifference to bodily suffering (his master's beatings reputedly meant nothing to him

as he considered his body as merely an outer shell), which gave him
some courage to deal with his own frequent ill-health. For Epictetus
strength, freedom and truth lay within the person, but this could only
be found when one surrendered fully to the will of god (more akin to
fate in the stoic world-view). While there is no doubt that Pascal too
readily identified the deterministic Stoic notion of the divine will with
the Christian God, his study of Epictetus did provide him with a
philosophical argument for diminishing the importance the things of
the world and provided a philosophical parallel to the Augustinian and
Jansenist emphasis on the subjugation of the corrupt human will to
the will of God.

It is no coincidence that these two philosophers intrigued Pascal,
for the difference between them reflects, in a broad sense, the contrast
between two different Christian anthropologies which had marked the
history of theological debate on the question of grace, one emphasizing the depravity of the human condition and the mark of sin, the
other stressing the dignity of humanity raised above sin by the grace
of Christ. In the *Pensées* we see Pascal trying to come to terms with
this paradox in the human condition, the simultaneous wretchedness
and greatness of human beings. We are proud of our humanity, yet in
what can we have pride if we are at the same time sinful, weak and
wretched? (*Pensées* 131).

Pascal's mistrust of a rationalist approach to questions of religion
can be traced therefore both to philosophical sources and to the
influence in his life of a Jansenist anthropology. But his views as found
in the *Pensées* do not amount to a rejection of reason but rather to a
qualification of the powers of reason. He is acutely aware that if
religion despises and rejects the principles of reason it will appear
absurd; yet he is equally convinced that if religion relies on reason
alone for its foundation and rationale it becomes like any other human
endeavour and what is mysterious and supernatural in it will be
destroyed (*Pensées* 173). For Pascal nothing is as consistent with
reason as to deny reason a role where it has no proper place; it was
therefore imperative to avoid the twin pitfalls of excluding reason
totally or allowing nothing but reason (*Pensées* 182 and *Pensées* 183).
This is why Pascal was so concerned to show that his belief in God,
while it could never be shown to have a convincing rational basis, was
nevertheless consistent with a reasonable and justifiable interpretation

of the human condition. His philosophical scepticism and parallel theological fideism did not mean that he wanted to abandon critical thinking in favour of a celebration of the irrational.

This nuanced approach allows us to understand why Pascal was mistrustful of the traditional 'proofs' for the existence of God. He is aware that people seldom believe in God on rational grounds alone. Therefore, he argues, the classical, metaphysical 'proofs' are actually detached from the way in which people approach the question; their very complexity means that even if someone is convinced by the argument as they hear it, as soon as they go away they are just as likely to doubt it as to believe it (*Pensées* 190). Pascal ridicules those Christians who think that the 'proofs' actually have any influence on the unbeliever; the proof from nature, for example, is fine for those who already believe and see God all around them, but is pointless for those who look at nature and see only 'obscurity and darkness'; if Christianity has to rely on such 'proofs' then it would appear to be a very feeble religion indeed (*Pensées* 781).

Reason therefore is limited; even when it is successful it is so only fleetingly because it does not provide the certainty that belief requires. The certainty which Pascal saw as fitting to religious belief was not that of logic or reason, but rather an existential certainty which encapsulated the whole person. This helps explain Pascal's famous though cryptic remark on Descartes: 'Descartes useless and uncertain' (*Pensées* 887) – 'useless' because the procedural method of doubt does not bring us close to the living God, the God Pascal himself experienced so intensely; 'uncertain' because the 'certainty' achieved by Descartes is a false certainty which does not explain the true human condition. Pascal remarked bitterly that he could not forgive Descartes for using God in his system (to help ground clear and distinct ideas) and then, in Pascal's view, casting Him aside when His role was complete. But if reason is not the way to God, then what is? How are we to achieve knowledge of our true condition? This question brings us to the centre of Pascal's Christian apologetic.

Humanity is a riddle. In a famous passage in the *Pensées* Pascal describes the disproportionate nature of humans in the midst of the enormity and minuteness of nature. On the one hand there is the vastness of the universe ('Nature is an infinite sphere whose centre is nowhere and whose circumference is everywhere', *Pensées* 199) amidst which we are nothing; on the other hand there is the tiniest mite whose parts can be examined until our imagination cannot fathom anything smaller; how strange that all the enormity of nature can be held in the tiniest of atoms. So what is a human person between such extremes? Compared to the infinite expanses of the universe we are nothing; yet compared to the tiniest, minute parts of nature we are enormous – to the tiniest mite we must appear as great as the whole of nature does to us. We are caught in the middle, belonging neither to the greatest nor to the tiniest, lost in midst of all, unable to grasp the extremes.

What Pascal brings out with these powerful metaphors is that there is only one point of reference by which we can gain some foothold between the enormity and the minuteness of nature and this point of reference is ourselves; but the riddle of human existence is that we are not transparent to ourselves and human existence is itself relative to all that is around it. Our intelligence cannot grasp the mystery of human existence. Drawing the moral from his metaphor Pascal concludes that our intelligence is to the world of the mind as our bodies are to the world of nature, in that it can never hope to grasp the extremes nor hold fast to some fixed reference point of truth in a turbulent sea of possibilities. In other words our own feeble minds cannot provide us with the ultimate answer to the riddle of our own existence.

Our inability to comprehend ourselves spatially and intellectually is complicated by our nature as spiritual and bodily entities. One would think, he reasons, that as we are made of mind and matter we could fathom what this means. Yet, our very own constitution is an impenetrable mystery to us. We do not understand how such a combination of mind and matter is possible, so our very self is in fact the thing which we understand least (*Pensées* 199). To some extent Pascal shares Descartes' mind/body dualism, but unlike Descartes he does not place his trust in the power of reason to overcome the paradox; for Pascal the solution to the riddle of human existence does not come from within ourselves. We have no answer to our own situation, which is one of being lost in the universe. We do not know our own place in the great scheme of things. We have lost our real home and gone astray. We turn here and there for answers but ultimately are no wiser. It is as if we are lost in the darkness of our existence with no way out (*Pensées* 400). This bleak vision of our situation is a penetrating existential analysis which anticipates the vision of Kierkegaard, Kafka and Camus; for Pascal we can find, as Sartre was to say almost two hundred years later, no exit.

Compounding this spatial and intellectual ambiguity is a moral ambiguity in the human condition. Pascal was acutely aware of the danger of relativism – that there is no unchanging truth because what is regarded as true and morally good changes with time, custom and location. He is aware of the relativist argument that there is no such thing as a 'natural' way to behave and that what is deviant to one group may be normal to another. Just as those on a ship leaving the harbour can have the illusion that it is the harbour which is moving rather than the ship, so do those who lead disreputable lives think that everyone else is out of step with them. Of course, we know that it is the ship that is moving and not the harbour, but where can we find such a fixed point when it comes to moral differences (*Pensées* 697)? This lack of a fixed perspective leads to a situation in which the most base crimes have been considered good at one time or another: everything from theft to incest has, at one time or another, been taken as morally acceptable. Thus Pascal arrives at the apparently relativist conclusion that 'nothing is just in itself, everything shifts with time' (*Pensées* 60).

Our inability to find a fixed point of reference in life leads us not to an examination of our predicament and a search for a solution, but more often than not, it leads us into diversion and escape. We attempt to distract ourselves from thinking about our real situation by launching ourselves into a frenzy of activity. But this results only in greater misery because it prevents us from coming to terms with the human predicament. We attempt to avoid it but we still suffer from it; therefore our misery increases rather than diminishes (*Pensées* 414). To be in a state of rest is intolerable for the majority of us because when the activity ceases we must come face to face with the loneliness, inadequacy, helplessness and emptiness of our lives. Afraid of the loneliness which quiet reflection brings, yet finding no fulfilment in the frantic activity of our daily lives, we end up bored, sad and resentful; at worst we become depressed, angry and filled with despair (*Pensées* 622). These sentiments could easily have come from a twentieth-century existentialist bemoaning the futility of life, and they indeed constitute an existential analysis of the human condition which is at the centre of

Pascal's apologetic. What he wishes to show is that when we strip away the trappings of our lives we are left with nothing but a void of despair which we are ourselves incapable of filling.

Our escape into distraction prevents us achieving our true dignity, for amidst our despair we have one faculty by which we can rise above our wretched condition: we are born to think. Pascal agrees with Descartes that our dignity as creatures lies in our ability to think, to reflect. We are compelled to think, one could say almost *condemned* to think, but we must learn to think correctly (*Pensées* 620). In a striking metaphor Pascal describes the fragility of the human person: 'Man is only a reed, the weakest in nature, but he is a thinking reed. There is no need for the whole universe to take up arms to crush him: a vapour, a drop of water is enough to kill him ... Thus all our dignity consists in thought. It is on thought that we must depend for our recovery, not on space and time, which we could never fill. Let us then strive to think well: that is the basic principle of morality' (*Pensées* 200).

While this recourse to the dignity of the human as a thinking being might appear to sit uneasily with his emphasis on the weakness of reason, we must take into consideration the very nuanced position which Pascal is adopting. For his tactic is to steer a middle course between rationalism, which believes that thinking can give us certainty, and scepticism, which believes knowledge to be finally unattainable and which ultimately leads to despair. Thinking – i.e. correct thinking as Pascal describes it – is our pathway to our solution, but it is not the solution itself.

Pascal held to a form of intellectual dualism in his clear separation of scientific and religious thinking; each has its own place and forms of thought but the processes of one cannot be transposed on to the other. The loser in this scheme is philosophy, which is not science in terms of investigation and verification, but nor should its pretensions to judge religion be allowed. Pascal's vehement theological rejection of philosophy is that it claims to provide knowledge of God without also acknowledging the sinfulness of humanity. Thus he attacks the arrogance of philosophers whose pride has led them to seek knowledge of God through reason, but who have never had the courage to come to terms with their own wretchedness (*Pensées* 449). Equally pernicious in his view are the atheists, who acknowledge only half the human equation: they can perceive the sad state of our condition but fail to see that there is a way out of the predicament, namely that salvation is at hand in Christ.

What both atheists and philosophical theists miss is that the ultimate solution to the human predicament is to be found not in philosophy nor in science but in the living God, for it is only in the God of Abraham, Isaac and Jacob that true happiness can be achieved. There is for Pascal a very simple answer to the problem of being a human being: we are wretched without God and happy with Him (*Pensées* 6). What could be more simple than that? Pascal's existential analysis of the profound need at the core of human life now finds its corresponding response in God's offer of redemption. Our salvation from our despair is not, for Pascal, a matter of abstract belief in a distant creator, but is rather a specific belief in the Christian God and the salvation offered by Jesus Christ. All the philosophical proofs and arguments of natural theology are, without Christ, 'useless and sterile' (*Pensées* 449).

But to bring people to this point Pascal must offer a further rationale, for as he is well aware the unbeliever is not easily persuaded by the cold logic of the 'proof'. This further step in Pascal's apologetic contains two aspects: first, an epistemology which is not dependent upon reason alone, and secondly, an explanation of why it is better to believe than not to believe.

We have seen that despite Pascal's scientific brilliance, he does not accept that reason can explain the human predicament, or that rational argument can lead to belief. For Pascal, true belief requires a commitment of the whole person which is based on an intuitive grasp of the whole of reality. The term which Pascal used to describe this ability to grasp the truth about ourselves existentially is 'the heart'. For Pascal our access to the truth comes not merely through our reason, but also comes through a much deeper appreciation of our plight; we can learn to appropriate the truth at the most fundamental level of our being, that is in our very 'heart' (*Pensées* 110). The heart can go beyond the limited intellectual knowledge provided by reason: in a famous phrase Pascal asserts that 'the heart has its reasons of which reason knows nothing' (*Pensées* 423).

The term 'heart' as used by Pascal requires some explanation, for it cannot be equated simply with feeling or with religious sentiment or love of God. The heart for Pascal is a metaphor for the fundamental ability to grasp the structure and meaning of reality; against Descartes, it is the 'heart' and not bare mental cognition which allows us to know the first principles such as space, time, and motion (*Pensées* 110). Descartes' error was to seek to establish these first principles on the basis of reason alone; Pascal argues that reason can take over once they have been established and apply them as necessary, but it cannot itself ground them.

Likewise in the realm of religious belief; faith comes through God moving the heart of the believer. Without this activity of God we are thrown back on to reason which is always duplicitous and can never provide certainty. Reason therefore must be balanced by feeling, but such feeling is not mere sentiment; it is rather the spiritual centre of our very selves. When Pascal asserts that 'the heart has its reasons of which reason knows nothing' he means that there is more to the mystery of humanity than can be fathomed by the intellect. The heart provides insight and existential apprehension; it is the locus of the activity of God which instills faith, and it is therefore through the heart that we *know* God. This alternative epistemology helps us understand why Pascal was so critical of those whom he saw as reducing the mystery of human existence to an object of scientific rationality; hence, we can comprehend his otherwise rather strange objection to Descartes, namely that he has probed too deeply into science (*Pensées* 553). To probe science too deeply, says the scientist Pascal, is to assume that reason can achieve that which it is powerless to do. Reason's greatest achievement, its 'last step', is to recognize that it does not have the final word, and that ultimately the truly important things lie beyond the limits of its competence (*Pensées* 188).

Pascal is seeking to establish that the profound need at the core of human existence cannot be met adequately with intellectual answers. Reason, though useful, is powerless to answer our deepest needs; it is helpful in justifying belief but that justification cannot be founded on reason itself. But if the answer to our predicament lies in belief in God, then how and why are we to come to that belief if it is not simply a matter of rational persuasion? The path to faith constitutes the last part of Pascal's apologetic argument, and it is here that we meet the argument for which he is best remembered, the Wager.

In line with his existential analysis of the human condition, Pascal divides humanity into three groups: 'There are only three sorts of people: those who have found God and serve him; those who are busy seeking him and have not found him; those who live without either seeking or finding him. The first are reasonable and happy, the last are foolish and unhappy, those in the middle are unhappy and reasonable' (*Pensées* 160). These divisions would appear to mirror Pascal's own experiences and journey to faith: the first group is where (presumably) he now belongs at the time of writing; the middle group reflects Pascal's state of mind before his intense conversion experience; the third group is constituted perhaps by those worldly friends whom Pascal knew from his gambling days. Of course for Pascal true happiness is a thing of the heart, because it is the heart and not reason which reaches out to God. Faith, for Pascal, is God perceived by the heart (*Pensées* 424). To move from the second or third category to the first is therefore to commit oneself to a new way of perceiving existence, to a new way of understanding oneself and to a new way of knowing God. It is the only way to overcome misery and know true happiness.

To bring the non-believers and the waverers to faith Pascal wants to affirm that only in faith do we find lasting happiness. The journey to faith is the journey to true happiness because the things of the world offer only diversion. It is essential to Pascal's tactic to establish that there is no ultimate happiness in this life: 'One needs no great sublimity of soul to realize that in this life there is no true and solid satisfaction, that all our pleasures are mere vanity, that our afflictions are infinite, and finally that death which threatens us at every moment must in a few years infallibly face us with the inescapable and appalling alternative of being annihilated or wretched throughout eternity' (*Pensées* 427). If therefore there is a true and lasting happiness to be found, why do people not reach out for it? According to Pascal it is because they are afraid that Christianity may be true (*Pensées* 12) and would therefore have to change their lives. But Pascal believes that if he can persuade people that it is worthwhile to believe, then at least they could move into the middle group of those who will search for true faith.

Why then is it worth it to believe? In the famous section of the *Pensées* on 'the wager' Pascal presents us with an inescapable choice: either God exists or he does not exist; which choice are we to make? The arguments of reason cannot resolve the issue because plausible arguments can be put forward for each possibility (for example, does the natural world around us show the beauty and majesty of the

Creator or the coldness of a world without God?). As reason cannot give us a definitive answer to this question, Pascal frames the issue in the terms of a personal dilemma. Our lives hang in the balance like the toss of a coin. As it spins in the air what do we choose – life with God and the promise of eternal happiness or the futility of endless misery (*Pensées* 418)?

He interjects into his own argument with the view of the sceptic that, as reason cannot offer us an answer, the best thing to do is not to wager at all. But this is a false option, for not to wager at all is effectively to wager against. Pascal presses his point: we must wager, for we have no option. So we must choose. But we do not merely have to guess, for we can calculate what the best outcome will be. If we call heads that God exists then we stand to win everything – happiness for eternity. But if we choose God and it turns out that he does not exist then we have lost nothing. It makes no sense therefore to wager against – we must make the choice for God (*Pensées* 418).

What exactly is this 'everything' that we have to gain if we wager in favour of God's existence? Although Pascal does claim that the one who gambles on God's existence 'will gain even in this life', the true prize of belief – the 'everything' of which he speaks – is eternal life with God. Due to the enormity of the stakes, Pascal goes so far as to say that it is unreasonable not to make the wager: as we are obliged to play (not playing is equivalent to choosing against) we must be renouncing reason if we hoard our life rather than risk it to gain something infinite. Hence he turns reason on itself: reason cannot give us certainty, and since it cannot give us certainty it would be unreasonable not to chose that which can – potentially – offer us the most happiness. It is, says Pascal, more reasonable to believe in God than not to. Pascal's ingenious tactic therefore is to expose the futility of all worldly attempts at happiness, while raising the stakes ever higher; eventually he hopes to push the listener to the point where belief is seen as the better part of an unavoidable choice.

Ingenious and persuasive as this argument is, it is not without its problems. One of the most obvious difficulties is that the persuasive force of the argument appears to rest on the assumption that belief or unbelief is tied to eternal reward or punishment, happiness or unhappiness. Although Pascal does argue that belief will make us happier in this life, the wager only becomes compelling when eternal stakes are on offer. In another fragment of the *Pensées* Pascal argues that the question as to whether the soul is either mortal or immortal has important consequences for ethics (because if the soul is immortal then we should do everything in our power to ensure eternal happiness for ourselves). He bemoans the fact that philosophers mostly ignore this consideration in discussing ethical issues (*Pensées* 612). There is clearly a link in Pascal's thought between eternal reward/punishment and virtuous behaviour in this life, but when the link between eternal happiness and an explicitly Christian profession of belief is weakened – as in many modern theologies which view God's grace as given universally to all human beings – then the argument loses some of its force. In addition, it does appear increasingly difficult to defend the concept of personal immortality in the face of modern advances in the study of consciousness. Even allowing that all things are possible to God, knowing what we do about the dependence of consciousness on the physical brain it is very difficult to imagine personal identity continuing when the brain has decayed. As in the case of Descartes, it is perhaps unfair to lay these difficulties at the door of Pascal himself, as they depend on later advances in theology and physiology, but they do constitute real difficulties for the wager argument as he formulates it.

A further difficulty occurs with Pascal's presentation of the way in which faith is to come about. He appears to suggest that opting for God's existence will make us better persons, more 'faithful, honest, humble, grateful, full of good works, a sincere, true friend ...' (*Pensées*, 418). Is he suggesting here that opting for belief in God will make one automatically virtuous, or is he saying that if one follows a virtuous life then one can grow into faith? Is it possible to take a risk on belief in God and then will one's way into a deeper faith? At this point we run up against the incomplete nature of Pascal's reflections, and a certain amount of contradiction is evident. On the one hand we have the wager, which appears to be a matter of decision and effort. Pascal advocates behaving *as if* one did believe, following religious practices such as using holy water and having mass said for one's benefit (*Pensées* 418) and we hear him defend the will as a major element in belief (*Pensées* 539). However, on the other hand we have his Jansenist belief in the depravity of the human will (*Pensées* 421, *Pensées* 662) and the well established theological principle that faith is a gift of God (*Pensées* 588) which cannot be decided by us. These difficulties are perhaps intractable and, finally, the incomplete nature of the *Pensées* forces us to suspend judgment. The crucial factor is that it is less important to establish precisely what Pascal's view was than to take up the considerable theological challenge that the wager involves. Like many great thinkers, Pascal leaves us less with clear-cut answers and more with a series of fascinating questions.

Pascal's thought has a very 'modern' ring to it, not least because of his existentialist approach to human beings and their situation in the world, but also because of his perception that extremes of dogmatism and Pyrrhonism (one of the most radical forms of scepticism, after Pyrrho of Elis, *c.* 375–27 BC) are to be avoided equally. His critique of the application of rationalist principles to religion foreshadows many of the views which some eighteenth-century thinkers were to adopt as they came to see the limitations of the powers of reason. In his view that the existence of God is something that can neither be proved nor disproved, Pascal anticipated Kant's critique of natural theology which was to prove so influential in modern theology. His emphasis on the intensely personal nature of the commitment of religious belief, his nuanced judgment on the use of reason, and his dogged insistence on the essentially alienated state of humanity make his thought highly attractive to the contemporary reader.

But despite Pascal's genius and his astute insights he was a tortured figure whose writings sometimes reveal depths of intense loneliness. His Jansenist despair at the human condition and his incapacity to take any comfort from the beauty of his natural surroundings do not appear to have been alleviated by his faith, and there is a certain poignant and plaintive tone in his admission that when he looks at the world all he sees is darkness (*Pensées* 429). His pessimistic outlook pushed him not only to the theological fideism which we have described but also to sometimes cut himself off from normal human contact. In a fragment from the *Pensées* imbued with pathos he protests that no one should become attached to him for he cannot satisfy them or make them happy. When he dies they will lose the object of their love, and their unhappiness will be his doing. It is better, he says, to love God, for God will not disappoint those who devote themselves to him (*Pensées* 396). As well as the sheer sadness of Pascal's apparent inability to understand the true value of human love, there is also is a dark

Kafkaesque quality to the bleak despair of his loneliness. He appears to suffer not simply from the loneliness of a person without lovers, friends or human warmth, but he is also pierced by the intellectual loneliness of a man who needs consolation and cannot find it, who desires a security which like the horizon is always receding. He seems to think that his pessimism, at least, is beyond redemption.

Pascal was acutely aware that the secure religious world in which everything had its proper place in the divine scheme, and in which the earth and humanity were fixed safely in the centre of the universe, was crumbling in its conflict with the rapid changes that were then taking place in the natural and human sciences. Reading Pascal – for all his emotion and occasional stridency – we cannot help but hear echoes of our own time; perhaps what we see in Pascal is a figuration of our own century, and our attempt to find a foothold in a changing and sometimes hostile world.

Notwithstanding these undoubtedly 'modern' aspects of Pascal's thought, and despite the undoubted personal integrity of his intellectual struggles, we cannot avoid certain awkward questions about the picture of Christianity and the evaluation of humanity which he promulgated. For instance, did not Pascal, in the intensity of his own personal life, project many of his own experiences on to humanity in general? This is not an unjustified and superficial psychological interrogation, for there are other important instances in the Christian tradition of important theological ideas growing out of intense personal struggle (the cases of Augustine and Luther are among the most prominent). We may therefore legitimately ask whether Pascal's emphasis on the weaknesses of humanity should be qualified by the knowledge that in Jansenism's teaching on human sinfulness – with its accompanying moral rigidity and pessimistic evaluation of those who are not touched by grace – he found a ready-made intellectual home for his own pessimism and self-disgust? Despite his brilliance Pascal appeared to see no alternative other than that between Jesuit casuistry and Jansenist austerity. In his mistrust of reason and human effort did he not – along with many others of course – ignore the Christian gospel's emphasis on God's compassion for the weak efforts of human beings? In the final analysis did he not simply want us all to be like him?

Perhaps some of Pascal's theological limitations may be explained by the distinct separation which he maintained between science and religion. It is somewhat surprising that a scientist of Pascal's ability would interpret the scriptures in a purely allegorical manner (e.g. *Pensées* 290–297), or that he would place such a naive faith in miracles (one of the most influential events of his life was the alleged cure of his niece from a serious infection by the application of a thorn reportedly from the crown of thorns). Did Pascal believe that the limitations of reason were such that all matters of faith – including scripture and miracles – were cocooned in a realm of their own and so safe from critique? An unfortunate legacy of religious intransigence is that the separation of religion from science which emerged in the early modern period was to be gradually accentuated in the following centuries until the two came to be seen as in perpetual conflict. Pascal's view of the relationship of science to religion varies little from that of the church leaders who had condemned Galileo earlier in the century, and although Pascal cannot be blamed for all the difficulties of subsequent conflicts, it is nevertheless true that with him a potentially crucial possibility for progress was lost.

As his health deteriorated Pascal became increasingly embittered by the ongoing Jansenist controversy. Towards the end of 1661 his sister Jacqueline died and the convent at Port-Royal was closed shortly thereafter (it was eventually destroyed under royal orders). Pascal bitterly resented what he saw as a capitulation to his enemies the Jesuits, but in the last months of his life he is reported by some sources to have accepted as final the judgment of the Pope on the Jansenist controversy. Pascal's last days were spent in the care of his family; he had already sold almost everything he owned and given the money to the poor. He died in August 1662 at the age of thirty-nine after a long and painful illness. As a testimony to his genius, only a few months before (in March 1662) Pascal came up with an idea for a fixed price carriage journey across Paris; if it had been realized this would have been the first urban bus route, but sadly Paris was not yet ready for such innovation and the scheme failed.

Apart from the attraction of a fascinating thinker, we need to recall why a study of Pascal, who did not share the Enlightenment ideal and who died well before the high-point of Enlightenment thought, is essential to an adequate understanding of the religious thought of the period. There are three reasons. First, and as we have seen in his critique of Descartes, Pascal's thought is a reaction to key elements of Enlightenment thinking almost from its inception. Secondly, Pascal also stands out as a forerunner to the existentialist opposition of Kierkegaard to the Enlightenment thinking so epitomized in the philosophy of Kant and taken to dizzying heights in the thought of Hegel. Thirdly, Pascal's genius in turning philosophical weapons to suit his own purposes, his attack on the pretensions of reason, and his Christian apologetic made him one of the major interlocutors of the eighteenth-century philosophes on the question of religion.

The first of these points we have already considered, and the second lies outside the scope of this work, so we shall look briefly at the third. One of the most intense eighteenth-century criticisms of Pascal can be found in *Letter XXV* of the second edition of Voltaire's *Letters Concerning the English Nation* (1741), although its contents have little to do with England. Voltaire comments upon selections from Pascal's *Pensées*, taking him to task on a range of issues, some of them trivial but most of them addressing key aspects of Pascal's thought. The main thrust of Voltaire's criticism concerns Pascal's view of the human condition and some points of his Christian apologetic. Voltaire's summary of his view of Pascal are a good synopsis of what many of the philosophes believed about Christianity as a whole: 'It appears to me that Mr *Paschal's (sic)* design, in general, was to exhibit mankind in an odious light. He exerts the utmost efforts of his pen, in order to make us all appear wicked and wretched ... I shall be so bold as to take up the pen, in defence of my fellow creatures, in opposition to this sublime misanthropist. I dare affirm, that we are neither so wretched, nor so wicked, as he declares us to be.'[5]

While admiring the genius of Pascal's mind, Voltaire believes that he has misused that genius to deduce falsehoods, a failure which Voltaire claims is shared by many works of Christian apologetic of the period; they are, he says, attempting to prevent a great oak from falling by surrounding it with reeds (a jibe at Pascal's description of man as a 'thinking reed'). Voltaire attempts to blow away some of these reeds by very matter of fact comments which nevertheless hide a philosophical anthropology antithetical to that of Pascal. Take one of Pascal's fundamental assumptions, that we human beings are a mystery, 'incomprehensible to ourselves'. Voltaire's response is to point to our place in nature and to basic facts of our lives – birth, the senses, air, food – which show that we are not a mystery but rather simply part of the way things are; to pretend that we are incomprehensible is to set up a false problem just to have the pleasure of giving our own solution to it. There are hints in Voltaire's response of the mediaeval notion of the great chain of being in which every creature has its proper place ordained by God and that the way things are is just the way they are; but it is a notion of order stripped of its theological foundation, even though Voltaire does pay lip-service to the role of religion. Voltaire's view of our place in nature is a naturalistic one; it is as if he is saying to Pascal, 'This is just the way we are and there is no point in asking superfluous questions which you cannot answer.'

Of course, in taking this as his point of attack Voltaire is sidestepping the real existential question about the meaning and purpose of human life which Pascal is raising. But he is doing this for a purpose and the purpose is that he does not share Pascal's theological anthropology and in particular his belief in original sin. But Pascal in this regard is a difficult opponent, for part of his genius was that he looked elsewhere than to theology – e.g. to the philosophy of Epictetus or Montaigne – for evidence about the human condition which he would then find expressed more fully in Christian doctrine, and this is what made him such a formidable opponent. When Voltaire responds to him, therefore, he is not responding simply to a claim from Christian revelation, but to something which is a partial truth at least about the human condition. When, for example, he talks about God inspiring us with the principle of self-love Voltaire is making the point that we are not as degraded as Pascal's Christian anthropology says we are. But there is also something unconvincing about Voltaire's attempt at a glibly naturalistic interpretation of our place in the world, for Pascal's pessimism does remind us of something uncomfortable about the human condition which we would more often than not prefer to forget. There is, in this dispute, some truth on both sides.

Another point of attack by Voltaire on Pascal is his rejection of the wager argument. Despite a rather prissy complaint that a gambling metaphor is unfitted to the dignity of the subject of the existence of God, Voltaire sees clearly the weakness in the wager argument. First, the wager presents us with a false dilemma; it is possible not to choose and to remain in a situation of doubt. Secondly, just because it is to my advantage to believe in something does not make the existence of that thing any more likely. Thirdly, Voltaire sees a theological weakness in the wager argument; if we are to believe on the grounds of attaining eternal happiness, this is not a very good argument to convince large numbers of people as scarcely one of us in a million can believe ourselves deserving of that reward. If you wish to convince me of the existence of God, says Voltaire, don't try to scare me; instead try to convince my reason, and the best way to do that is to listen to 'the voice of all nature' (the argument from design being a very popular eighteenth-century alternative to more theological approaches to God's existence).

Voltaire attacks Pascal on other less crucial issues as well. On Pascal's famous question as to where are we to find a harbour in morals, Voltaire responds in the same manner as Kant was to do later: in the universal maxim of the golden rule. Against Pascal's belief that activity is distracting and that our true nature is to be found only in repose and silence, Voltaire points out that if we were all happy with only ourselves then the propagation of the human race would be in trouble, and that unease with repose is what drives us to be active and useful to ourselves and others. Against Pascal's claim that the discrepancies in the genealogies of the Gospels of Matthew and Luke show that there was no conspiracy in their compilation, Voltaire retorts by pointing out that this argument is akin to a lawyer who announces that his client has contradicted himself. In response to Pascal's claim about Christian origins that histories based on the witness of those prepared to become martyrs for their beliefs are more credible, Voltaire asks why it is that the historian Josephus does not mention the events surrounding Christ and the early Christians. Against Pascal's defence of the Jews as God's chosen people who were the vehicle of Christ's coming Voltaire offers a view of the Jews as a barbarous and ignorant race, an anti-Semitic view which sits very uneasily with his self-proclaimed toleration.

All of these points – some more convincing than others – are part of Voltaire's strategy to undermine Pascal's apologetics; he was prepared to chip away at it little bit by little bit until, he thought, there was nothing remaining. Notwithstanding the brilliance of Voltaire's critique of Pascal's apologetic it constitutes a failure of the imagination on his part that he did not see the depth of insight which Pascal had into human beings and the fear which can be induced by an acute awareness of what it means to be a conscious being in such a puzzling and uncertain universe. Perhaps Voltaire did have such insight, but allowed it to be clouded by his zeal in countering Pascal's Christianity; and perhaps this is why Voltaire's critique, even though so much of it is correct, appears somewhat stale today. On reading it one gets the impression that somehow he missed the point; but then the modern reader, unlike Voltaire, has the benefit of seeing Pascal through the lens of other great thinkers who struggled with the same problems. Hume, Kierkegaard, Schopenhauer, Nietzsche and Kafka are all in many respects the heirs of Pascal, even if they do not share his conclusion that faith in the God of Jesus Christ is the only safe harbour in the storm of life.

But not only Pascal's analysis of the human predicament remains important. So too – despite the disaffection of Voltaire and other eighteenth-century philosophes with it – does his approach to religious belief. In post-Enlightenment religious thinking, where a purely rational approach to religious belief is found wanting, the alternative of a faith commitment remains, and as long as the existential questions about the human condition explored so vividly by Pascal remain with us, the possibility of a religious response to those questions will remain as well.

5

The Distant God of Deism

In Chapter 3 we saw that in the thought of Descartes, reason was characterized by the attempt to base knowledge of empirical reality on eternal truths established *a priori*. For Descartes, and other rationalists of the seventeenth century, reason discovered truths which, as Ernst Cassirer puts it, were 'held in common by the human and the divine mind'.[1] The activity of pure *a priori* speculation produced certainties which, due to their incontestable nature, could only be certainties grounded in the mind of God. In this seventeenth-century assumption that the human mind can, as it were, reach into the divine mind, we can see traces of the mediaeval theological and philosophical principle that our own activity and knowledge is grounded in the fact that we are creatures of an intelligent, creator God. What makes us like God is our use of reason, so that while we may know the divine nature by means of analogy only, our own faculty of reason nevertheless functions as a sort of palimpsest on which the traces of the eternal divine reason are forever inscribed. However, as we saw in the case of Descartes, portraying the relation between divine and human reason in this way can call into question the need for the divine reason at all, as once assured of our own powers of reason we may decide not to look for any further grounding.

This seventeenth-century concept of reason underwent a subtle but decisive shift in the eighteenth century. Reason came to be seen not so much as a way of penetrating to the eternal truths of the divine mind, but rather as a way of investigating the here and now of the empirical world. It is perhaps not surprising that such a shift would occur, for not only is it difficult to remain for long in the realm of pure speculative enquiry, but with the many new methods and discoveries in the natural sciences the process of reasoning was being changed by the pressure of activity. As Cassirer remarks, the eighteenth-century concept of reason differs from that of the previous century in that reason now 'does not consist in enabling us to transcend the empirical world but rather in teaching us to feel at home in it'.[2] Reason is no longer equated with established *a priori* certainties but rather with an activity of investigation, a process of discovery in which the homely comfort of Descartes' warm stove is exchanged for an unmapped territory into which the thinker must journey without any pre-established certainty of where the journey might end.

This shift in reason's self-understanding had implications for the role of religion in interpreting the world and for the way in which God's relation to the world was viewed. In short, the late seventeenth and eighteenth centuries saw a development in which many of the central beliefs of revealed religion – key doctrines of Christianity such as the Trinity, the divinity of Christ, original sin – were often cast aside in favour of a religion based on what could be known through the use of reason alone. This restriction of belief to that which is accessible to the enquiring human mind resulted in a religion in which God is seen not as the biblical Father but as the Supreme Being, the impersonal Creator, a God who is a necessary requirement for the maintenance of the laws of nature but is little interested in worship, doctrine, churches and other religious trappings.

The term 'deism' (from the Latin *Deus*, God) is conventionally used to describe the views of a range of thinkers who loosely subscribed to such a rejection of revealed religion yet who consistently held to the existence of a Creator. It is a notoriously imprecise term which cannot capture the myriad differences between these thinkers themselves, between them and certain forms of Christianity, and between them and some barely undisguised forms of atheism. Occasionally – as in Voltaire's *Philosophical Dictionary*, for example – the term 'Theist' seems to equate to what we would consider a deist. Yet, despite the fluidity of the term, it has not yet been superseded by anything more accurate and can serve our purposes here to describe a new form of religious thinking in Western culture which emerged alongside the mainstream of Christian theology and which saw itself as rooted more in the new freethinking culture of contemporary Europe than in the stolid history and traditions of Christianity. To understand deism and its significance in the new climate of the eighteenth century it is helpful to begin with one of its precursors, a thinker who in the Enlightenment was considered an atheist both by many of the critics of Christianity and by many of its defenders, the seventeenth-century philosopher Spinoza.

Baruch Spinoza (1632–77) was an Iberian Jew whose family fled to The Netherlands to escape persecution. While his family were Orthodox Jews, Spinoza's own theological beliefs were far from conformist and he was shunned by his community. While supporting himself as a lens-polisher he developed a unique philosophical system, published posthumously as the *Ethics*. Spinoza's *Ethics* is in reality both a metaphysical explanation of the whole of reality combined with an ethic developed in conjunction with that view. While the ethic is of enduring worth, it is his philosophical-theological metaphysics which is of most interest in our context.

Spinoza's system shares with Descartes the principle that the deepest knowledge of reality is to be gained by reasoning alone (that is, as distinct from empirical observation). So as to copperfasten his system Spinoza employed the style of Euclidean geometry, using theories and axioms to argue step by step to his conclusion and to relate the parts of his system to each other. To a modern reader who picks up Spinoza's *Ethics*, this philosophical method may seem curious in the extreme, but, while it is no longer particularly rewarding to follow this logical progression each step of the way, it is important to note that Spinoza wanted to present a watertight system because of his fundamental belief in the unity of all things. Spinoza held to a rigorous monism (everything is essentially one) with obvious consequences for his philosophical method: if everything is connected then it must be possible to *demonstrate* logically that everything is connected, hence the Euclidean style.

What is of most interest to us in our study are the implications of Spinoza's monism for the relation of God to the world. Consider the following two passages from the *Ethics:*

> ... and consequently thinking substance and extended substance are one and the same thing, which is now comprehended through this and now through that attribute ... And thus whether we consider nature under the attribute of extension or under the attribute of thought or any other attribute, we shall find one and the same

order and one and the same connection of causes: that is, the same things follow in either case.[3]

and

... the human mind is a part of the infinite intellect of God, and thus when we say that the human mind perceives this or that, we say nothing else than that God, not in so far as he is infinite, but in so far as he is explained through the nature of the human mind, or in so far as he constitutes the essence of the human mind, has this or that idea.[4]

The rejection of Cartesian dualism in the first quotation is immediately evident, but Spinoza goes so far as to say that thought and matter are essentially the same thing considered from different perspectives. This is more than a rejection of dualism or a statement of the interdependence of entities; it is to say that mind and matter are *the same thing viewed separately*. If we now look again at the second quotation – which asserts that to know the human mind is to know the divine mind – we begin to see emerging the implications of a monistic metaphysics. For if mind and matter are the same thing considered from different angles, and the human mind is to be equated with the mind of God, how then do we distinguish God from matter? For Spinoza the answer to this radical question is that we do not, indeed cannot make such a distinction. When he writes, 'except God, no substance can be granted or conceived',[5] he states precisely what the above passages imply, namely that God, mind and matter are all one unity. Spinoza is a thoroughgoing pantheist (from the Greek words for 'all' and 'God') who believes not merely that God is in everything but that *everything is God*.

One of the consequences of pantheism is that it becomes very difficult to reject the charge of atheism, and during Spinoza's lifetime this charge was indeed levelled at him. The abiding problem is that it becomes virtually impossible to retain anything of the orthodox idea of God as omnipotent, personal, and transcendent if God is simply to be equated with everything that exists. To most observers there is little difference between pantheism so defined and simply pointing to the contingent world and calling it God, which to all intents and purposes is no God at all. Spinoza's pantheism thus resulted in a form of fatalism in which he – to the scandal of his contemporaries and later generations – denied free will, immortality, and moral responsibility with its attendant attitudes such as regret and remorse.

Spinoza became something of a beacon to the freethinkers of the Enlightenment; an independent who had the temerity to look at nature and call it God. This 'hideous hypothesis', as the ironic David Hume – an admirer of Spinoza – was later to call it, was not readily adopted by the leading thinkers of the eighteenth century. Nevertheless, there is no doubt that Spinoza was a forerunner of those who would look at nature and call it nature, with no reference to its possible divine design or origin. However, before the outbreak of such overt atheism there came the half-way-house of deism in which the rationalist approach of Spinoza to God was employed but the distinction between nature and the divine was conserved. In Chapter 7 we shall see some of the scientific reasons why this distinction was maintained, but it is first necessary to see what was distinctive about the deists themselves.

The term 'deist' came into wide use towards the end of the seventeenth century chiefly through its use in Pierre Bayle's famous *Dictionary*; there the term was employed in an article on Calvin's follower Pierre Viret who had described as deists those who believed in a creator God but who rejected Christian revelation and the divinity of Christ. Although the term was sometimes employed as equivalent to 'atheist', by the time that Doctor Johnson compiled his *Dictionary* in the middle of the eighteenth century it had been established in the meaning attributed to Viret, which was to become the conventional meaning, namely as referring to those who rejected specific revelation (especially that of Christianity) but who nevertheless held to belief in God on grounds of reason.

In earlier tendencies towards deism, however, there were to be found more nuanced ways of looking at the relationship between rational religion and the traditional sources of revelation, in particular the scriptures. In the middle of the seventeenth century the Cambridge Platonists – Ralph Cudworth, Benjamin Whichcote, Henry More and others – advocated a rational religion which conformed to the truths revealed in the scriptures but which spurned enthusiasm and the irrationality which they encountered in much of the Calvinism of the day.

While the first use of the epithet is to be found in continental Europe, it was in Britain that deism as such was to develop. The first acknowledged deist was Lord Edward Herbert of Cherbury (1583–1648), brother of the metaphysical poet George Herbert. Lord Herbert's ideas were to have considerable influence in the growth of deism in the Enlightenment and consequently in the emergence of atheism. In his *De Veritate (On Truth)*, first published in 1624, Herbert defended what he called 'Common Notions' in religion which 'all men of normal mind believe'. Herbert believed that these notions can be demonstrated rationally to belong to the intellect. As universal notions they should then be evident in all reasonable religion. But while this appears to be the method of rationalism, it is not always convincing; Herbert's writing sometimes gives rise to the suspicion that he has observed empirically that certain practices are very common and then tried to justify them in terms of his method. Indeed, a key impetus behind Herbert's rational religion was his observation of the plurality of religious beliefs and practices, not only in post-Reformation Christianity but also in the context of the new worlds and cultures (e.g. India, the Americas) being opened up by trade and exploration.

Amid this plurality of bickering churches and polymorphous religiosity Herbert sees five Common Notions. In outline these are:

(1) there is a Sovereign Deity;

(2) this Deity must be worshipped;

(3) piety is closely linked to virtue, to good living;

(4) wrongdoing must be expiated by repentance;

(5) there is reward or punishment after this life.[6]

Each of the Common Notions contains further refinements which defend and expand upon the general concept. For example, under the first and basic notion that there exists a Supreme Being, Herbert delineates eight qualities of God, among which are that God is the cause of all that is good, and that God is the end of all things, and that God is eternal, just and wise. This is a form of natural theology based on the analogy between human values and the divine nature, i.e. 'that what exists in us in a limited degree is found absolutely in God'.[7] In its classical formulation in scholastic theology, most notably in Aquinas, such a natural theology is viewed as a complement and support for revealed truth. Herbert, however – in a move which was later to become characteristic of Enlightenment thinking across a range of disciplines – wishes to show the underlying unity of his subject under the messy diversity of its outward form. In appealing to rationalist grounds to achieve this goal, one necessarily calls into question the need for specific revelation and brings his rational religion into conflict with some central Christian doctrines (how, to take the clearest example, could the Christian triune God be reconciled with the one Supreme Deity?). Herbert himself (perhaps for reasons of prudence) did not deny that revealed truth exists, but he did chip away at what was left to specific revelation; for example, he considered the ten commandments to be Common Notions which could be deduced rationally. This claim may seem innocuous to us but in the early seventeenth century it could be taken as heretical (there is some slight irony in the tale that the rational Herbert, unsure whether to publish *De Veritate*, decided he had received a positive sign upon hearing a loud noise in a cloudless sky).

Herbert's *De Veritate*, therefore, laid down the principles which later deists were to draw upon. Its importance, however, does not lie in Herbert's own explicit ideas on the composition of rational religion; many of his specific points were to be rejected by later deists, for example the essential link between piety and virtue (in what seems a bizarre quibble to the modern mind, it was commonly thought that atheists could not lead morally good lives – Herbert himself sidestepped the issue by refusing to believe in the existence of atheists). The importance of *De Veritate* is that it made it possible for subsequent thinkers to profess belief in God, yet to abjure revealed religion and established Christianity; the liberating effects of such a possibility for thinkers immersed in the daring discoveries of the new scientific age should not be underestimated.

In 1695 the great English philosopher and political theorist, John Locke (1632–1704), published a defence of Christianity entitled *The Reasonableness of Christianity*. Locke argued that although religion is not contrary to reason, any divine revelation claimed by religion must be subject to the judgment of reason. The basis of these ideas had been developed in Locke's *magnum opus, An Essay Concerning Human Understanding* (1690). There Locke unfolded his theory of the mind as a *tabula rasa* on which the raw data of experience is registered. Locke's empiricism – i.e. the view that most of our knowledge derives from our experience – was to be one of the two poles (the rationalism of Descartes and those who followed him was the other) within which the Enlightenment disputes about epistemology were to occur.

Book IV of the *Essay* contains what is the core of Locke's theory of religion. In chapter 10 of Book IV Locke argues for the existence of God. That he does so on a rationalist and not empiricist basis (his precise arguments need not concern us) gives the lie to the assumption that he was an empiricist *tout court*. But consistent with his overall epistemology Locke rejected the Cartesian assumption that we can have an innate idea of God. For Locke, God, as he puts it in Book II, is a complex idea which we build up in the mind by taking ideas we already know – e.g. 'existence and duration, knowledge and power, pleasure and happiness'[8] – and projecting them to infinity (a theory to be put to much different use by Ludwig Feuerbach in the nineteenth century). We receive the simple ideas from the senses and the mind organizes and 'enlarges' them until we arrive at the greatest complex idea of all, that of God.

However, for Locke, the number of things which we can know by reason are limited to the existence of God, the truths of geometry, and the certainty of our own existence (in a swipe at Descartes, Locke says – with typical English pragmatism – that anyone sceptical enough to doubt their own existence should enjoy the experiment until hunger intervenes and brings them back to reality). Reason for Locke has a wider scope. It entails our judgment on that which we can take to be more or less certain – this we can call knowledge; and it also entails judgment on that which we can accept as being probably true, without certain knowledge that it is so. We can accept the probability of truth from our own experience and that of reliable witnesses, as long as there is something within our own experience with which to make sense of the other's claim. In chapter 15 of Book IV of the *Essay* Locke says that if he sees someone walking on ice it is something which he knows to be true, and if someone else reports seeing another walking on ice he knows enough from his own experience to accept it as true. However, he then recounts the tale of the Dutch ambassador to Siam who related to the King of that country that in Holland in winter water can get so cold that people walk on it, and it can become strong enough to bear an elephant. The King – unable to comprehend something so beyond the bounds of his own experience

– retorted that he had taken the ambassador as an honest man, but would from this point on consider him a liar.

Faith for Locke is thus best understood as a trust in the powers of our own reason. Even though he does admit that there are things which we learn from revelation which do not come from reason, they must be subjected to our reason before we can accept them. Indeed we should not and could not do otherwise if we are to be true to our own selves, for our reason always judges, and if we find something in revelation which is contrary to reason then it must be rejected. Reason is a gift from God and is therefore our final arbiter, and even faith must be in conformity with it.

So, Locke's epistemology of religion clearly expounds the basic principle of all rational religion, namely that belief must be in conformity with reason. It is evident that such a theory of knowledge would have consequences for what is to be considered the truth of religion. In seventeenth-century England inter-religious strife was widespread, with the various Christian sects each claiming to possess the definitive divine revelation. For Locke, a lover of truth 'for truth's sake', such bickering was pointless. Not only does the variation in the degree of probability of our knowledge (witness the King of Siam) lead to a diversity of opinions which should be respected, but the competing claims to divine authority validated by faith should themselves all be subject to reason.

In chapter 18 of Book IV of the *Essay* Locke deals with the question of faith and reason. While he is respectful of the truth of revelation, respecting its validity, he nevertheless argues that for it to be accepted by us it must be subject to our reason; it is impossible for faith to convince us of something which is contrary to reason because to admit this would be to undermine the principles and foundations of all our knowledge. Indeed the certainty of reason is greater than the certainty of revelation: it is more certain to us that the three angles of a triangle equal two right angles when we can demonstrate it through reason than if it were passed to us as revelation, just as our knowledge of the Flood through revelation – while still knowledge – is not so certain as that of Noah who was actually present. Or, again, says Locke, whatever God has revealed is true and must be the object of our faith; but what actually counts as having been revealed by God, *that* must be judged by reason.

Thus, on the premises of his empirical philosophy, Locke could argue for religious toleration, not only because the variety of our opinions is a result of the inescapable diversity of our experience, but also because the certainty of revelation to which various sects laid claim was itself ultimately secondary to the truth of reason grounded empirically. Nothing that comes under the title of revelation can shake the 'plain knowledge' that we get from our own experience.

Locke's attempt at defending the rationality of Christian belief shows that – while the high point of deism was still to come in the eighteenth century – there was already in the latter part of the seventeenth century enough concern among the orthodox to warrant formal responses to the new ideas. For example in 1677 Bishop Stillingfleet published his *Letter to a Deist* in which he bemoaned the fact that while deists believed in God they did not truly believe in Christianity. Stillingfleet sought a *via media* between a religion that was irrational and one that was merely rational; faith was a rational act which secures belief through assent to the 'facts' about Christ recorded in the Bible. While Stillingfleet like many others had a pre-critical understanding of the historical veracity of the scriptures, he was perceptive enough to see that from the perspective of the orthodox Christian, deism was ultimately not Christianity at all.

As we shall see many times in this narrative, ideas did not stand still for long during the Enlightenment; Locke's attempt to defend both the 'reasonableness' of Christianity and hold to an empirical epistemology opened a gap between revealed religion and that which may be derived from reason without special revelation. Through that gap came the horses and carriage of deism, initially in the form of the Irishman John Toland (1670–1722). Born into a Catholic family in the north of Ireland, Toland ran away to England as a young man and became a Protestant, of a sort. He was a brilliant scholar who was known in Oxford as 'a man of fine parts, great learning, and little religion'. However, 'little religion' did not necessarily mean no religion, for Toland believed in the existence of a Supreme Being, the reality of which could, he thought, be established on broadly rationalist principles. The religion of which Toland had little was that of traditional Christianity in its different forms; he ridiculed clergy of all denominations, but his favourite target was the naive faith of the Puritans in the literal truth of the Bible. Toland became a popularizer of deistic ideas and had a marked effect on the spread of the new religious thinking, but it was through one book in particular that his influence was most felt.

In 1696, one year after Locke's *The Reasonableness of Christianity* appeared, Toland published his *Christianity not Mysterious: Or a treatise Shewing that there is nothing in the Gospel Contrary to Reason, Nor above it: And that no Christian Doctrine can be properly call'd a Mystery*. The basic premise of the work is explained in the subtitle: Christianity is a naturalistic religion which requires no mysterious explanation, and the requirements of the Christian gospel can all be decreed by the use of reason without recourse to divine revelation. It is hardly surprising that Toland's book caused an uproar; it was attacked by theologians of all persuasions, condemned by the Irish Parliament and even burned by the hangman.

Only one year separated Locke's *Reasonableness of Christianity* from Toland's *Christianity not Mysterious*, but while the distance in time was not great, the distance in thought was. Peter Gay has commented that 'Locke had tried to prove that Christianity was acceptable to reasonable men; Toland that what was mysterious and miraculous about Christianity must be discarded – in that single amendment the essence of revealed, dogmatic religion evaporated.'⁹ While we must allow for Gay's somewhat hyperbolic expression, there is no doubt but that learned people seized on the possibility that one could be 'religious' and still not believe *everything* that traditional Christianity taught. In an intellectual climate in which critical biblical scholarship was virtually unknown and unconventional religious thinking of any sort looked on with suspicion, religious belief was generally presented as a unitary package in which the dubious and the simply unbelievable were intermingled with the basic truths of faith. To an intelligentsia which had little freedom to voice criticisms of religion, treatises such as that of Toland were a means by which they could continue to believe in God while justifying the futility of disputes between the Christian sects. One now had some at least of the intellectual tools by which one could fashion a solid and rational religion, free of claim and counter-claim of divine authority, without believing literally in biblical miracles, the divinity of Christ, or the veneration of idols.

One of the most influential deists in the early part of the eighteenth century was Toland's contemporary Matthew Tindal (1657–1733).

His *Christianity As Old as the Creation: Or, The Gospel A Republication of the Religion of Nature* (1730) was known as 'the deists' Bible' for its clarity of statement and its popularity among the advocates of the new thinking. Tindal was greatly influenced by Locke and took the major premises of his thinking from Locke's distinction described above between that which can be known by reason and that which is revealed. Tindal drew more radical conclusions from this epistemology than Locke had been prepared to do, arguing – as the title of his major work reveals – that the truths of Christianity have always been available to rational people from time immemorial. Hence, if the basic truths of religion can be known rationally, religion has no need of revelation at all.

Not far under the surface of the rejection of revealed religion by Tindal and other deists lay a barely disguised anti-clericalism (although it is important to note English anti-clericalism was never so virulent as that of France, for example). Openly to doubt the necessity of revelation was not simply to entertain a radical but abstract theological hypothesis; it entailed an implicit rejection of the whole structure of established religion, the usefulness of a professional class of clergy, and the value of church benefices, etc. In England after the revolution of 1688, to attack revealed religion was to attack the established Anglican Church, and to attack the church was in effect to attack the state as well.

To defend the established religion a number of repressive laws were passed in the latter half of the seventeenth century, amounting to a situation in which any attack on Christianity could lead to punishments ranging from a fine to loss of public office and withdrawal of basic rights such as the right to purchase land; a second offence could lead to imprisonment. This was indeed the fate of Thomas Woolston (1670–1731) who, having lost his post at Cambridge for his heterodox views, was finally convicted of blasphemy for questioning the miracles of Jesus. He was fined and sentenced to a year in jail, where he died in 1731, having been unable to meet the fine.

The fear of public punishment did not cause the leading deists to abandon their radical thinking but it did force them into a series of evasive manoeuvres to avoid the direct charge of blasphemy. They resorted to pseudonymous authorship, irony, the use of the dialogue to express dangerous views at second hand (a common tactic of the provocative thinker), and a variety of other methods to avoid prosecution. One of the deists most brilliant in utilizing these tactics was Anthony Collins (1676–1729), a friend of Locke, who having published a series of free-thinking tracts, explained his methods in *A Discourse concerning Ridicule and Irony in Writing* (1727). Other deists, most notably Tindal, referred to themselves as 'Christian deists'. It is difficult to say, when one considers the deists' attacks on revelation, what this apparent oxymoron could mean. It could be interpreted, along the lines of the title of Tindal's most famous work, to mean that Christianity correctly defined (i.e. as defined by deists) was in reality the most ancient and rational of religions, but given the ever-present threat of the blasphemy laws it is reasonable to assume that calling oneself a 'Christian deist' was a tactical move to deter accusations of heresy. This was certainly a judicious step by a man one of whose works had been condemned by Parliament and burned by the hangman.

As well as the maintenance of order in one of the pillars of the establishment, it is also possible to discern another reason for the authorities' attempts to suppress religious freethinking at the time, namely the concern with public morality. For the average citizen of three hundred years ago religion and morality were closely intertwined to an extent that would seem oppressive to most twentieth-century Western people. The church was the guardian of public morality and ethical precepts were more often than not biblically based, so that for a freethinker to question the necessity for churches or the authority of biblical revelation was not simply to cast doubts on doctrine but also on the very grounds of morals. Tindal's *Christianity as Old as the Creation*, for example, attacked the morality of leading figures from the Old Testament. This was scandalous enough in itself but he then went on to charge the Christian clergy with oppressing people by means of a legalistic morality using the example of these self-same figures. But if morality can be determined rationally, as Locke had argued, then the rules and regulations of the churches – based on biblical example and precepts – were at best superfluous and at worst the perfidious weapons of priestcraft. In this respect thinkers such as Tindal were ahead of their time for it was difficult for both secular authorities and the public alike to accept that morality was not necessarily dependent upon revealed religion.

Thus, biblical criticism, which most deist publications attempted, was a risky affair; Toland, for example, while indulging in a form of comparative cultural criticism by advocating that the Bible be read like any other book, was also careful to say that morality could be established on rational premises. For him the duties and responsibilities of a good Christian were essentially those of a good citizen. He and other deists were struggling with the question of how morality can be grounded in conjunction with rational religion. Indeed one of the great projects of the Enlightenment was the attempt to establish ethics independently of religious authority. This attempt culminated, as we shall see, with Kant but it was partially prepared for by the early rationalist religious thinkers such as Toland.

The leading moralist among the deists was Anthony Ashley Cooper, the Earl of Shaftesbury (1671–1713) a protegee of Locke and a friend of Bayle. In his *Inquiry concerning Virtue* (1711), *Characteristics of Men, Manners, Opinions and Times* (1711) and other writings Shaftesbury advocated a naturalistic morality which celebrated human nature and the positive aspects of human company and society. Shaftesbury rejected both the secular pessimism of Thomas Hobbes (1588–1679) – his bête noir, who had likened human relations to a state of perpetual warfare – and the Christian doctrine of human nature stained by original sin. In contradiction of Christian warnings about the sin of pride, he advocated the virtue of self-love which naturally gives rise to love of others and is ultimately beneficial to all (a view echoed again through the Enlightenment by Voltaire, Adam Smith and others). He ridiculed Hobbes' misanthropy by asking why, if Hobbes had such a low opinion of human motivation, he had bothered to spread the good news about his own philosophy at all. Much like many modern socio-biologists, Shaftesbury thought that there was altruism in our nature and that we do not need the reward of heaven or the threat of hell in order to be virtuous.

Like Pope, whom he influenced, Shaftesbury revered nature. 'The state of Nature was the reign of God'[10] wrote Pope, echoing Shaftesbury's lyric claim that divine providence has wreathed nature in smiles. If only we could open our eyes to the beauty and harmony all around us then we would neither hate our neighbours nor look to miracles and scriptures for the truth about religion. Indeed such attempts to persuade us to believe may actually do damage by giving

us a false image of God, who may only be truly known through contemplation of nature. Religion, however, if it is not too negative or
morose can be useful in leading us towards the contemplation of
nature and may actually help develop in us that 'moral sense' which is
the true foundation of virtue and happiness.

For Shaftesbury, to know nature is to be moral, for to know nature
is to esteem order, beauty and harmony which inculcate in us the
virtues. Further, to know nature is to know God; it was inconceivable
to him that anyone who took the wondrous beauty of nature seriously
could disavow belief in a Creator. Yet in his assertion that to know
nature is to be moral, Shaftesbury opened the possibility that the
atheist could be as moral as the believer. As morality was not dependent on revelation it was equally accessible to all. The legacy of
Shaftesbury to the Enlightenment was thus that he made possible a
purely naturalistic and atheistic morality – a view which he himself, it
must be emphasized, did not share – in which morality is founded on
our relation to ourselves, other human beings and the natural world
and not directly and primarily to God, the church or the scriptures.

Shaftesbury was much admired by leading thinkers in the early
eighteenth century and the main reason for this would appear to be his
belief in the innate goodness of human beings and his celebration of
our natural affinity with others which were perceived at the time as
refreshing alternatives to a negative Christian emphasis on our sinful
nature. The emphasis which his form of deism places on natural
sensibility and emotion is an excellent example of how complex the
notion of reason in the Enlightenment is, for no one could be further
than he from the stereotype of cold rationality. The deism which he
advocated was a simplified religion, but is was a warm and attractive
one too.

Throughout the eighteenth century there was an ongoing polemical
battle between the English deists and their orthodox counterparts,
although the nuances of the arguments mean that it was sometimes
unclear in which camp a particular protagonist sat. The orthodox
numbered among their luminaries the philosopher Bishop George
Berkeley (1685–1753), Bishop Joseph Butler (1692–1752) and the
leading Anglican divine Samuel Clarke (1675–1729). In the Boyle
Lectures of 1704/5 Clarke attacked certain aspects of deism while
defending orthodoxy on rationalist grounds. He argued that some-

thing must have existed from eternity and that we can call that something 'God'; indeed Clarke believed that our knowledge of God's existence was as close to mathematical certainty as made little difference. While his views were much closer to orthodoxy than many of the deists, this did him little good, however, for he was sacked from his church living for being thought an Arian. Clarke was very famous and influential in his time but is little remembered today; however, his place in history is assured as the butt of a famous witticism by Anthony Collins, who remarked *a propos* of Clarke's somewhat tortuous rationalist arguments that no one had doubted the existence of God until Clarke tried to prove it.

Bishop Butler's ethical theory, which attempted to find a middle path between rationalism and Shaftesbury's 'moral sense' approach, and his reaction against deism are of abiding interest. Butler's ethics – as we find it in his *Fifteen Sermons* (1726) – proceeds on the principle that we may endeavour to follow nature but that nature may mean many things, and not all of them will direct us towards doing the good; some of our 'natural' impulses may indeed be evil. But as well as all our desires and impulses, says Butler, we possess what he call a 'principle of reflection' which should help us to discern those impulses which are moral from those which are not. We cannot always, as Shaftesbury had it, look to the outcome of an action to see whether it was virtuous (Shaftesbury believed that virtue produced happiness) for that may not always be the case; instead we had to look inward to the rule of conscience to determine whether what we do is moral or not.

Butler agrees with Shaftesbury that we have natural bonds of affinity with our fellow human beings, but we cannot always rely on this to impel us to a moral course of action; the conscience, on the other hand, is for Butler a permanent guide to moral conduct. Conscience is what prevents our 'self-love' from slipping into mere indulgence of our desires and it reminds us that happiness is not the basis of virtue, for who are we to decide whether or not a certain action will lead to more or to less happiness? Conscience helps us to regulate a legitimate self-love with the benevolence which we feel towards others; but if conscience were not there self-love would become indulgence and our benevolence towards others would suffer. Religion, in this scheme, does not provide a foundation for morality but functions to remind us at all times of the priority of conscience. And this morality is 'natural', for it is not based on revelation even though religion can aid in its realization; there is more than a hint in Butler of what was to be more fully developed later in the century in the thought of Kant (see Chapter 9).

Butler's counter-attack against the deists is contained in his *Analogy of Religion* (1736). In the *Introduction* to the analogy Butler quotes an observation from Origen (*c*.185-*c*.254) that 'he who believes the Scripture to have proceeded from him who is the Author of Nature may well expect to find the same sort of difficulties in it as are found in the constitution of nature'. In other words if God is the origin of the scriptures and of nature then we should not be surprised if both of them cause us difficulties. The reason that Butler adopted this approach was that the deists asserted that it is plain from the wonders of nature and the very existence of a world that there must be an Author of Nature, but that it was quite problematic that the scriptures – filled with error and difficulty – were the revelation of this selfsame God. Anyway, if we had the certain evidence of nature, what additional information could we require, especially if the reliability of the available information was doubtful?

Butler bemoans the fact that the deists and others in his time appear to have come to the conclusion that Christian revelation is meaning-less. But by means of his analogy between nature and revelation he aims to 'show, what too many need to have shown to them, that the system of religion, both natural and revealed, considered only as a system and prior to the proof of it, is not a subject of ridicule, unless that of nature be so too'.[11] To proceed along this dangerous trajectory he needs to have agreement on a crucial point, namely the existence of God which, he says, has been shown by excellent arguments, from the witness of tradition and from general consent. He also argues in favour of the immortality of the soul; he considers this to be important to his argument because he thinks that while one could conceivably believe in immortality and be an atheist, if one denies immortality then one is denying the rationale and end of the Christian religion also.

If we accept this much, says Butler, we then have to look at the actual world and ask whether the difficulties we encounter in explain-ing it are easily glossed over. We may ask, why, if the world is ordered by God, is there so much unhappiness, evil, injustice and misery? The reality of the world does not coincide with our desires and were we to have designed it we would have made it a happy and peaceful place where we would not encounter the miseries which afflict us. But the world is not like this and yet, even amidst these problems and difficulties, we accept that it was so ordered by God. By analogy, then, can we not accept that divine revelation, which also has its problems, puzzles and inconsistencies, could be of divine origin? If both nature and revelation are problematic and yet we accept one as coming from God, then why not accept the other as well?

Against deists who already accept the existence of God, this is a clever argument, for they are forced to admit that the premises for their own belief through the evidence of nature are no more reliable than the premises for belief through recourse to revelation. However, Butler's adoption of a *via negativa* to argue that both nature and revelation cause difficulties for the believer plays straight into the hands of the atheist who can then simply say that neither is convincing. In the end Butler's argument in *The Analogy* belongs in the context of the deism controversy and does not stand the test of time. What is of more interest is the fact that he touched on the weak point of deism, its naive optimism about the goodness of the universe and the often too glib inference of the existence of God from the evidence of nature. Butler was not a pessimist in the mode of Pascal but he was no Shaftesbury either; he was a realist and in his realism he saw the flaw in the benign and confident deism of his day. It is unlikely that he would have been surprised by Edmund Burke's observation at the end of the century that no one bothers to read Collins, Tindal, Toland and the other deists any more.

But Butler was enough a man of his time that he shared with the other leading English defenders of orthodoxy, such as Samuel Clarke, and with their deist opponents the principle that reason was paramount in theology: whatever one believed, it should be capable of rational defence. Eventually this shared assumption was itself to be questioned by sceptics, pietists and, of course, the activism of John Wesley. English deism, however, had already had a considerable influence beyond its own shores. The ideas of a multitude of thinkers, both on the European mainland and in the United States, to whom forms of deism could be ascribed, had their roots in the thought of the pioneering English thinkers. In the later chapters we shall see the sceptical and idiosyncratic deism of Voltaire, the romantic deism of Rousseau, and of course the religious thought of Kant.

One key figure, however, who embodied deism in its clearest form was the English/American writer and political theorist Thomas Paine (1737–1809). Although the high point of deism in England had long past before Paine's work appeared, his deism is deserving of our consideration both because of the clarity and vehemence of his argument and because of the impact which it had in the United States. Paine's desire was to defend rational religion against atheism, but in the climate of the time his theological views earned him more condemnation than thanks.

Paine was born in Norfolk in the east of England, and until the age of thirty-seven he had no impact on public life, working as a customs official and as a maker of stays for women's corsets. Although these years resulted in the death of one wife, the breakup of his marriage to another and the failure of his business, Paine had become a self-educated man, spending most of his income on books and pamphlets. In 1774 he was fortunate enough to be introduced to Benjamin Franklin, who gave him a letter of introduction to his son-in-law in Philadelphia. In America Paine wrote for various newspapers and magazines, putting into print many of his radical ideas on slavery, government, taxation and – most importantly – the right of America to strike for its freedom from Britain. Paine had an enormous influence on the movement for American independence but that, and the story of his work on behalf of the French Revolution, is not the aspect of Paine's work which most concerns us. For Paine was also an avid deist and launched such a strong attack on Christianity that he earned the distinction of being described by a twentieth-century President of the United States, Teddy Roosevelt, as 'that filthy little atheist'. Raised in the simplicity of Quakerism, Paine was to attempt to simplify his religion even further by reducing it to a few basic, rational truths.

Paine advocated deism in America towards the end of the eighteenth century when its heyday in England was long since past. However, the importance of his principal anti-Christian diatribe, *The Age of Reason* (1794), was that it was one of the first American attacks on religion in its traditional form and that it was a seminal work against what Paine called 'the adulterous connection of church and state'.[12] Furthermore, it advocated a natural religion as a possibility for all people, not simply for the intelligentsia: even among the Deists few were prepared to advocate wholesale rejection of formal Christianity, fearing a concomitant collapse in public morality. Paine proclaims at the beginning of *The Age of Reason* that he does not believe 'in the creed professed by the Jewish Church, by the Roman Church, by the Greek Church, by the Turkish Church, by the Protestant Church, nor by any Church … My own mind is my own Church'.[13] This individualism is characteristic of Paine's well-known egoism, but is also an appeal to an austere individual honesty in religion. Paine railed against what he called 'mental lying', believing that if people professed to believe in public what they rejected in private it was the basis of failure in other areas of morality also. He thus rejects on ethical grounds the propensity of more aristocratic thinkers to leave the lower classes happy in their ignorance.

Paine's attack on Christianity in *The Age of Reason* follows fairly conventional deist lines: he points out the inconsistencies in the Bible and the vices of some of its leading figures; he points to the varieties of religions and their competing claims to be the one true religion; he highlights the contrast between the good moral character of Jesus and the immorality of his followers in the churches; and, he attacks the unreliability of the resurrection witnesses, whose testimony we are expected to accept, saying that anything which is to be believed by all should provide evidence which is available to all. In general, like his predecessors, he attacks mystery, miracle, prophecy, incarnation and any Christian beliefs which are not accessible to common sense reasoning.

This much granted, what form of religion does Paine advocate? To the rhetorically posed challenge as to whether we can then dispense with revelation, Paine responds: 'THE WORD OF GOD IS THE CREATION WE BEHOLD and it is in *this word*, which no human invention can counterfeit or alter, that God speaketh universally to man.'[14] Here then is the evidence that is available to all, unlike the meagre and unreliable evidence of what passes for revelation in Christianity. Paine goes on to query how the message of Christianity could ever hope to be passed on to every human being when human languages are so diverse and understanding consequently so difficult; the natural world, however, is different, for creation speaks a 'universal language' which cannot be forged, copied, lost or censored. So do you want to know God, asks Paine; do you want to see His greatness, mercy or wisdom? If so, all you need do is look around you; if you want to read the word of God 'Search not the book called the Scripture, which any human hand might make, but the Scripture called the creation.'[15]

To know God through reason focussed on nature was, for Paine, true religion. Indeed, in contrast, Christianity was closer to atheism, for it pretended to worship God while all the time worshipping a man, Jesus Christ; Christianity in Paine's view is not deism, but 'Manism'. Spurning all forms of traditional religiosity and worship Paine enjoins us to listen to and study the works of 'the Almighty Lecturer' and to imitate Him in all things 'moral, scientifical and mechanical'. This is the true theology from which we gain all our knowledge of science.

Paine's trust in the possibility of deducing the existence of God from the evidence of the world appears naive in the light of our knowledge of the criticisms which Kant had already brought to bear on such claims, criticisms of which Paine was unaware. His faith in the mechanical deity was already dated in the latter part of the eighteenth century. It was therefore ironic that when the revolutionary hero Paine returned to the United States from France in 1802, he found himself vilified as the Godless author of *The Age of Reason*. In Europe by the beginning of the nineteenth century the great religious debates of the Enlightenment had receded into a more genteel toleration, but in the new republic of the United States deism still appeared as Godless heathenism. Perhaps Paine's orthodox opponents gained some satisfaction from his ignominious end: having being buried in obscurity, Paine's remains were in the process of being brought back to England from America in 1819 when they were washed overboard and lost forever.

In Europe, meanwhile, deism had long passed its highpoint. While the impact of English deism was significant in France (in the next chapter we shall see the sceptical deism of Voltaire) and had some impact on the later-flourishing German *Aufklärung* (including Kant), there were countries where deism did not take hold among those who had begun to investigate religion rationally. In the Netherlands, for example, advances in science which might have given rise to attacks on revelation and consequently to the rise of deism were instead integrated into the context of a natural theology. Any hint of the theories of the deists ran into the brick wall of orthodox Calvinism. Perhaps the most interesting European country where enlightened ideas took hold among religious thinkers, but where deism did not, is Switzerland. Samuel S. B. Taylor has traced the emergence of a liberal and rational form of theology among urban Swiss Protestants, where previously a rigid Calvinism had been dominant.[16] According to Taylor, the vigorous form of reaction against religious dogmatism and intolerance which had been evident in England and France did not occur in Switzerland partly because 'academic circles in Geneva and elsewhere in the Protestant cantons espoused a rational philosophy and established an intellectual climate receptive to further philosophical advances, and alien to the intellectual rigourism of earlier years'.[17] Among the educated there was a general impetus towards reform and a scepticism – fed by an active media – emerged in many areas of life. In the high academic standards of the *Académie* of Geneva with its focus on rational education, reform-minded theologians found a focus for an investigation of religion which did not begin from the presumption that Christian revelation must first be rejected for reason to flourish.

Among the leading liberal theologians such as Jean-Alphonse Turrettin and Jacob Vernet there was a tendency to emphasize morals and to thereby simplify Christianity while avoiding the more thorny questions of doctrine. This emphasis suited the outlook of the intellectuals and it was 'the creation of an enlightened intelligentsia composed of a wealthy, educated and governing elite that enabled the Enlightenment to take root in the cantons with minimum strain and without major conflict with the church'.[18] The result was that the Swiss Enlightenment was not anti-clerical in the way that the leading French or English thinkers were, and it was not necessary for the educated laity to develop a form of rational Christianity independent of the prevailing orthodoxy. Taylor sums up the reason why deism did not develop in Switzerland when he says: 'In every way the Protestant church was rationalist but within the confines of Christian faith which it saw as supported and not destroyed by reason ... Religion and Christian Revelation were supremely logical and rationally defensible. No confusion was therefore possible with deism, which eliminated Revelation.'[19]

The example of Switzerland is instructive because it indicates that

Enlightenment rationality did not necessarily lead to deism; it could lead instead to an orthodox form of rational faith. Among the more radical of the freethinkers and philosophes, however, rational religion meant precisely the rejection of any links with orthodox Christianity. Why then were so many of these revolutionaries reluctant to go all the way towards atheism and reject all forms of religious belief as illusory, as so many philosophers and scientists were to do in the nineteenth century?

There would appear to be two main reasons why deism emerged as a half-way-house between orthodox Christianity and outright atheism. The first is that in the dawn of the new science in which the universe was seen to be governed by laws which were rational and consistent, it was inconceivable to most people that an ordered cosmos could have arisen without the help of a Designer; hence the new scientific discoveries of Newton and others enabled freethinkers to reject traditional Christianity, but also impelled them towards deistic forms of belief.

The second reason has to do with morality. As an intimate link between morality and religion was more or less taken for granted by everyone – mainly through the perseverance of the vivid reward and punishment imagery of heaven and hell in Christian piety – few of even the most radical thinkers could envisage a purely secular ethics which would replace the clearly successful role of the Christian churches in this regard. Plainly, it was religion which made the majority of people do good and avoid evil – particularly the latter – and a situation in which the traditional deterrent of eternal punishment was done away with would undoubtedly lead to a deterioration in ethical standards. Hence the idea of a Deity continued to serve a useful social function, even for those who were in the process of divesting their enlightened minds of what they considered as nonsense. Voltaire's famous quip that it is very useful if one's servants and one's wife believe in God (thus encouraging honesty and fidelity), should be seen in this regard, as indeed should his further ambivalent comment that if God did not exist it would be necessary to invent Him. Whether one took the view of Voltaire that religion was necessary for the preservation of the morality of the masses or that of Kant who (as we shall see) attempted to establish the existence of God as a correlate of an autonomous morality and thereby justify moral goodness, the end result was the same: the existence of some form of Deity was intrinsically linked to the preservation of morals. In the eighteenth century, at least, only a few radical thinkers were prepared to leap over this boundary into the realm of pure disbelief.

The consequences for some other central pillars of orthodox doctrine should be obvious. Jesus Christ was revered as a particularly wise moral teacher, but not as the second person of the Trinity, God incarnate. This anti-christology gelled well with the rejection of original sin and the emphasis on a secular morality based on the golden rule which, it was clear from the knowledge of other cultures, was not the exclusive property of Christians.

As the truths of religion were readily available through use of reason, there was less need for ancient documents such as the scriptures. When Lessing made his famous remark that there was an 'ugly great ditch' between history and reason he was simply articulating something which so many of his contemporaries took for granted, for how could the modern age depend on unreliable, conflicting and partial witnesses when there was a critical tool at hand to go directly to the truth without the help or hindrance of these unreliable mediators. In publishing the *Fragments* of Reimarus, Lessing was placing his trust not only in his predecessor's biblical scholarship but also in the principle that the way to the truth of religion lay not in uncritical acceptance of the documents of the past but in the correct use of reason.

The whole concept of a supernatural revelation became problematic during the Enlightenment. Revelation appeared to leave more problems than it resolved: is it not an affront to reason; is it not unnecessary because God is fully revealed in his creation; how can there be one true religion if there are many conflicting claims about what is truly revealed; which authority do we follow in deciphering revelation; is it not simpler for more rational people to agree on a few established principles which we can all know? These and many other similar questions were at the forefront of the Enlightenment debate over rational and revealed religion, and they left a host of problems which still concern theologians today.

Is deism then to be understood as a particular historical development of interest only to historians of the period or is it more akin to a permanent tendency within religious thinking, for is there not always a tension in religion between a natural theology and the claims of a specific, supernatural revelation? On the one hand there is no doubt but that deism arose in a particular historical period as a response to the changing relationship between orthodox Christian belief and an increasingly independent group of thinkers influenced by new scientific developments. In this regard deism is best viewed as a passing phase which was superseded by both the rise of atheism in the late eighteenth and the nineteenth century and by theological developments – particularly after Schleiermacher – which made Christianity more acceptable to sophisticated minds. However, on the other hand, there appear to be reasonable grounds for suggesting that deism is always with us. For example, in secular societies there are many people who continue to say that they believe in the existence of God, yet abjure any connection with formal Christianity; among theologians and scholars of religion faced with a plurality of religious traditions each with its own claims to be true, is there not always present the convenient thought that all of this human religiosity is an attempt to worship the one Divine Being? In short are there not reasons why deism could be seen as an attractive option for modern people interested in such matters?

Even if such a modern form of deism does exist it is born of different parents from those of its Enlightenment counterpart. Deism in the seventeenth and eighteenth centuries was the child of what Gibbon in his *Decline and Fall of the Roman Empire* called an 'involuntary scepticism' about all matters religious. When previously unquestionable dimensions of Christian doctrine – such as the biblical miracle stories and the doctrine of original sin – came into conflict with modern scientific rationalism, it is not surprising that a hybrid would emerge which would bear characteristics of both Christian belief and the cult of nature. In the intellectual climate of the Enlightenment, where revealed religion was seen as going beyond the parameters which reason would allow, it is unsurprising, perhaps even inevitable, that something akin to deism would arise.

6

From Scepticism to Atheism

We saw in Chapter 4 how in the seventeenth century Blaise Pascal used the methodological scepticism of Descartes to argue for religious belief as the only truly viable solution to the human predicament. This was a brilliant move by Pascal to turn the tables of scepticism on itself, but it was not one which was to prove convincing to the majority of freethinkers in the following century. As the emergence of deism demonstrates, those scholars, scientists, and men of letters interested in the new forms of thinking had first of all to leave behind the world of old ideas, and for them this meant above all leaving behind the world of revealed religion. In this chapter we shall see how this abandonment of revelation in favour of the natural religion of reason eventually gave way to a more radical form of scepticism resulting in atheism. This movement from natural religion to atheism was not a neat, linear progression; nor can we say with certainty that it was inevitable. Both deism and fideistic scepticism, like many forms of protest, opened up the possibility that they too would be superseded by something more radical.

When the freethinkers of the eighteenth century looked back to the previous century for the intellectual roots of their religious scepticism, it was not to Pascal they appealed, but to the Huguenot Pierre Bayle (1647–1706). Like Pascal, Bayle was sceptical about the powers of human reason both in religious and secular matters, but from the perspective of the French philosophes his greater religious tolerance appeared as a marked contrast to Pascal's rigid Jansenist anthropology.

Bayle's Calvinist background, more than any philosophical influence, helps explain his view that reason could never establish the God of Christianity; hence deism held no attraction for him. He was in agreement with Pascal that while scepticism undermined rational religion it did not of necessity lead to atheism. Yet Bayle himself was suspected of atheism, even in the more tolerant surroundings of Holland, where he lived in exile after his conversion to and subsequent rejection of Catholicism. Among the reasons why Bayle had the privilege of coming under attack from both Catholic and Calvinist theologians were his arguments in favour of religious tolerance and, perhaps most importantly, his scandalous suggestion that an atheist could lead a good moral life. The latter issue, strange as it may seem to some modern ears, deserves our attention for it marks one of those important shifts in thinking which so characterized the tempering of the intellectual power of religion in the Enlightenment.

Bayle's scepticism had its roots both in the method of Descartes and in the Calvinist mistrust of the powers of human reason. Hence, his scepticism combines both the intellectualism of rationalist thinking and the moral pessimism of Calvinism. It is not only our scientific theories, histories and metaphysical speculations which are open to doubt, but also our ability to lead good, moral lives. One has only to look at a Christian community to see that all the failings of humanity in general are present there; so, as only a few are truly Christian (Calvin's elite), the vast majority of human beings find themselves together in their intellectual and moral failure. What makes people behave well is not love of God (if it was there would be many more true Christians) but fear of one's fellow citizens and the judgment and punishment of the law. Bayle concludes from this that for a society to function well it does not have to be composed of Christians; indeed, atheists who are virtuous should cause us no more surprise than Christians who commit crimes.

The scandal of this assertion was that it appeared to undermine the fundamental Christian belief in the necessity of God's grace for living a virtuous life and consequently to sever the connection between religious belief and social cohesion. At a time when religion was viewed as the foundation of a stable society this was a dangerous claim to make. It was difficult – if not impossible – for many people in the eighteenth century to understand how society could function without the controlling influence of religion. The question of Dostoyevsky in the following century was no less in the minds of the political, religious and intellectual leaders at the time of the Enlightenment: if God does not exist then is everything permitted?

The inability or unwillingness of many thinkers to contemplate the severing of the apparently unbreakable bond between religion and moral and social stability led to some strange paradoxes. The case of Voltaire is instructive. The leading philosophe, and gadfly of all established, uncritical belief during the high-point of the Enlightenment found it impossible to separate religion and morality, for others that is. Two of Voltaire's most famous witticisms – that if God did not exist it would be necessary to invent him, and the caustic view that it is very useful if one's wife and servants believe in God as it prevents love affairs by the wife and theft by the servants – are indicative of the difficulty which many of the leading critics of religion had in explaining how morality could survive without religion (even Kant, as we shall see, found this a major problem). The man of reason did not need God to help him behave morally, but everyone else did. Thus Voltaire peddled the double-thesis that religion should be eradicated from society and that belief in God is necessary for the preservation of everyday morals. Such a paradox betrays not only the inability of many Enlightenment thinkers to appreciate how religious and other beliefs are deeply embedded in a social, cultural and historical matrix, but it also shows how Enlightenment rhetoric on the universality of reason was not always carried through consistently into other areas. The monarchist Voltaire certainly had little confidence in the ability of the masses to govern themselves or to maintain social cohesion without religion.

It is to Bayle's eternal credit that while remaining a religious believer he was prepared to argue in favour of religious tolerance for atheists at a time when they were regarded as a threat to the state as well as to the church. He distinguished between 'speculative atheists' like Spinoza and *de facto* atheists who showed their lack of attachment to God by their degenerate lifestyle. (It was to a great extent Bayle's defence of Spinoza in his infamous *Dictionary* that led to the suspicion that it was his own 'speculative atheism' which was really being defended.) In his *Philosophical Commentary on the Words of Jesus 'Constrain Them to Come in'* (1686) – a treatise on toleration – Bayle advocates tolerance for Christians of all denominations, Jews, Muslims, heretics and, most scandalously, atheists. He put forward, for example, the politically expedient view that tolerating different sects would impel them to compete to show their loyalty to the state.

From our perspective, however, the most interesting argument is that based on Bayle's understanding of conscience. It had been generally accepted in Christianity since the time of Augustine's dispute with the Donatists that orthodox believers should do everything in their power to compel heretics to return to the fold of truth. Indeed, part of the rationale behind the burning of heretics was that as they had proved to be unregenerate and were doomed to hell anyway, it was better that they should go there quickly before they had the opportunity to imperil the souls of the orthodox.

The concept of truth underlying this view of heresy is that truth lies outside the individual conscience and is something to be adhered to irrespective of what one's private opinions are. After the Reformation, with the Protestant emphasis on the interiority of religious truth, the necessity of the believer to adhere in conscience to one's faith took on greater importance. It was, therefore, only a short step for an original and courageous thinker like Bayle to see that what one believed was what one's conscience told one was the truth, and that when this was recognized any attempt to determine a purely objective truth independent of the conscience of the individual was doomed to fail. If the truth of religious belief lies within the conscience of the individual, then – even if all others consider that belief to be heretical – there is little point in blaming the 'heretic' as he or she can believe in no truth other than that which they hold in conscience. Even if a belief is actually erroneous (Bayle uses the example of a collector of old medals who thinks he has a priceless collection when actually they are worthless) it must be recognized as true for the person who holds it. When the inviolability of conscience is recognized, toleration is the only adequate response. Bayle further argues that as conscience is placed in us by God then to go against our conscience is to go against God: 'The law that forbids a man to blind himself to the light of his conscience is one from which God can never dispense us since, if He were to do so, He would be permitting us to scorn or to hate Him.'[1]

This thoroughly modern argument along the lines of freedom of the individual conscience – along with Locke's *Letter on Toleration* – provided a major part of the intellectual foundation for the place of religious belief in modern democracies. Bayle's preference for the sincere and righteous atheist over the sinful or idolatrous believer helped lay the foundation for the emergence of a secular morality in the late eighteenth and nineteenth centuries. It is not surprising that his tolerance of unbelief was grist to the mill of the philosophes in their attacks on what they considered to be the hypocrisy and oppression of established religion.

Bayle continued his sceptical attacks on all forms of intolerance and dogmatic certainty in his *Historical and Critical Dictionary* (2 vols, 1695 and 1697). Bayle's keen interest in history and the question of interpretation had led him to keep an account of errors and misrepresentations which he had encountered in the works of others. Eventually this collection came together in a remarkable dictionary which was written in the style of the Jewish *Talmud*: relatively short entries on topics or figures of no great importance were expanded upon in a series of footnotes and notes on the footnotes until what had begun as a relatively innocent looking and straightforward account turned into a prolonged and scathing demolition of accepted ideas.

In this manner Bayle ranged through biblical criticism, Greek philosophy, Newtonian science, political commentary, and a host of other topics, often leaving a trail of controversy (and sometimes reputations) in his wake. The *Dictionary* was a huge success and provoked widespread controversy. Some entries appeared particularly scandalous to the pious; for example, the defence of the rights of atheists and the entry on King David which wickedly recounted his immoral behaviour while ostensibly describing his good character. The *Dictionary* was an inspiration to the philosophes in the eighteenth century, and the literary tactic employed throughout the great French *Encyclopédie* of appearing to say one thing while really saying another owes a great deal to Bayle.

Bayle's influence was enormous, including a direct impact on the growth of atheism in the eighteenth century. Even if Bayle himself took the path of scepticism to reach fideistic conclusions, many of those thinkers who followed him shared his sceptical methodology but employed it to reach an agnostic or atheistic viewpoint. The difficulty for the Enlightenment thinkers influenced by Bayle was plain: if one agrees with Bayle's sceptical views on rational religion then one cannot be a deist; however, if one equally holds to the Enlightenment conviction that to believe something for which one has no rational ground is folly, then atheism is the only path remaining.

One striking example of a direct influence of Bayle on atheism is via Lord Shaftesbury's *Inquiry Concerning Virtue* in which Shaftesbury drew on Bayle to 'divorce morality from any necessary connection with religious belief'.[2] Shaftesbury's work was subsequently translated into French by the leading philosophe and atheistic editor of the famous *Encyclopédie*, Denis Diderot. Michael Buckley comments: 'Voltaire, and much of Europe with him, feared that moral anarchy would follow a denial of God. Bayle and his disciple Shaftesbury contested this thesis and advocated the possibility, which Diderot would later espouse, that the persuasions of atheism need not threaten ethical convictions and political stability.'[3]

The difficult problem of the relation of religion to morality had another important dimension which exercised the minds of many thinkers, Voltaire in particular. This was the issue of the moral status of the universe itself and, of course, the goodness or otherwise of the Creator. After Newton had made clear the basic laws of physics which governed the universe, it was commonly agreed among the intelligentsia that the Designer of these laws was wise and good. But the very consistency of the laws of physics frequently resulted in natural disasters which called into question the goodness of the Designer who had put those laws in place. If the creator was truly good, then why were these laws not more benign?

One event in the middle of the eighteenth century shocked Europe and resulted in a searching examination of the undoubted note of optimism which had characterized the new scientific and cultural ethos; this was the Lisbon earthquake of 1755. The earthquake occurred towards midday on 1 November, All Saints Day, when the churches were crowded and many people were killed by the collapsing buildings. Almost 30,000 people died in a very short space of time and it was the sheer magnitude and unexpectedness of the event that was so shocking. To understand fully why the earthquake had such an intellectual impact we have to understand the way in which many of the philosophes and others viewed the question of evil.

Christian theology had traditionally attributed the origin of both moral (i.e. human) and natural evil to the sin of Adam and Eve in the garden of Eden. It was because of this act or rebellion that the redemptive death and resurrection of Christ was necessary, and it was to overcome the effects of original sin that Christ instituted the church and the sacraments. Christianity had always lived in the tension between its belief in the essential goodness of humans as creatures made in the image and likeness of God, and their utter depravity as the offspring of Adam and Eve; the tensions between Augustinians and Pelagians, Erasmians and Lutherans, Jesuits and Jansenists clearly illustrated this. To the philosophes, however, humanity was characterized by the dignity bestowed by reason and the doctrine of original sin was an affront to this dignity. Thus, to fight *for* reason they felt that they had to fight *against* the doctrine of original sin and what they saw as its attendant pessimistic anthropology. Ernst Cassirer can therefore claim with some justification that the 'concept of original sin is the common opponent against which all the different trends of the philosophy of the Enlightenment join forces'.[4]

For the leading Enlightenment thinkers the shadow of Pascal hung over their attempts to develop a more optimistic anthropology. We have seen how Pascal subtly provokes those who are irreligious into agreement with his basic assessment of humanity as both glorious and degenerate, and then issues a challenge to them to provide a better explanation for this paradox than that offered by Christianity. If Pascal's paradox about the human condition and the weakness of reason posed an ongoing challenge to the Enlightenment's reflection on the human person, then the dilemma for the intellectuals of the time was to find a way to explain how, in a world governed by rational laws, apparently pointless evil could exist.

Furthermore, to paraphrase Voltaire against himself, it was not enough for those who opposed the Christian explanation to say merely that man was not born wicked but became so, they also had to say how he became so in a universe based on reason. Throughout his life and work Voltaire returned again and again to this challenge of Pascal's paradox, for Pascal had articulated the problem of evil as a problem at the very heart of what it meant to be a human being. His challenge to philosophy and to any non-theological interpretation of the human condition was to explain how the being in which reason was incarnate could also be so depraved.

While Pascal framed this question unreservedly in what we would now term existential terms and saw the only solution in accepting the paradox and taking the leap of faith, there were still those followers of Descartes who took up the challenge of actually attempting to offer a justification of the presence of evil in the world. The high point of the rationalist solution to the problem of evil was that developed by the

German philosopher Gottfried Wilhelm Leibniz (1646–1716), who in his *Theodicy* (1710) attempted to demonstrate that this world is the best possible world that God could have created (the precise details of Leibniz's argument need not concern us). An alternative was to take the path of the young Voltaire to place one's trust in the Designer of the universe and get on with living life to the full; this form of practical deism was essentially a convenient way of ignoring the problem. Perhaps it was the previous hedonistic complacency of Voltaire rather than any misplaced optimism which caused him to react with so much vehemence to the events of Lisbon.

In an immediate response to the earthquake, Voltaire had written a poem, *The Lisbon Earthquake*, subtitled *An Inquiry into the Maxim 'Whatever is, is Right'* in which he raised the issue of the moral justification of the event. Were the citizens of Lisbon more deserving of punishment than those of London or Paris? How can such an event be justified by saying that it is outweighed by greater goods? How could it be considered a rational part of the best of all possible worlds? Voltaire rebuts the response that the laws of nature operate irrespective of ethical considerations by posing the question: could God not have created general laws of the universe in which earthquakes and similar events did not happen? He concludes by saying that we may hope that all may be well in the future, but that to believe that it is so now is nothing but an illusion. Cassirer comments that 'as a result of the earthquake of Lisbon, Voltaire expressly retracts his [earlier] glorification of pleasure'.[5] It appears equally probable that the event and the poem *The Lisbon Earthquake* mark the beginning of Voltaire's disenchantment with the Supreme Being.

It was the meeting of Leibniz's high rationalism with the disillusioned deism of Voltaire which gave rise to one of the most effective satires in the history of literature, Voltaire's novel *Candide* (1759). Voltaire was essentially an optimist about the human condition and about the world in which we live, but never to the point of naive confidence in everything being for the best; now, stung by the meaninglessness of the Lisbon catastrophe, he turned his considerable wit and venom on the Leibnizian theory that this world is the best of all possible worlds. In the novel the eponymous hero finds himself cast from the safety of his castle home into a world where he suffers a series of horrific misfortunes. Throughout the ordeal of his travels the innocent Candide is guided by the constant refrain of his tutor, Dr Pangloss (a teacher of 'metaphysico-theologo-cosmolonigology') that all is for the best in this best of all possible worlds. By the end of his travails Candide is becoming wise to the absurdity of this claim. The novel ends with Pangloss listing the misfortunes of Candide in order to repeat his Leibnizian theory that it was for the best that all this happened because otherwise Candide would not now be sitting in his garden eating candied fruit and pistachio nuts. The well-known cryptic response of the by now doubtful Candide – that all of this is very fine but we must tend to our gardens – can be read in two ways. One common interpretation of this remark is that Voltaire is advocating that we should withdraw from the world and lead private, circumspect lives. A more likely interpretation, and one which is more in line with Voltaire's overall intention of ridiculing Leibniz's theodicy, is that we should trust not in fate or metaphysical justifications of a harsh reality, but in our own actions and abilities.

In his lifetime Voltaire was by far the most famous and influential of the philosophes, but having been twice imprisoned in the Bastille as a young man (once for writing satirical verses against the court and once for provoking a duel) he decided that discretion was the better part of a philosopher's valour and spent most of the rest of his life on his estates on either side of the French/Swiss border. On the French side he could produce his plays, which were banned in the Calvinist cantons of Switzerland, while the Swiss border was nearby should he again offend the French authorities.

His wariness of French authority is evident as early as his *Letters Concerning the English Nation* (one of the earliest important works of the Enlightenment and written after Voltaire was exiled to England following his release from the Bastille) in which he held English government, commerce, manners, intellectual freedom and religious toleration up for adulation. While the situation of the minority was undoubtedly better in England than in France, Voltaire overstated the level of tolerance (and conveniently ignored the draconian oppression in Ireland) in order to heighten the effect by comparison with his native country.

This exaggerated polemic was characteristic, for it was not Voltaire's love of religion which led him to advocate tolerance, but his dislike of bigotry and his barely disguised hope that all the Christian denominations would perish together. Throughout his long career Voltaire made a point of attacking Christianity to the extent of committing himself to its destruction. Voltaire's anti-Christian polemic is best exemplified in his *Philosophical Dictionary* (1764). In a highly idiosyncratic manner he combined fable, invention, history, observations on the natural world and philosophical acumen to ridicule Christian beliefs while simultaneously informing, delighting and at times scandalizing his readers. In entries such as 'Abbé', 'Bishop', 'Faith', 'Love of God' and 'Religion' he exposed the pretensions of prelates and popes while never losing an opportunity to strike at Christianity as such.

Some articles take an unusual detour from what one might expect their content to be in order to make a polemical point. The article on 'Climate' is typical of this tactic: in place of the expected discussion of weather patterns and the like, Voltaire discusses the manner in which climate affects religious belief. He ranges from a discussion of the pleasure of bathing in the Ganges and the reason why Muslims do not eat pork, to the origins and spread of the custom of circumcision. By thus employing a crude form of comparative religious studies, Voltaire brings religion down from the exalted heights of metaphysical truth to the lowlands of custom and culture. This form of criticism was a powerful weapon in the philosophes' battle to bring religion under equal scrutiny and criticism with all other forms of human culture and behaviour.

Voltaire's increasingly vehement anti-Christian campaign – during which he coined his famous phrase *Écrasez l'Infâme* ('crush the infamous one', i.e. Christianity) – came to a head in the 1760s with the Calas affair. The son of a Huguenot family in the south of France was found dead, and local rumour had it that he was killed because he wished to convert to Catholicism. The young man's father, Jean Calas, was arrested and executed on the basis of flimsy evidence motivated more by religious hatred than the due process of law. The event disgusted Voltaire because it proved to him the evils generated by religion: whether the son wished to convert or not and whether the father was guilty or not, one of the two had been killed unjustly for reasons of religious motivation.

It was events like the Calas affair and the abiding memory of the St Bartholemew's Day massacre of Huguenots (an event whose anniversary each year made Voltaire physically sick) which made

France the battleground between the established power of the church and the emerging secular spirit. In other European countries such as England and Holland, where the power of the church had been tempered by the power of the state, there was less bitter antagonism. From the time of the revocation in 1685 of the Edict of Nantes, the Catholic Church held enormous power as the first of the 'three estates' (i.e. 'levels' or 'orders') of French society (the second estate being the nobility and the third estate being the rest of the population who belonged to neither the clergy nor the nobility). Given the power, wealth and influence of the church it is therefore not surprising that France was the cradle of the atheism which was about to emerge among the intelligentsia. It is not known for certain whether Voltaire himself finally cast off his deism in his latter years, but his bitter anti-religious rhetoric would seem to suggest that he did move towards atheism.

Not all philosophes shared Voltaire's agonizing over theodicy. As long as Voltaire continued to view the problem of evil within the parameters of deism and the paradox of humanity as described by Pascal, then it would remain an intractable problem. However, if one no longer believed in God or the Supreme Being, the problem of evil effectively disappeared and with it the necessity for a theodicy. This is how Arthur M. Wilson, in his definitive biography, presents the position of Denis Diderot: 'But it is characteristic of Diderot, with his strictly naturalistic conception of a universe that he thought could be explained without having to predicate God, that the Lisbon earthquake presented him with no intellectual problem whatever.'[6] By the middle of the eighteenth century naturalistic interpretations of the universe which took its existence and laws at face value without attempting any further philosophical or theological interpretation were becoming current among the philosophes. Two figures in particular stand out, Diderot and the German materialist Baron Paul d'Holbach (in this chapter I shall consider Diderot and treat d'Holbach in connection with the theme of Science and Religion in Chapter 7).

Diderot's great achievement was to have initiated and seen through to completion one of the greatest achievements of the eighteenth century – and perhaps one of the greatest of human intellectual accomplishments – the enormous and hugely influential *Encyclopédie*.

From 1750 until 1772 Diderot laboured tirelessly in the face of adversity and setback to edit twenty-eight volumes of articles and plates. Until 1758 he was assisted as co-editor by Jean d'Alembert (1717–83), but following D'Alembert's withdrawal due to the difficulties which the *Encyclopédie* was encountering with the French authorities Diderot took on sole responsibility as editor.

Some knowledge of the history of the *Encyclopédie* is necessary if we are to understand its impact in the area of religion, an impact which was more indirect than direct but was no less important for that fact. In an era in which scientific discovery was increasing and influencing diverse areas of life from religion to medicine to agriculture, there was a general need for and interest in works of reference. The early part of the eighteenth century saw a number of Lexicons and Dictionaries, one of the most notable of which was the seven volume *Cyclopedia* in English by Ephraim Chambers. In the mid-1740s a Parisian publisher named André-François Le Breton began a project to translate Chambers' work into French. After two false starts he eventually appointed as editors the well-known mathematician d'Alembert and the relatively unknown author Diderot. Under their influence what had begun as a task of translation quickly became a plan for an original work in French.

The *Encyclopédie* was aimed at what twentieth-century business jargon might describe as the 'upper end' of the eighteenth-century market: aristocrats, wealthy men of letters and higher members of the clergy. The risky but successful requirement that subscribers pay in advance both succeeded in funding subsequent volumes and freeing the enterprise from dependence on the contributions of a few wealthy individuals or, worse, state subvention. When the *Prospectus* for the first edition was published there were over one thousand subscribers in the first six months; this figure may appear small by comparison with twentieth-century publishing figures but it was a significant achievement in the context of the time. The first edition eventually had four thousand subscribers and when one considers that many of these were from abroad (as French was the dominant language of culture and diplomacy) and that the fame of the work, due to its often controversial contents, led to its being widely known and discussed, it is clear that its impact went well beyond those individuals wealthy enough to subscribe.

The *Encyclopédie* was categorized according to topics arranged alphabetically, with the aim that it be as comprehensive as possible and that there be a minimum of repetition. There were a large number of contributors whose articles (for the most part) were acknowledged with the addition of their names, a practice uncommon at the time. The *Encyclopédie* is notable for the efforts of the editors to have contributors who were the experts in their fields and for the efforts of the contributors to go to great lengths to find the most accurate and up to date information for inclusion (for example, on the development of procedures in industry the *Encyclopédie* was an invaluable source of accurate information through both its articles and the detailed drawings and prints).

The articles followed no single line of thought on major matters such as politics and religion, tending to reflect the views of the contributors rather than any strict editorial policy. With the benefit of hindsight we can, for example, see that in matters of politics the contributors were relatively conservative and most of them were monarchists of one hue or another. Nevertheless, given that the contributors were drawn primarily from the ranks of the philosophes and their friends it was inevitable that certain articles would offend the political or clerical establishment. In an age when state censorship was imposed on all significant publications the challenge to the editors was to advance scholarship and critical thinking while ensuring that they did not stray over that line which would result in suppression of the whole endeavour. This was an ever-present danger for the aim of the editors was not merely to provide a work of reference but to change the way people thought; despite the plurality of views expressed in its twenty-eight volumes, the *Encyclopédie* was to all intents and purposes one very long manifesto of free thinking.

If the *Encyclopédie* can be said to have a directing spirit it was that given to it by d'Alembert's introduction to Volume I, *The Preliminary Discourse*, which showed the influence of Bacon, Descartes and Locke among others. In it d'Alembert described the growth of human knowledge throughout history as a gradual progression of learning constructed in a Lockean manner from the building blocks of pure experience, the binding thread of his argument being that the contemporary period formed the apex of an intellectual progression which had been slowed in recent centuries by the sclerotic carapace of late scholasticism. D'Alembert defined the spirit of the age as the attempt to understand everything and to take nothing for granted. In a reference to the religious Inquisition of previous centuries – but with an eye clearly on the circumstances of his own time – he observes that 'the abuse of the spiritual authority, conjoined with the temporal, forced reason to silence; and they were not far from forbidding the human race to think'.[7]

D'Alembert lauds Francis Bacon for making the move from the scholastic study of general beings to the empirical study of individual objects, and Locke for reducing metaphysics to what he calls 'experimental metaphysics', or what later ages would call simply science. While praising Descartes he nevertheless makes the standard criticism of his time that Descartes was mistaken in admitting the existence of innate ideas. This thoroughgoing empiricism which explicitly denied innate ideas, combined with a highly political view of intellectual history unsympathetic to religion, placed d'Alembert under theological suspicion, for his theories could be interpreted as an attack on some key theological doctrines such as the innate religious basis of morality and the existence of the soul.

The *Preliminary Discourse* marks a watershed in the intellectual history of the eighteenth century and thus of the West as a whole, for it is nothing less than a manifesto for a new form of thinking which was already occurring in practice but which nevertheless required justification and defence. It was a manifesto for freedom from intellectual authority, but not in the sense in which it is often understood today (as the freedom of the individual person to say and do whatsoever she wishes); it was rather a defence of the right to free investigation and a right to follow the conclusions of that investigation wherever they lead, even if that meant the critique or even rejection of beliefs held by many to be beyond doubt. It was a manifesto which would lead inevitably to conflict with religious authority.

The suspicions of both Jesuits and Jansenists – otherwise implacable enemies – towards the *Encyclopédie* came to a head in a somewhat comical, but nonetheless momentous theological controversy at the Sorbonne in the winter of 1751/52 in which a young cleric, the Abbé de Prades, submitted a thesis as part of the requirement for candidates attempting to gain the teaching licenciate in theology. The thesis was entitled *Of the heavenly Jerusalem*, and being

longer than the stipulated length was printed in very small typeface.[8]
Perhaps it was due to this fact, or to the lethargy of the professors, or
even to the unlikely possibility that there were theologians at the
Sorbonne sympathetic to the new radical thinking, that the Abbé did
very well in the examination without his thesis coming under detailed
scrutiny. When, after the examination, the thesis was published some
theologians and others did read it closely, only to discover that it
contained much that the church considered heretical, including an
attack on the miracles of Jesus and a defence of rational religion. The
embarrassment of the professors of theology was matched only by
their outrage that such a blasphemous work could find its way into the
citadel of orthodoxy.

Much of the methodology employed by de Prades in his thesis was
a reflection of d'Alembert's *Preliminary Discourse*. When it was further
discovered that de Prades had contributed an article to Volume II of
the *Encyclopédie* it was enough to convince the orthodox that the
editors were launching an attack on religion. On the basis of these
accusations the project was banned by the King for a period in 1752
but soon recommenced with the aid of some powerful people at court
(including the King's mistress) and relatively benign censorship.

By 1756 six volumes had been published and it was possible to
discern that the suspicions of the theologically orthodox were well
founded. In the first volume, for example, the article *Athées* by the
Abbé Yvon employed what was to be a common tactic of contributors
on matters theological, namely to use heterodox tools – in this case
Spinozan rationalism – to reach safely orthodox conclusions. He also
made the point that open hostility between Catholics and Protestants
contributed to atheistic beliefs, an insight which it took the Roman
Catholic Church another two hundred years to reach officially (at the
Second Vatican Council when it acknowledged that believers must
often take responsibility for the spread of atheism).

In Volume II Diderot himself engaged in scriptural exegesis in his
article on the Bible, casting doubt on the doctrine of inspiration. In
various articles which touched on theological matters it was a common
trick of the contributors to refer to the superstitious practices of the
pagans or of other major religions, thus avoiding direct critique of the
religious practices of Christianity but nonetheless leaving the readers
to draw their own conclusions.

Another common tactic was judicious use of cross referencing, allowing the editors to refer historically to, say, the errors to be found in the classical myths, while by means of a well-placed cross reference making it plain that the same conclusions could be drawn about Christian beliefs. Sometimes Diderot himself becomes wickedly provocative as when, discussing the verb 'to adore', he says that it has two uses, religious and secular: in the former one adores God and in the latter one adores one's mistress. Again, in the article on 'Fornication' Diderot begins by observing that it is a term in theology. The purpose of such clever and effective satire was not merely to entertain, but to lead the readers to the conclusion that religion was not a privileged zone of mystery which due to its divine origin was beyond the remit of historical or scientific investigation. The aim was to bring religion into the light of reason, so that its origins, practices and beliefs could become one more area of normal scientific investigation. There was also the abiding aim to mitigate the political and cultural power of the church.

Some contributors eschewed circumlocution and took more direct risks. In Volume I d'Alembert's article *Aveugles* ('the Blind') roundly praised a previous publication of Diderot's – the *Letter on the Blind* (1749) – for which he had spent more than three months in prison. Diderot's crime had been to write a fictitious account of the death of the English mathematician Nicholas Saunderson, an account considered by the authorities dangerous enough to religion to merit imprisonment. Diderot attributed to Saunderson the view that he could only believe in that which he could touch (i.e. being blind he cannot see the wonders around him and therefore can only accept for certain that for which he has concrete evidence). Diderot puts into the mouth of the dying Saunderson the words: 'If you want me to believe in God, you must let me touch him.'[9] This challenge is consistent with the practical nature of Diderot's lack of religious belief and again indicates the influence of Locke's empiricism on the philosophes.

Diderot pushes this point further to attack the argument for the existence of God based on the observation of order in the natural world, the so-called argument from design. Saunderson's interlocutor is the clergyman Holmes, who attempts to persuade the blind man that while he may lack sight he has only to feel the organs of his own body to understand the wonder of their design. Saunderson's reply is simple but crucial: even if the human body is extremely well designed, there is no necessary inference to be drawn about the possible existence of a 'sovereign supreme being'.

Saunderson applies Occam's Razor to the problem of the origin and nature of the world: if it is a 'difficult knot' then we have difficulty enough in attempting to discover the physical laws which might underlie it without introducing a Supreme Being as an attempted solution, for this 'solution' will itself soon become an even more difficult knot. While Holmes attempts to defend his view by calling on the respect for the design argument shown by authoritative figures such as Leibniz, Newton and Clarke, Saunderson replies by admitting that the universe is ordered but challenges Holmes as to his assumption that it was always so. Surely such order may have come about out of a much less ordered world?

Diderot is here struggling with an embryonic version of an evolutionary view of the world, and he has Saunderson conclude with an eloquent passage which shows how far Diderot had come towards a form of dynamic materialism: 'What is this world? A complex whole subject to revolutions which all indicate a continual tendency to destruction; a swift succession of beings which follow each other, thrust [themselves] forward and disappear; a transient symmetry; a momentary order ... [W]e shall all pass away without being able to assign the real extent we filled in space, nor the precise time that we shall have endured. Time, matter, space are perhaps only a point.'[10]

It is important to note here that Diderot is defending the idea that the world contains its own dynamism. This is a very different understanding of materialism from that of Descartes, for whom matter was inert and required external causation (i.e. God) to set it in motion; in Diderot's materialism God is not necessary for the world. Thus Michael Buckley can justifiably make the momentous claim that 'Diderot's Saunderson introduces a critical transition in Western thought with his dismissal of transcendence and assertion of the virtualities of dynamic matter. He introduces atheism.'[11] Buckley goes on to make the important point that Diderot's understanding of the material world as containing within itself the driving principle of change was not merely the idle speculation of a philosopher but was at the time becoming an accepted theory in diverse branches of the natural sciences.

While the *Letter on the Blind* shows Diderot's emerging atheism, his imprisonment made him a more cautious man; many of his most interesting and original works were published after his death. This caution was encouraged by the continuing difficulties he experienced with the publication of the *Encyclopédie*. In 1757 d'Alembert's article *Genève* appeared in Volume VII. The resulting controversy, combined with other contentious publications of leading philosophes, helped to spur a vehement reaction against liberal religious thinking. Rather than face this storm d'Alembert resigned, leaving Diderot to continue alone as editor. In March 1759 the *Encyclopédie* was placed on the *Index* of forbidden books and further publication was forbidden by the political authorities.

This was the low point for Diderot and perhaps the point at which the forces of religious orthodoxy – particularly in the form of the Jesuits – might have triumphed. That they did not do so and that the *Encyclopédie* was gradually permitted to resume publication can be put down to a number of factors: the success of the early volumes and the demand for continued publication, the fact that the ecclesial and political centres of power did not reflect the general mood of tolerance among the intelligentsia, and not least the astonishing determination and tenacity of Diderot himself. Diderot pushed the project through to completion against great odds, including the devastating discovery that his publisher was secretly censoring passages which he thought risky enough to warrant the attention of the authorities and thus endanger the whole project. However, the expulsion of the Jesuits from France in 1765 removed one major obstacle and the final volume was published in 1772.

The significance of the *Encyclopédie* is that it is indicative of the emergence of an independent, secular and empirical scientific method, rejecting the assumption which had governed intellectual and political life since the Gregorian reform of the eleventh century, namely that all matters of 'secular' knowledge were subject to the divine knowledge gained through revelation and invested in the authorities of the church; theology may once have been the 'queen of the sciences', but it was no longer so.

Part of the hatred of the philosophes for the scholasticism which had preceded them can be attributed to their infuriation at the fact that religious authority (in Paris this was primarily in the form of the

Jesuits at the Sorbonne) automatically assumed that new discoveries in the sciences should be subject to the test of religious orthodoxy. From the point of view of the philosophes, if the study of anatomy was retarded by theological reservations about dissecting the bodies of the dead, or geological theory on the age of the earth was subject to biblical chronology, or belief in the power of God to do miracles took precedence over the laws of nature, then religion must be the enemy of truth and of progress.

This was essentially a conflict of world-views, between an a-historical religious consciousness which saw itself as the protector of the divine truth which had been vouchsafed to it, and the emergence of a method of investigation which adhered to the Cartesian principle that nothing – including Christian beliefs – could be presupposed. It was a situation in which the post-Enlightenment theology of the past two hundred years – which has attempted to develop a critical theology which takes full cognizance of the major philosophical challenges – had yet to be born, and in which the early success of the empirical scientific method was evident to anyone disposed to see it. It cannot therefore be surprising that the philosophes saw all religion (save perhaps the minimum of a rational religion) as being little more than obfuscation and superstition.

Arthur M. Wilson recounts a short parable from Diderot's *Pensées philosophiques* which reveals this outlook (as well as showing Diderot's wit and his views on the theologians of the time): 'Lost in an immense forest at night, I have only a little light to show me the way. Along comes a stranger who says to me: *Friend, blow out your candle the better to find your way.* This stranger is a theologian.'[12] The metaphor of light is indicative of the philosophes' self-understanding and their view of the darkness brought about by the theologians; religion stood for darkness and the past, reason – the 'little light' – stood for the present and future of enlightened knowledge.

For Diderot and many others, the *Encyclopédie* – with its freedom of expression, its meticulous attention to detail and its attempt to describe true *knowledge* as opposed to 'superstition' – was the incarnation of the new word, the word of certainty built on methodical doubt. This word was not pre-existent, born before all time, but was being born anew every minute through investigation, observation, analysis, trial and error. Thus while the individual authors of the entries in the

Encyclopédie held varying views on religion – and despite the fears of the Jesuits they were not always the enemies of belief – the enterprise as a whole effectively served to undermine the authority of religious truth by offering an alternative vision of knowledge. Of course, this juxtaposition of the inherent rationale of the *Encyclopédie* with a negative understanding of religion is quintessentially modern: that which can be measured, described, categorized and tested is real, all else is at best fancy, at worst dangerous nonsense. Diderot's pithy remark that 'religion retreats as philosophy advances'[13] neatly encapsulates the attitude of the philosophes to the struggle in which they were engaged.

One leading thinker who did more than most to cause the retreat of religion, and whose thought proved perilous not only to eighteenth-century theology but also to Enlightenment confidence in reason, was the Scotsman David Hume. In this chapter we shall concentrate on Hume's thoughts on religion; we shall deal with his epistemology in connection with Kant (Chapter 9), on whom it had a significant impact.

In his essay *On Miracles* (Section X of *An Enquiry Concerning Human Understanding* (1748)) Hume attacks an important plank of eighteenth-century Christian apologetics, namely the claim that miracles, particularly the miracles recounted in the Bible, are guarantees of divine revelation. Hume follows a similar line of attack to that developed by an Anglican apologist against the Roman Catholic doctrine of the real presence of Christ in the Eucharist; the argument may be called the argument from *historical probability*. It begins with the common-sense statement that our experience is usually reliable, but that it it not an infallible guide – sometimes things turn out quite differently from what we have expected. This leads Hume to the view that the wise person makes belief proportional to the evidence available. Depending on the circumstances, we can trust our experience with more or less certainty. In many cases our experience allows comparatively little certainty, and we must weigh up the possibilities very carefully. What we end up with is seldom absolute certainty but a greater or lesser degree of *probability*.

Hume applies these principles to the instance of human testimony. While we may often rely on the testimony of others about events of which we do not have direct experience, doubts may arise and we must therefore test the reports of witnesses against our own experience and whatever other evidence may be available, for, Hume argues, 'the ultimate standard, by which we determine all disputes, that may arise concerning them, is always derived from experience and observation'.[14] In other words, when in doubt about something we have been told, we have to check things out for ourselves.

Now, Hume goes on, suppose we hear of something unusual that differs from our normal experience; it will surprise us because we are accustomed to the more usual way of seeing things (this idea of being accustomed to the way things relate to each other is part of Hume's overall epistemology). We now have a tension between our tendency to rely on the witnesses and our experience that this unusual occurrence cuts across the evidence to which we are accustomed. Hume resolves this tension by claiming that we must follow the evidence to which we are accustomed and dismiss the unusual occurrence. Why? – because we can reason only according to probability and in this case the evidence rests more with our usual experience. Of course if further evidence were to emerge which persuaded us that the testimony were true, then we would change our view; in the absence of such evidence, however, it would be unreasonable to do so.

Hume applies this reasoning to miracles. A miracle is by definition a violation of the laws of nature; we know these laws through repeated and constant experience, therefore a miracle is by definition a violation of this experience. Hume concludes that 'as a uniform experience amounts to a proof, there is here a direct and full *proof*, from the nature of the fact, against the existence of any miracle'.[15] In other words, we have no reasonable grounds for believing something on the testimony of others which goes against all 'uniform' experience. Into this category Hume puts the claim that a man can rise from the dead (an obvious reference to the Christian belief in the resurrection).

It is important to note here that Hume is not saying that a miracle can *never* happen; he is saying that it is so unlikely to be hardly worthy of serious consideration. Hume develops his argument in a number of ways. First, that there has never been a miracle so well attested and described by witnesses of such admirable character that it dispels all doubt and can be taken as certain by all. Secondly, human beings enjoy the surprising and the wondrous and are therefore somewhat predisposed towards the 'agreeable emotion' which something out of the ordinary provides. This should alert us to be suspicious of all such stories – the miracles of religion included – which are interesting diversions from the mundane but which cannot be judged real on the basis of the evidence. Thirdly, miracles appear to be more common among less developed cultures; Hume, like so many of his contemporaries, saw his age as being more rational, more enlightened and less prone to the mysterious or supernatural than almost all previous eras. But are there not stories of miracles from recent times also? Even if there are, counters Hume, it just goes to show that there are deceivers in all ages and the reason that they appear to flourish less now than before is that their lies are sown in less fertile soil. Fourthly, Hume provides an argument from comparative religion. There are many religions, virtually all of which claim miracles; but not all these religions can be equally true, therefore their miracles cancel each other out.

Hume concludes that Christianity was founded upon miracles and to this day cannot be believed without accepting the miraculous. For those who say that they live by faith, and not by miracles, Hume retorts that they can do so only through being determined to believe something which is contrary to well-established experience and custom. In other words, faith itself is a sort of miracle and therefore susceptible to the same objection. Hume's critique of miracles thus offers a useful correction to any overly naive theology which would base its apologetics on miraculous divine intervention. Even when his critique is corrected by the observation that it is a somewhat positivistic view of religious history, it nevertheless continues to pose a problem for certain core religious beliefs such as the Christian belief in resurrection.

Let us now turn to Hume's other important contribution on the topic of religion, his *Dialogues Concerning Natural Religion*, published after Hume's death in 1779. The theological classics of British Deism, Toland's *Christianity not Mysterious* (1696) and Tindal's *Christianity as Old as the Creation* (1730) had argued for a rational, natural religion, free from 'superstition' and believing only that which can be established by reason alone. Hume's rejection of a universal reason grounding such a religion is illustrated in his earlier essay *The Natural History of Religion* (1775) where he argued against a common origin of religion in favour of a multitude of responses to the manifold experiences of human beings in the world. The unknown causes of the forces which threaten and destroy us become the objects of our hopes and our fears; they lead humans to postulate the existence of deities, and to worship these deities in myth and ritual. This is the path to religion of the majority of people, even though Hume does allow that a rational religion may be possible for the wise.

Hume's *Dialogues* present a discussion on religion between Cleanthes (the defender of deism, which was already in terminal decline as Hume wrote), Demea (the defender of orthodoxy who, like the mediaeval scholastics, defends the classical attributes of God and the argument from design) and Philo (the character closest to the views of Hume, who simply wants to take the world as it is and draw no conclusions from it about the deity). Philo argues from the thesis that all ideas are grounded in sense impressions to the conclusion that the nature of God is beyond the limits of human knowledge. Our analogical language of perfections attributed to God says nothing about the nature of the deity, but reflects only those attributes which we ourselves hold in high esteem.

In the *Dialogues* Hume provides a compelling rejection of the argument from design (the teleological argument), that is, the argument that the order which is observed in the world implies the existence of an intelligent Creator. Cleanthes (the deist) views the world as analogous to an artifact of human manufacture, such as a machine. But, retorts Philo, the world is clearly more like an animal or a vegetable than it is like a watch or a knitting loom, so that maybe the cause of the world is something analogous to these living things. Cleanthes falls into Philo's trap by replying that the world is not truly like a vegetable or animal, for Philo's point is that it is not very much like a machine, a vegetable or an animal. In fact we can draw no conclusions about the origin of the world from the way we find it; in Hume's words, 'we have no *data* to establish any system of cosmogony'.[16] We may be able to draw conclusions about the rationality of human beings from the artifacts which they produce, but about the world as a whole we can draw no such conclusions. There is nothing in our experience which allows us to draw conclusions about the origin of *everything*. Hume's sceptical conclusion is that a 'total suspense of judgment is here our only reasonable resource'.[17] The upshot of this part of Hume's argument was that it constituted the final blow to the deists' confidence in the Supreme Intelligence behind the wondrous laws of nature.

But it was not just the God of the deists who was the target of Hume's critique. According to Pamphilus, who introduces the *Dialogues*, the whole discussion does not call into account the existence of God, but only our ability to describe the nature of the deity. However, the disputants' acute differences of opinion on the matter of the ability of reason to say anything about God *in se* depicts how fragile is the thin line between the question of knowledge of the nature of God and the question of belief *in* God. The concept of religion expressed in *The Natural History of Religion* and the ingenious ending of the *Dialogues* – where Pamphilus decides that the views of Cleanthes (the defender of natural religion) are closest to the truth, even though Philo has the best arguments, when taken together with the posthumous publication of the *Dialogues* – shows that Hume was well aware of the radical implications of his reasoning. To call into question the ability of human reason to describe the nature of the deity does not leave the likelihood of the existence of God intact, as the *Dialogues* ostensibly professes.

What Hume succeeds in doing is to drive a cognitive wedge between reasoning within the bounds of experience and the reasoning of natural theology which seeks to go beyond that experience and draw metaphysical conclusions from it. In the practical matters of politics, trade, or even morals, he writes, we can rely on common sense and experience, however, 'in theological reasonings, we have not this advantage ... We are like foreigners in a strange country, to whom everything must seem suspicious ...'[18] Philo, the character in the *Dialogues* who most closely reflects Hume's own views, offers a précis of his epistemology of religion. In Philo's words against the orthodox Demea: 'Our ideas reach no farther than our experience: We have no experience of divine attributes and operations: I need not conclude my syllogism: You can draw the inference yourself.'[19] Many did, and most notable among them – as we shall see – was Immanuel Kant.

Despite the clear evidence that leading thinkers were moving as close to atheism as made no difference, it would, however, be a mistake to interpret the eighteenth-century critique of religion by philosophers and other intellectuals as indicating a general decline in religious practice or the presence of widespread atheism. Explicit atheism was confined to a few radical thinkers and after the decline of deism even some of these retained the possibility of a god as an epistemological hypothesis. The great mass of people still held to a mixture of religion and superstition and most likely had little knowledge of, or interest in, the esoteric theories of a few philosophers. There is nevertheless evidence that in some Catholic areas there was a decline in at least the ostentation and frequency of religious devotions.[20] However, we should not make too much of this as the great decline in religion associated with the industrialization process of the nineteenth century was still to come. In some Protestant countries there were religious revivals – most notably Pietism in Germany and the Methodist revival in England – which clearly counter any naive misunderstanding of the eighteenth century as godless.

What then are we to make of the sceptical approach to religion of many important and influential thinkers? Three broad characteristics of eighteenth-century thought are of particular importance in so far as they were initially part of the world view of a limited number of educated people only, but gradually became part of the popular consciousness: these are the concepts of reason, history and scientific methodology. *Reason*, in both its rationalist or empiricist forms called into question the truths of religion either by elevating the power of the human intellect so that no external revelation was required (this was the basic principle of rational religion), or being sceptical about the power of reason to know anything beyond experience (this was the basic principle of Hume's critique of both rational and revealed religion).

The acute awareness of *history* which characterizes the eighteenth century enabled the critics of religion to view Christianity not as the culmination of Western civilization but as one period (albeit a long one) which was now coming to an end. In this interpretation of history between the glories of Greece and Rome and the achievements of the new rational age lay a great period of darkness and obfuscation. The religious wars of the previous two centuries only served to show that this great world-dominating religion was as much a human product as politics, literature, art or fashion.

The model of *scientific enquiry* in which test and experiment became the new criteria of orthodoxy, enabled a whole body of accurate knowledge to emerge which was fully independent of religion. The natural sciences provided an understanding of the workings of nature which had increasingly less need for divine intervention, while the nascent human sciences allowed for the development of non-religious anthropologies which would reject the Christian view of humanity as tainted by original sin, dependent for everything on the grace and mercy of God and living in hope of heaven and fear of hell. Feuerbach, Marx, Nietzsche, Freud, Russell and Sartre were yet to come, but the roots of their atheistic doctrines were firmly planted in the age of Diderot and Hume.

New Light or Old?: Science and Religion

The topic of the relation of science to religion in the Enlightenment is an enormous and highly complex one, which we cannot hope to cover fully here. What is possible, however, is to gain an insight into how progress in science could be interpreted as inimical to religion and how the hostility which has marked so much of the recent history of science and religion has its roots in certain Enlightenment attitudes and assumptions. One important factor which will become apparent is that it was not always scientific discovery or the personal views of scientists which caused conflict with religion, but rather the philosophers and writers who took scientific theories or achievements and interpreted them to suit their own polemical purposes. As indicative of the major areas of importance I shall concentrate in this chapter on two representative topics, the enormously influential work of Isaac Newton and the issue of materialism, which came to prominence in France in the middle of the eighteenth century, yet continues to be of interest in discussions on science and religion today.

The great figure whose achievements dominated science in the late seventeenth and early eighteenth centuries, and provided both the model and the impetus for the role of science in the Enlightenment, was Isaac Newton (1642–1727). Voltaire attended Newton's funeral and his astonishment at the honour shown the great scientist never left him. Alexander Pope's famous couplet does not exaggerate the esteem in which Newton was held:

Nature and Nature's laws lay hid in night,
God said, *Let Newton be!*, and all was *Light*.

Newton was born in Lincolnshire and became, at the age of 26, Lucasian Professor of Mathematics at Cambridge, where in all he spent over thirty-five years. He moved to London in 1696 and was president of the Royal Society for almost a quarter of a century. Among his many achievements were several advances in mathematics, including the discovery of the calculus (also discovered independently by Leibniz), important work on optics, and copious writings in theology. His enduring importance, however, comes from the publication in 1687 of his scientific masterpiece, the *Philosophiae naturalis principia mathematica* (Mathematical Principles of Natural Philosophy), which one of the foremost of Newton scholars has called 'the most influential scientific book ever written'.[1] Leibniz himself commented: 'Taking mathematics from the beginning of the world to the time of Newton, what he has done is much the better half.'[2] In the *Principia* Newton presented his theory of motion and explanation of the orbits of objects in the solar system; most importantly he extrapolated his theory to postulate the theory of universal gravitation: every tiny piece of matter in the universe attracts every other, the force of the attraction between two given bodies is proportional to the product of their masses and to the inverse square of the distance between them.

Every schoolchild, of course, knows the tale (probably invented by Voltaire) of Newton's insight into the problem of gravity when he saw the apple fall to the ground; this simple story reveals something quite important about the methods of science that Newton himself always emphasized, namely that his conclusions were based on careful observation of the phenomena (i.e. *a posteriori*) and not simply by deduction from rational principles (i.e. *a priori*). Where Cartesian philosophy had viewed scientific phenomena as primarily uncertain possibilities which could only be counted as reliable once the correct axioms were known, Newtonian science began with observation and analysis of the phenomena and proceeded to describe them mathematically; Newton's achievement, of course, was that he went beyond the merely descriptive to attempt to explain the phenomena. Thus his method is not Cartesian deduction (drawing conclusions from established principles), but rather empirical induction (moving from particular facts towards the possibility of general laws).

Sometimes Newton's work tended towards the more rational – such as in the *principia* – where mathematics was used to develop theories which were then shown to be consistent with the observed phenomena, and at other times – such as in the *Opticks* – he began with experimentation and moved to theoretical explanation. These approaches were not contradictory, but were rather the model for a new science, for Newton 'was proposing by example a *new pattern* for science, one in which mathematics and experimentation both play a part – with the emphasis placed on description and prediction, rather than on guessing at the causes of things'.[3]

For Newton the underlying first principles of everything, so beloved of the Cartesians, were unknowable. Consider his remarks in the *Principia* on the theory of gravity: 'But hitherto I have not been able to discover the cause of this property of gravity from phenomena, and I frame no hypotheses; for whatever is not deducted from the phenomena is to be called a hypothesis; and hypotheses, whether metaphysical or physical, whether of occult qualities or mechanical, have no place in experimental philosophy.'[4]

This reluctance on Newton's part to countenance the cause of gravity is ascribed by John Henry to his interest in natural magic, namely the belief that there are hidden powers in nature, powers which can be tapped and described, but the ultimate source of which is unlikely to be discovered.[5] Newton demonstrated the action of gravity, but he was not prepared to form unscientific speculations on its cause. He combined a scepticism about our ability to unearth the ultimate cause of gravity with a confidence in our ability to describe its effects, and his reluctance has been vindicated for there are many aspects of gravity which remain to be explained. So even if this caution stemmed partly from the influence of his interest in magic, it made perfect sense scientifically, and enabled Newton (and others) to go on investigating the phenomena without falling back on the error of the Aristotelian Scholastics, namely, attempting to fit the phenomena into a pre-determined conceptual framework.

The inductive method employed so successfully by Newton had been advocated already by Francis Bacon (1561–1626), but Newton's spectacular successes constituted a definitive break with the mediaeval epistemology of science which, despite Descartes' attempts to overturn it, was still influential into the eighteenth century, particularly in continental Europe. The Newtonian view of nature is commonly described as that of a machine operating according to well-defined laws and the task of science is to uncover those laws. In his book *Religion in an Age of Science*, which is becoming something of a contemporary classic on the topic, Ian G. Barbour outlines some key areas where the mediaeval, Newtonian and twentieth-century views of nature differ.[6]

There are six factors listed by Barbour which differentiated the Newtonian world-view from the dominant preceding view. First, the mediaeval view saw nature as a fixed order, which allowed for some changes and a direction to history, but was essentially static; the Newtonian view allowed more potential for change in the elements which constitute nature but the underlying structure still remained unchanging. Secondly, the mediaeval world-view was teleological, in that everything was seen as having a purpose dictated by God, and the aim of life was the fulfilling of that purpose; the Newtonian world by contrast was deterministic, ruled by causality and not by any built-in purposiveness. Thirdly, where the mediaeval view saw the world as composed of 'substances' which existed independently and were kept in existence by God, the Newtonian view saw nature as composed of discrete 'particles' which are capable of being known and analysed. Fourthly, in the mediaeval world, nature and society were understood as ordered hierarchically, with the human person standing at the centre of the earth and the cosmos, bolstered by the power of the church to mediate between heaven and earth; the Newtonian view rejected this hierarchy in favour of a reduction to the simplest components and laws which then had an effect throughout the system. Fifthly, the mediaeval world-view was dualistic, with the material serving the higher purposes of the spiritual; the Newtonian view maintained a dualism through the influence of Descartes, but it was more immanentist, with the rational replacing the spiritual as the controlling principle.

Barbour sums these factors up in a sixth point: the dominant mediaeval metaphor was that of nature as a kingdom and the dominant Newtonian metaphor was that of nature as a machine. While schemas such as this one can result in over-simplification of complex realities, there is no doubting that when the above factors are considered together they do portray a new paradigm of understanding. Newton's world is a world of order, determined in its parts and as a whole. Because it has shown itself to be a world of order it is *capable of analysis*. This is the single most important conceptual factor differentiating the world of Newton from that of the Middle Ages; even allowing for Newton's belief that 'first principles' (i.e. the fundamental laws, structures and components of the universe) could never be known, through the tool of mathematics his scientific method allows the world as we see it to be analysed and explained. Gone is the mediaeval fear of investigating the realm of divine power and in its place is the conceptual basis of modern science (or, to be more precise, modern science up to the discovery of quantum mechanics, at which level the laws of Newtonian physics appear not to apply).

Newton's achievements gained him widespread fame and a host of followers. His methods of analysis seemed so successful that many scholars in various disciplines thought that the model of Newton's mechanics could simply be transposed to theology, philosophy, medicine and other areas. This assumption was wholly in error, but Newton's success in explaining the forces which ruled the motions of the planets stoked one of the guiding premises of the Enlightenment, namely the belief that comparable laws could be discovered for the study of human nature and human society.

On the continent Voltaire enthusiastically lauded Newton's achievements to the French, seeing them as the basis for a new religion, the optimistic deism of the first decades of the century. For Voltaire, Newton epitomized the scientific and political sophistication of the English which he so admired; in his *Letters Concerning the English Nation* he wrote of Newton that it was his good fortune ' ... not only to be born in a Country of Liberty, but in an Age when all scholastic Impertinencies were banish'd from the World. Reason alone was cultivated, and Mankind cou'd only be his Pupil, not his Enemy.'[7] In Voltaire's view the mechanical picture of the world implied a Divine Mechanic behind it all, and this was enough for him to enlist Newton into his army of thinkers who, in his opinion, shared his hatred of organized religion and its attendant clericalism.

Newton's own views on religion were, however, more subtle than the proselytizing Voltaire was prepared to admit (or, perhaps, was aware of). While, as we shall see, the new science of Newton did open up the possibility that nature – and the human being as part of nature – could be studied independently of theological considerations, this possibility of the autonomy of the natural world was not one which appealed to Newton, who had deep theological interests and who was less prepared than many of his admirers to abandon mainstream Christianity. Newton devoted much of his later life to theology, undertaking a detailed investigation into the history of religions and the early centuries of Christianity; he became convinced of the truth of biblical Christianity and its God, but rejected the Trinity, holding a position close to Arianism (the belief that the Son is not co-equal with the Father). Newton's theological endeavours should not be considered as incidental to his science for, as John Hedley Brooke points out, 'Newton was deeply concerned with the action of God in human history.'[8] Thus Newton himself was not the scientist/deist whom one could meet in the writings of Voltaire, but a convinced Christian, albeit a heterodox one.

Newton was too methodical a scientist to allow his theological concerns to dominate his empirical investigations; he was not to be swayed by any misplaced unease about attempting to understand the ultimate secrets of the universe, for these were known by God alone. This, however, does not mean that he did not seek to discover the action of God upon nature. His own theories allowed him the possibility of such discovery, for there were some things for which he could find no satisfactory scientific explanation.

Newton's belief that an intelligent creator had fashioned the solar system was based on the fact that all the planets orbited the sun in the same plane, and on the additional fact that there is a single sun sufficient for all the planets (rather than one sun or none);[9] but nevertheless some difficulties remained. One difficulty was the orbit of the planets, for which his calculations could not fully account; in particular for the fluctuations in the orbit of some planets caused by the orbits of others (the planets Uranus, Neptune and Pluto were unknown to Newton).

Another difficulty was provoked by the law of universal gravitation, namely, that given the operation of gravity with no countering force why were the stars not forced together into one huge mass? (Newton, of course, was unaware of theories of the evolution and expansion of the universe, such as the 'Big Bang' theory.) Here then was concrete evidence for the divine activity: God did some fine-tuning on the planetary orbits to keep them consistent, and by an act of will kept the stars safely in their places. As regards gravity Newton was reluctant to offer an explanation of precisely how it operated, but he kept open the possibility that it too was controlled by God, and not due to a force inherent in matter itself.

Newton's view of the divine activity was consistent with his theology as a whole; he spent a great deal of time and energy attempting to reconcile his scientific knowledge with the Bible. He believed in the existence of God and in the continuation of divine activity after the creation, and did not share the deistic view that God had made the world and then left it to its own devices. While this is a wholly orthodox view, Newton's application of the divine activity to the particular instances of planetary orbits and stellar stability led some later commentators to talk of his view of a 'God of the gaps', namely a God who is invoked whenever science fails to account for all the phenomena.

This accusation is probably unfair to Newton himself, although it was always tempting for Christian apologists to point to the apparent failures of science to explain everything and say that God was required after all. This tactic could, of course, lead to very great embarrassment when science progressed towards a solution to the previously unsolved problem and God was apparently left redundant. Added to this, Leibniz's comment in his correspondence with the Newtonian Samuel Clarke that God must 'be so much the more unskillful a workman, as he is oftener obliged to mend his work and set it right'[10] showed that recourse to a 'God-of-the-gaps' would prove a very weak weapon for Christian apologetics.

Leibniz's critique of Newton at this point was based on theological principles; he feared that if God were considered to be adjusting the world from time to time then this had to be done either 'supernaturally' (in which case almost anything could be called a miracle, which would be absurd) or 'naturally' (in which case God is no longer above the world, resulting in Spinozan pantheism, equally heterodox). With the benefit of hindsight we can see that Newton's position owes a great deal to his incomplete explanation of the universe, whilst Leibniz's theological concerns are equally comprehensible in the context of the time.

Despite the theological dangers described by Leibniz, appeal to the God-of-the-gaps was a constant temptation for eighteenth-century apologists, and can be seen to be closely linked to a defence of divine power and the rejection of an 'active principle' in matter (i.e. a physical property of matter which would enable attraction at a distance). The God-of-the-gaps, however, was symbolically laid to rest in the early part of the nineteenth century when the French scientist Pierre-

Simon de Laplace succeeded in accounting for the complexities and anomalies in the orbits of the planets. When asked by Napoleon about the place of God in his theory, Laplace famously replied: 'Sir, I had no need of that hypothesis.'

Newton's own beliefs should lead us to reject any simplistic view that in the Enlightenment science was always the enemy of religion. Further, under Newton's influence, Anglican divines – such as Samuel Clarke in his Boyle lectures on 'The Being and Attributes of God' – explored the view that the new scientific appreciation of the beauty and harmony of the world indicated the ultimate beauty, harmony and wisdom of the Creator.

Nevertheless there was a fundamental tension in such a position, which when pushed to its limit opened up the possibility of a purely naturalistic interpretation of the new science. The dilemma can be stated simply by reference to Newton himself. To maintain what he saw as the necessary accord between his faith and his science Newton required evidence of the divine activity in the world; he thought that such evidence was contained primarily in the workings of the general laws of nature. However, by explaining those laws Newton left the way open for the very idea which he had wished to avoid, namely that the mechanisms of nature could be explained without recourse to divine activity. Simply put, if the theories and observations of science could explain nature then why postulate the intervention of anything beyond nature? This, in addition to his innate scientific caution, was precisely why Newton was reluctant to speculate on the causes of gravity: there was no evidence to justify the claim of direct divine intervention, but to place the power of gravity in matter itself was to question the need for any external Power at all.

Thus, this problem of the nature of matter – on the surface a purely scientific issue – turns out to be of crucial significance in understanding what was at stake between science and religion in the Enlightenment. It is possible to trace the issue through four distinct stages of its development. First, there was the dominant view before Descartes when, for the Scholastics, Aristotle was the unquestioned authority. Following Aristotle the Scholastics explained causality in terms of *forms*; (this is not to be understood in Plato's sense of Forms as perfections of which actual things in the world are poor copies, but rather as a mark of particularity within individual things which gives

them their own distinguishing characteristics). In this view everything in the world is composed of formless matter (i.e. made of the
same 'stuff') and a particular mark or form which shapes this 'stuff'
into particular rocks, trees, dogs, human beings, etc. (Of course for
the Christian Scholastics, the properties of matter and form alike
were not inherent in a naturalistic sense but were endowed as such by
God.)

When we apply this to causation, as in Aristotle's famous example of
the potter making an urn, the potter can make the urn not only because
he has the ability to do so but because the clay has within it the potential form of an urn (i.e. it is capable of being made into an urn in a way
that, for example, blood is not). The limitations of this explanation
should be obvious: it cannot apply to all possible circumstances (how
could it explain, for example, the effect of magnetism, which operates
at a distance without any apparent physical contact?). Thesedifficulties
led the Scholastics to postulate the existence of increasing numbers of
occult forces, i.e. forms hidden within things but unknowable.

The second stage is the Cartesian reaction to this emphasis on
occult forces. We recall that for Descartes the distinguishing mark of
matter is that it is extended (i.e. that it has physical dimensions).
Matter itself is inert and its motion depends on the initial impetus
given by God at the creation, motion sustained by the action of God.
This means that from a Cartesian perspective all force of matter on
matter must be caused by *contact*; it is impossible for one body to act
on another at a distance without material contact between them. This
principle led Descartes to assume the existence of invisible vortices,
that is, screw-like particles which emanate outwards from one body
and connect with the vortices emanating from another body.

This theory forms the basis of, for example, his (to modern ears)
rather strange explanation of magnetism as due to the interlocking of
such screw-like particles[11] (it is perhaps somewhat ironic that modern
theories on the activity of photons and gravitons are saying something
quite similar and, to most of us, equally strange). So, while Descartes
wished to escape from the clutches of occult forces his theory of
matter forced him to rely on an equally improbable and somewhat
crude mechanical explanation.

The third stage comes with Newton's rejection of the Cartesian
solution, for the very sound reasons that it had not been developed

inductively through experimentation but deductively from assumed principles; nor could the theory account for all phenomena, such as chemical reactions, in which there is physical contact but in which the elements frequently change radically (a common example being how two gases – hydrogen and oxygen – combine to form a liquid, water). Newton's alternative was somewhat surprising and caused some of his contemporaries to accuse him of returning to the theory of occult forces.

In his *Thinking Matter: Materialism in Eighteenth-Century Britain* John W. Yolton shows the complexity of Newton's views, which appear to have changed with time. In 1693, in a letter to Richard Bentley, Newton was calling the theory of action at a distance ('without the mediation of something else, which is not material') 'an Absurdity'. Twenty years later, however, in the second edition of his *Opticks* (1713) he was prepared to argue – at least in the cases of gravity, magnetism and electricity – that the 'small particles' of bodies had powers by which they could act at a distance.[12]

How can we account for this change in Newton's views? First, a partial explanation is to be found in his interest in the occult qualities inherent in nature. Secondly, Newton was initially reluctant to give any hostages to fortune which might associate him with the Aristotelians, for to do so would have been to discredit his own scientific credentials. Thirdly, both scientifically and theologically he was prepared to countenance, but never fully defend, the theory of active matter: this is due to the fact that he had no adequate scientific explanation for the cause of the phenomenon of action at a distance and, also, admitting to an active principle in matter opened up the theologically dangerous possibility that the principle was a property of matter itself and therefore not necessarily of divine causation.

Newton had been influenced enough by Cartesian dualism to hold that if mind could act on matter in the human person then surely God, who was all 'mind', could act on matter as a whole. Thus, he was caught in something of a double-bind and it was not one which others were slow to exploit; Leibniz – in the third of his letters to Samuel Clarke – accused Newton's theory of gravity of either advocating an occult quality in the Scholastic sense (somewhat of an insult) or else being a perpetual miracle. Newton would have been infinitely more likely to admit to the latter accusation than to the former, but that then left him open to Leibniz's other criticism of the interfering God who was an inadequate craftsman.

To be fair to Newton, while his God ruled the world this God was never the distant Divine Mechanic of deism. It was always the God of the Bible whom Newton had in mind; this was the God of whom he could say in the *Principia* that 'We know him only by his most wise and excellent contrivances of things, and final causes; we admire him for his perfections; but we reverence and adore him on account of his dominion: for we adore him as his servants; and a god without dominion, providence, and final causes, is nothing else but Fate and Nature ... But, by way of allegory, God is said to see, to speak, to laugh, to love, to hate, to desire, to give, to receive, to rejoice, to be angry, to fight, to frame, to work, to build ... And this much concerning God; to discourse of whom from the appearances of things, does certainly belong to natural Philosophy.'[13]

The fact, known to us, that Newton was essentially correct in his staunch position of defending the reality of the phenomenon of gravity while refusing to be drawn into a firm position on its cause, only serves to highlight the manner in which science and religion were intimately linked in the early Enlightenment. The movement of science away from theology and towards autonomy in its own sphere was only just beginning. This historical background should make clearer the fourth stage in this sketch, the emergence of a more explicit atheistic materialism.

According to Barbour's definition, scientific materialism makes two assertions: first that 'the scientific method is the only reliable path to knowledge', and secondly that 'matter (or matter and energy) is the fundamental reality in the universe'.[14] While these assertions are not always explicitly made by all the thinkers in the eighteenth century who tested the waters of materialism, there was undoubtedly a great deal of discussion on the nature of matter. As in most areas of contention, the result was different shades of opinion rather than any clear-cut agreement. Among German thinkers of the late seventeenth and early eighteenth century, for example, there were several materialists of different hue. Influenced by Hobbes' atheism, Spinoza's apparent pantheism and Locke's speculation in his *Essay Concerning Human Understanding* (Book 4, III, 6) that God could add the faculty of thinking to matter, philosophers argued for various materialistic doctrines, such as the materiality of the soul, the existence of the mind but not of the soul, the dependence of thought on matter, the eternal nature of the world, the identification of God and the world, and various forms of determinism. It is clear that not all of these theories were compatible and perhaps for this reason materialism did not have the same major impact in other countries as it did in France. What these various materialist theories have in common, however, is that they cast doubt on fundamental tenets of religious orthodoxy such as the immateriality of the soul (which was a necessary condition of the doctrine of immortality). Any doctrine which suggested that there were not two distinct substances – matter and spirit – was considered dangerous to religion, hence several German thinkers who toyed with materialist ideas were accused of atheism.

In England Hobbes was the foremost materialist of the seventeenth century and some accused Locke of materialism; later, a rudimentary form of materialism was present in the deist John Toland's *Letters to Serena* (1704). It was the potentially materialistic implications of Locke's empiricism which so disturbed the young Irishman George Berkeley (1685–1753) – later Bishop of Cloyne – who at the age of twenty-five published his *A Treatise Concerning the Principles of Human Knowledge* (1710). Berkeley was convinced that Locke left the way open for materialism and atheism by his acknowledgment that, despite his own professed beliefs, he had no philosophical argument to counteract the claim that there might be nothing more to thought than physical processes. Berkeley could see that Locke was vulnerable to the sceptic's claim that all knowledge of reality could be placed in the same category as colour, smell and other intangible 'ideas', and he set out to frame a counter-argument which would secure our knowledge of objects in the real world and prove to be a defence of religion at the same time.

Berkeley's brilliantly original solution – to put it simply – was to radicalize Locke's empiricism by denying the existence of matter and thereby denying the whole problem of the relation between 'real' objects and our perception of them. But if all we have are our ideas are they not caused by some thing, do they not come from an object somewhere 'out there'? Not necessarily, says Berkeley, for causation does not come from inert material objects but only from the will, and the only will that can be the cause of everything is the will of God.

Therefore God places in our minds the correct ideas which we think correspond to 'objects'; but such objects are illusory and everyone lives in a sort of wonder world of the divine creation where we are truly in the mind of God.

If this sounds bizarre to the modern ear, that is because it is. Most people today – as advocates of common sense – would probably respond to Berkeley like Doctor Johnson did when it was put to him that the rock on the ground might not exist; he kicked the rock and thought he had clearly refuted Berkeley. The only thing he made clear was that he had neither understood the depth of the empiricist's problem nor the wonderful ingenuity of Berkeley's solution. Whether philosophers consider Berkeley to be a thoroughgoing idealist or a radical empiricist, his solution to the dangers of materialism is indicative of the challenge which materialism posed to orthodox Christianity in the Enlightenment.

Among the English materialists of the eighteenth century the most noted was the chemist Joseph Priestley (1733–1804) who paradoxically combined materialism and determinism with his own idiosyncratic Christian theology; Priestley is a good example of the alliance which could be forged between science and religion, especially where authority was relatively weak as it was in the Dissenting tradition to which Priestley belonged. In his *Disquisitions Relating to Matter and Spirit* (1777) and consistent with his rule that Christianity should expunge everything which is superfluous (and this included a great deal which most Christians would consider essential, such as the Trinity), Priestley rejected the concept of the soul and attributed mental functions to the organic structure of the brain. This was daring for the time and Priestley's religious unorthodoxy and political sympathy for republicanism attracted the attention of the mobs; his equipment was destroyed in a riot and he eventually emigrated to America. As a materialist and a Christian (he was influential in the origins of Unitarianism) Priestley is an intriguing figure; however, as Yolton points out, Priestley's materialism was not influential in England and the train of thought stimulated by Locke's musings on the possibility of thinking matter died out as the century progressed.[15]

This was not the case in France as the high point of materialism in the Enlightenment came in that country in the middle of the eighteenth century. One source of ideas for radical thinkers was the

Mémoire of Jean Meslier, a parish priest who lived a life of quiet rural obscurity. However, the priest's quiet life hid a hatred of the church and Christianity which only became apparent on his death in 1729, when a manuscript was discovered which rejected Christianity, propounded a vehemently materialist philosophy, and attacked the corruption of both church and state.

Meslier saw religion as a tool of the powerful, keeping the poor in their place (an insight which later gained him the favour of Marxists). His *Mémoire* contained a long and detailed rejection of the central planks of Christian apologetics, and advocated in the place of religion a naturalism based on atheism, materialism and a mechanistic understanding of the universe. Meslier is a sympathetic figure, for his rejection of religion would appear to have been impelled by the self-serving complicity of church and state in France at the time. Meslier's work was certainly influential; portions of his manuscript circulated clandestinely and Voltaire published part of it in 1762.

By that time, however, materialist philosophy had come out in the open through the work of the century's most notorious materialist, Julien Offray de La Mettrie (1709–51). La Mettrie was a physician who delighted in being provocative. In 1745 he published his *Histoire naturelle de L'âme (The Natural History of the Soul)* and followed this in 1747 with *L'Homme machine (Man as Machine)*; the titles of these works explain their basic rationale. In *The Natural History of the Soul* La Mettrie equated the 'soul' with aspects of the body's central nervous system; against the Cartesian premise of the independence of the cognitive faculty from the physical component, he argued that thought is dependent upon the brain, his aim being to show that what was considered to be the soul could actually be explained in purely physiological terms. He argued philosophically from the Lockean premise that there is nothing in the mind that was not first in the senses to the conclusion that the mind itself can be explained purely in terms of sensations; when the mind contains only sensations and depends on the physical brain to function, then the possibility of an immaterial soul disappears.

The ire of the censors was raised by this evident atheism and La Mettrie had to flee to Holland. When *Man as Machine* was published in 1747 his notoriety was assured. Thomas Hankins summarizes La Mettrie's theory of humanity: 'In his human machine there was no essential difference between conscious and unconscious behaviour, no freedom of will, no rational soul, and no moral good beyond the perfectibility of the mechanism.'[16] What La Mettrie had done was more or less to apply to humans what Descartes had said about animals, that they were mechanically functioning entities without any controlling spiritual dimension. In the Cartesian view humanity is distinguished from the animals by the unity of matter and spirit (in Cartesian terms, body and mind); if, as for La Mettrie, 'spirit' is but a product of material processes then this distinction which allows for the unity in the case of humans disappears and with it inevitably comes materialism and the rejection of religion.

The materialism of La Mettrie draws on the materialist current in seventeenth-century thought and turns it into a total system; his views also owe a lot to Epicurean philosophy with its atomism, scepticism about metaphysical theories, and advocacy of pleasure. It is therefore unsurprising that La Mettrie's patent atheism and the perceived amorality of his views led to great notoriety – even some of the philosophes found his amorality offensive to their bourgeois values – and he spent much of the remainder of his life in the sanctuary of the court of Frederick the Great in Berlin. His importance lies not only in that he was one of the first explicit materialists and had a considerable influence on those who followed him, but that his methodology of explaining psychological factors as naturalistic places him among the progenitors of modern psychology. In his vision of the human animal no religious or spiritual elements are required to explain its function or to give it meaning; in this regard he is a major forerunner of all modern naturalistic anthropologies.

La Mettrie was not alone in exploring the possibilities of materialism. Although not actually a materialist, Etienne-Bonnot de Condillac (1714–80) developed Locke's empiricism into a strict sensationalism (the doctrine which goes beyond empiricism to the point where all innate ideas and power of reflection is dispensed with and all that remains are the sensations produced by external objects). But, of course, as soon as one opens up this possibility then one is also faced with the question as to whether the mind can be reduced to a physiological function of the body?

This problem was raised by Claude-Adrien Helvétius (1715–71) in his *De L'Esprit (On the Mind*, 1758), which took as a model the

Newtonian explanation of the physical world and asked if the same could be done for human behaviour. Helvétius defended a deterministic view in which humans are the product of education, environment and circumstance. He advocated that as conditions determine all psychological traits, the state should take over education, creating a public morality through conditioning; the realm of morality – previously the domain of the church – would become the domain of the authorities, a suggestion unlikely to gain a following among the bourgeoisie, whose growing independence of spirit tended to mistrust external moral control from any quarter.

De L'Esprit caused a furore in France for its reductionism and what was seen as its lax morality. Despite its impact and the notoriety which it caused at the time, a modern commentator has called it 'a confused and unconvincing book';[17] however, its importance lies not so much in the success or otherwise of its argument but in the fact that it opened new possibilities at a time when what would come to be known as the human sciences were being formed. The attempt of Condillac, Helvétius and others to apply Newtonian methods to human behaviour, thought and morality – by searching for laws which governed them – was an important part of the way in which the study of humanity was separated from religion and theological suppositions. Even if this often resulted in the form of theories and interpretations which were not themselves convincing, its historical importance rests in the fact that it was attempted at all.

While French materialism was based more on philosophical principles than on scientific discovery, the materialist point of view occasionally received a boost from science. One of the most famous such occurrences in the eighteenth century was a series of experiments done by the Swiss naturalist Abraham Tremblay (1710–84). Beginning in 1742 he conducted experiments on the fresh water polyp, an organism about which there was some doubt as to whether it was a plant or an animal. Polyps had previously been thought to be plants, but Tremblay had observed a digestive system, indicating that they were animals. He experimented by chopping the polyp into two, and to his astonishment the animal regenerated like a plant into two polyps; he continued to chop and each time a part of the polyp would develop into a whole organism.

Today, with the knowledge which molecular biology has of cell

structure and of DNA (the genetic 'code' which carries the instruc-
tions for each life form), this process is much less of a puzzle, but at
the time the remarkable thing about this discovery was that it
appeared to deny the concept of there being an indivisible 'soul' in
each creature. Tremblay became famous throughout Europe, as
materialists leaped on the opportunity to argue that there was no soul
or guiding immaterial principle of life, and that therefore the power of
life was inherent in matter itself.[18]

Therefore what the works of La Mettrie, Condillac and Helvétius
and others show is that in the mid-part of the eighteenth century in
France radical thinkers were beginning to interpret scientific data as
raising the possibility of a de-theologized and purely physiological
description of living things, including the human being. This
materialist anthropology was not without its own inner tensions, for
much remained to be discovered about the workings of the body. For
instance, purely mechanistic explanations of physiology were inadequate because they could not account for the vitalism of life; matter
appeared to require something other than itself to become the moving
and changing world of living creatures which we see around us. The
philosophes who favoured materialism were reluctant to return to
Cartesian dualism with its theological overtones, such as the possibility of an immortal soul. Requiring the concept of a spirit which
could animate matter they reverted instead to the ancient Stoic
concept of an all-pervading spirit (*pneuma*) which infused matter with
the vitality of life.[19] Thus all matter has a Heraclitean character,
changing, living, almost breathing; the 'soul' becomes part of matter
itself, not something extrinsic to it, nor something given only according to divine volition, and matter itself is considered 'soulful'. So the
concept of a 'living principle' animating matter avoids the problem
of purely mechanistic explanations and allows for vitalism without
theological connotations.

This more dynamic form of materialism can be seen in the writings
of d'Holbach and Diderot, where it serves a clearly anti-religious
purpose. The Baron Paul Henri Dietrich d'Holbach (1723–1789) was
a wealthy German who spent most of his life in Paris; he was perhaps
the most overtly anti-religious among the philosophes. His house was
a regular meeting place of the philosophes, contributors to the
Encyclopédie, and assorted hangers on. On Thursdays and Sundays he

held formal dinners at which were discussed the weighty topics of interest to the group. The food at these dinners was reputedly excellent but if they provided a forum for stimulating and enlightened conversation it was lost on one eminent visitor, the English man of letters Horace Walpole (1717–97), who dined regularly at d'Holbach's. Having been introduced to the company by David Hume, Walpole met there Diderot, d'Alembert and other leading figures. In a letter of 2 December 1765 to George Selwyn, Walpole comments on d'Holbach's gatherings and gives us a passing insight into the thinking of some of the philosophes on the question of matter: 'I forgot to tell you that I sometimes go to Baron d'Olbach's (*sic*), but I have left off his dinners as there was no bearing the authors, and philosophers, and savants, of which he has a pigeon-house full. They soon turned my head with a new system of antedeluvian deluges, which they have invented to prove the eternity of matter. The Baron is persuaded that Pall Mall is paved with lava or deluge stones. In short, nonsense for nonsense, I like the Jesuits better than the philosophes.'[20]

On another occasion Walpole is so bored by the conversation of the Abbé Raynal (1713–96), author of a widely read *Histoire ... des deux Indes (History of the two Indies, 1772)* – a book viewed at the time as a radical critique of colonialism, the best parts of which were actually written by Diderot – that he pretends to be deaf, only to chat as normal to the other guests later. According to Walpole, Raynal never forgave him for this slight.

Irrespective of the standard of conversation at his dinners, d'Holbach was a radical thinker who propounded a fully atheistic and materialist philosophy. Like Hume he was known as an atheist who was moral, something which was generally not considered possible by eighteenth-century society (in this regard Rousseau probably used him as the model for the noble atheist Wolmar in *La Nouvelle Héloise*). The reference by Walpole to d'Holbach's attempt to prove the eternity of matter demonstrates succinctly the link between his atheism and materialism, for if matter could be shown to be eternal, then the need for a creator God disappears.

Throughout the 1760s and 1770s d'Holbach published a series of attacks on Christianity and the church, focussing on the superstitious nature of doctrine and belief, the corruption of the clergy, and the complicity of the church with the state. He protected himself from censure and probable imprisonment by anonymous publication, although his militant atheism was well known to his close associates. If the atheism of Diderot was akin to the attitude of a man who cannot be bothered to pursue the dragon because he has more important things to attend to, that of d'Holbach was of a knight who wishes to drive the beast to its deepest lair and slay it.

In 1770 d'Holbach published (as usual under a pseudonym) his *Système de la nature (The System of Nature)*, an argument in favour of a full-blown atheistic materialism. The *Système de la nature* defends the view that matter is eternal, and requires no external cause (divine or otherwise) to move. Nature is governed by laws which, acting upon matter, result in the changes and adaptations we see in the natural world. Humans are a part of this nature, and all their so-called 'higher faculties' (reason, thought, freedom, morality) are simply products of matter arranged organically. There is, of course, no such being as God and no such thing as sin or as an eternal soul. The influence of La Mettrie's physiological materialism is evident in d'Holbach's anthropology, and he draws on Hobbes, Spinoza and Epicurus among others to produce what amounts to almost a compendium of arguments for materialism. For d'Holbach there is no Divine Providence operative in the universe, no divine plan to unveil and therefore no point in speculating on the universe as a great mystery designed for our purpose. D'Holbach's vehement materialism is not simply an anti-clerical tirade, but an attack on all religious or pseudo-religious explanations which would imbue the universe with a higher purpose and meaning.

The *Système de la nature* is a somewhat boring book in its dogmatic tone and turgid style, but it nevertheless caused a storm when its contents became widely known, for it amounted to a denial of the validity of Christian revelation, the immortality of the soul, divine Providence, and even the God of deism. In its materialism it goes further than simply attacking religion; d'Holbach also has no time for the metaphysical premises of Cartesianism, the theory of innate ideas or an extrinsic morality divorced from concrete human need.

It is little surprise that the state, the church and the deists among the philosophes all reacted against it; luminaries such as Voltaire, Frederick the Great and d'Alembert attacked it. The objections were not necessarily due to the concerns of the protagonists to protect theological orthodoxy, for the idea that matter might contain within itself the potential for movement and for thought was still abhorrent even to many freethinkers. Thus, Voltaire, for instance, despite his hatred of Christianity, defended deism because – among other reasons – he found the atheistic defence of thinking matter 'most absurd'.[21] Despite these attacks and the limitations of its own rather dogmatic argument, the *Système* proved an influential work. It was the eighteenth century's most famous public avowal of materialistic atheism and its historic importance lies not so much in the details of its argument but rather when and where it appeared, and the fact that it raised the possibility of a completely different world-view from the Christian or pseudo-Christian views which had prevailed until then.

D'Holbach and Diderot were close friends and on many things their views were similar. Diderot too was an atheist and materialist, but his materialism differed from that of d'Holbach in that it was less dogmatic and more dynamic in its appreciation of the interconnections between life and matter and between the different features of reality as a whole. His atheism and materialism were not public knowledge during Diderot's lifetime for his masterpiece on the topic *Le Rêve de d'Alembert (d'Alembert's Dream)* was not published until 1831, although many in his circle were aware of its existence. There is no doubt that *d'Alembert's Dream* is one of the great texts of eighteenth-century thought, notwithstanding the fact that it was not part of Diderot's published *opus* in his lifetime. Diderot had explored his theories on science in previous publications, including articles in the *Encyclopédie* and the anonymous *Pensées sur l'interprétation de la nature* (1753) but in *d'Alembert's Dream* his speculations come together into something approaching a comprehensive world-view.

The work was written in Paris during the hot summer of 1769. It has a tripartite structure; in the first part there is a conversation between two philosophers (Diderot and d'Alembert) where the former defends materialism and the latter objects; the second part (from which the title of the whole is taken) recounts the dream of the opponent of materialism (d'Alembert) which is achieved by the ingenious device of having the dreamer's mistress jot down his ramblings and recount them to the doctor whom she calls to his bed-side; the final part is a short conversation between the mistress and the doctor on the morality of some sexual issues including the audacious question of humans cross-breeding with other species.

The key technique in *d'Alembert's Dream* is that the opponent of materialism reveals in his sleep that he has actually accepted his friend's arguments and come round to the very position which he ostensibly rejects. What then is this position? *d'Alembert's Dream* is characterized by its speculative audacity which reveals that Diderot was a long way ahead of his time in the biological materialism he was prepared to imagine. He propounds a theory of matter in which the distinction between living and non-living matter is effaced, and in which thought is itself a product of matter; he searches for a rudimentary theory of evolution, in which the relation between species is fluid and humanity is seen as intimately a part of nature, without any unique privilege or divine spark; he rejects much conventional morality, seeing – like Helvétius and d'Holbach – the ethical solely as that which is useful for the human organism; he describes a theory of reproduction which is not far from the scientific truth, and has a concept of time which would be at home in the following century. What is striking about Diderot's speculations – and why *d'Alembert's Dream* appears so resoundingly modern – is that they appear to anticipate scientific developments at a time when Diderot did not have the accurate information which would allow him to turn speculation into knowledge. One could say that he was lucky, but this would be unfair; what is more likely is that the breadth of Diderot's knowledge gained through his immersion in the *Encyclopédie*, together with the daring of his imagination, allowed him to anticipate things on which he could only make a very well-informed conjecture.

One of the interesting things about *d'Alembert's Dream* is that unlike d'Holbach's *Système* it is not directly an anti-religious polemic; it is rather Diderot's exposition of his own world-view. Diderot always had an eye on what posterity would make of him and *d'Alembert's Dream*, in its lack of direct anti-religious argument, looks forward to the time when religion would no longer be the powerful opponent it was in eighteenth-century France. Reading d'Holbach's *Système* today it reads very much as a treatise from the past, but this is not the case with Diderot's masterpiece which, despite its scientific shortcomings, comes across as a modern document. This is because it takes for granted what modern theology has accepted: that theological presuppositions do not determine the validity or otherwise of the results of scientific enquiry and that the autonomy of science is a prerequisite for its success.

Materialism as we see it emerging in France in the eighteenth century is a combination of ancient materialist philosophy, anti-religious polemic, half-formed scientific hypotheses and brave conjecture. Its importance lies not in its intellectual sources or in the scientific accuracy (or otherwise) of its theories, but in the fact that it was an attempt by significant thinkers to formulate a completely new philosophy of life and to re-evaluate the way we understand the world. Above all, it was an attempt to re-define the human being: in the writings of Diderot, d'Holbach and others, the creature of God, the pilgrim with the immortal soul, the player in the great drama between heaven and earth, gives way to the creature of nature, separated from the beasts by the power of reason, the object of study who can turn that reason outward on to the world and grasp its laws, and inward on itself to become transparent to itself. We see here the beginnings of the major alternative world view to religion, which continues to be the rationale of Western society (and increasingly of other societies) down to this day and will probably continue to be so for some time to come.

The materialist world-view operates like a giant Occam's Razor, accepting only the immediate, empirical, material world, and refusing to consider the possibility of any immaterial entity (spirit, soul or divine being). This materialism – in its overt political form in Communist states and in a more covert form in capitalist countries – has been a major challenge to religion during the past two centuries. Whether, and to what extent, the world-views of religion and scientific materialism are compatible, if at all, is a question which deserves more detailed attention than we can give it here; what is certain, however, is that the French materialists saw religion as the great barrier to scientific progress and themselves as initiating its demise. In all of this, however, a word of warning is in order. The views of the French materialists were not mirrored throughout Europe and to say that there was a clear and straightforward conflict between scientific materialism and religion throughout the Enlightenment would be to paint a false picture.[22] The case of Joseph Priestley, for example, shows that other alternatives were possible and it is certainly true to say that the materialist outlook of the Parisian philosophes was not the only influential view in their own time.

The debate over matter was not the only place where religion and new scientific or philosophical concepts might find themselves in opposition. One area which caused increasing conflict was in the question of the authority of the Bible in the study of history. In his enormous *Histoire naturelle, générale et particulière (Natural History, general and particular,* 1749–1803*)* Georges-Louis Leclerc, Comte de Buffon (1707–88) raised several contentious questions regarding the history of the earth and the development of species, including the human species itself. The following short passage from Buffon's preliminary discourse on method (Volume I of the *Natural History*) shows his understanding of the scientific method and the place of humans in his study:

> The first cause of things will remain ever hidden from us, and the general results of these causes will remain as difficult for us to know as the causes themselves. All that is given to us is to perceive certain particular effects, to compare these with each other, to combine them, and, finally, to recognize therein more of an order appropriate to *our* own nature than one pertaining to the existence of the things which we are considering ... The first truth which issues from this serious examination of nature is one which perhaps humbles man. This truth is that he ought to classify himself with the animals, to whom he bears resemblance by all that he has that is material.[23]

Buffon's aim is to observe and clarify the relevant phenomena and then to include the human animal in that classification. This step was revolutionary at the time because it was purely naturalistic; there was no reference to biblical authority at all. Thus irrespective of his conclusions, Buffon set himself on a different course to the religious orthodoxy simply by his methodology. He proceeds to develop a method of classification of animals and plants based on the principle of similarity and dissimilarity, thus allowing him to divide them into their particular species, genus and class.

In a second discourse, 'On the History and Theory of the Earth', Buffon argued on geological grounds – e.g. changes and variations in the thickness of the earth's rock formations, the evidence showing that dry land had once been under the sea – that the movements of water and rock which had caused these geological changes must have taken place over very long periods of time under the influence of 'a uniform and constant cause'. Such an interpretation of the age of the earth, together with his investigations on the development of species, led Buffon to the conclusion that the earth was much older than anticipated and that human beings were a relatively recent arrival among the species; in addition he speculated that the earth was created from a comet coming out of the sun. This, of course, conflicted with aspects of the creation story in the book of Genesis (e.g. that the earth was created before the sun). It was also clearly opposed to the date of the earth's creation commonly accepted among Christian apologists, which had been calculated, using the biblical genealogical tables, at 4004 BC by the Anglican Archbishop of Armagh, James Ussher (1581–1656).

Perhaps Buffon's greatest contribution to natural science lay in his estimation of the enormous amount of time over which the earth had existed; although he was not the only one to raise the possibility of the earth being much older than commonly assumed, he raised probing questions based on the evidence. For example, from the evidence that the fossilized remains of life forms commonly found in the tropics in Buffon's time could also be found near the poles, Buffon concluded that the earth had cooled and that this process had taken about a million years.

Although Buffon was not ostensibly anti-religious, his advocation of the separation of the spheres of science and religion would indicate that he was aware of the potential conflict raised by his investigations: he did not publish his estimate that the earth was one million years old, but as Norman Hampson points out, 'from the theological point of view his account of the appearance of man 70,000 years after the creation of the earth was just as scandalous'.[24] The scandal consisted of the fact that the Christian churches interpreted the Bible as being a literal description of the creation and of human history, and if this suggested that the earth was about 6,000 years old, then no scientist had the right to contradict it.

To grasp fully the reason for the widespread hostile reaction of Christian orthodoxy to such scientific investigation, it is important to note that while the post-Reformation Protestant churches held to the *sola scriptura* principle and the Roman Catholic Church, following the Council of Trent, held to the two-source theory (scripture and tradition), these differences were essentially about the authority to interpret scripture and about the sources of Christian doctrine and practice; the literal truth of the Bible was accepted by all the major denominations. Therefore, as Werner Jeanrond comments, 'Lutheran, Reformed and Roman Catholic orthodoxies were thoroughly united in their rejection of the emerging scientific and rational world-view ... What was at stake for them was the inherited biblical view of cosmos and time, i.e. the foundation of all thoughts and beliefs since the emergence of Christianity in the context of the Graeco-Roman world.'[25] Stuck with biblical literalism and doctrinal integralism in which the truth of Christianity as a whole stood or fell with each of its parts, the Christian churches were for the most part incapable of responding creatively to scientific advances which conflicted with their own orthodoxy.

Thus, while Christianity, in the aftermath of its own internal conflicts retrenched into ever more fixed orthodoxies, scientific investigation was ploughing another furrow. There were advances in almost all the branches of science. The Swede Carolus Linnaeus (1707–78) developed a model of botanical classification (later criticized by Buffon), as well as the system for naming plants which is still used today; the French naturalist Jean-Baptiste Lamarck (1744–1829) developed an early form of the theory of evolution; Joseph Priestley discovered the gas later known as oxygen; the French chemist and geologist Antoine-Laurent Lavoisier (1743–94) – truly representative of the Enlightenment in the breadth of his interests and achievements – was the founding figure of modern chemistry; the Swiss Albrecht von Haller (1708–77) and others made important progress in the study of physiology and anatomy; there was an increasing interest in archaeology and ancient history, fuelled by the discovery of the ruins of Pompeii and Herculaneum; Montesquieu (1689–1755) argued in his *L'Esprit des lois (Spirit of the Laws,* 1748*)* that the laws governing human behaviour and customs varied according to climate, thus contributing to the birth of sociology.

These advances were by no means necessarily inimical to religion, but as the century advanced and the scientific method proved so successful, there was always present the possibility of viewing nature not as a fixed creation but as an autonomous, evolving process which might not give up all its secrets, but was accessible enough to be a suitable object of rational investigation. It was then inevitable that what was applied to the natural world would eventually be applied to human beings as part of that world (Lamarck, for instance, contributed towards the rise of the nascent human sciences by including human beings as objects of investigation in his zoological studies).

If humans were part of nature, subject to the same forces and effects as all other life forms, then the Christian anthropology of the human as the creature of God (with an immortal soul, marked by sin and restored by grace, etc.) was called into question, on the principle that if nature was governed by laws which could be discovered by the correct scientific procedure, the natural explanations offered by science could be taken as a wholly adequate explanation requiring no further religious interpretation. Pope's famous line in his *Essay on Man* that 'the proper study of mankind is man', is indicative of the expansion of the scientific method to include not simply the natural world but the human being also. From being a spiritual pilgrim on the journey to heaven or to hell, residing in a world that is not its true home, the human person had become an intricate part of the natural world. In the Enlightenment we were brought right down to earth, and a naturalism of the human sciences, just as much as of the natural sciences, became a constituent part of the world-view of science as the eighteenth century progressed.

For those in the eighteenth century who were influenced by Locke, the human being was the locus of virtually limitless potential; as the mind was a *tabula rasa*, a blank page receptive to the impact of education, knowledge and an open culture, the possibilities for human development seemed increasingly positive. The Marquis de Condorcet's (1743–94) *Equisse d'un tableau historique de progrès de l'esprit humain (Sketch for a historical picture of the progress of the human mind, 1797)* was the eighteenth century's most optimistic statement of the belief in progress. According to Condorcet, 'We shall find in the experience of the past, in the observation of the progress that the sciences and civilization have already made, in the analysis of the progress of the human mind and of the development of its faculties, the strongest reasons for believing that nature has set no limits to the realization of our hopes.'[26] Condorcet's *Sketch* was written in the second half of the century, when the evidence of a certain amount of actual progress was evident, but his words have the tone of wishful-thinking about them. Whatever hope there might have been for rational and steady progress towards the elimination of want, sickness and war came to an abrupt end with the 'terror' which followed the revolution of 1789, and in which Condorcet himself died.

Although we could not in this chapter treat all aspects of the relations of science and religion in the Enlightenment we can still profitably conclude with some general remarks on the topic. The Enlightenment saw the end of two important pillars of the mediaeval edifice of knowledge which are crucial to understanding the strain under which religious thought came during the eighteenth century: one was the Aristotelian synthesis (i.e. the belief that all knowledge could be unified and encompassed in one intellectual structure, in this case the thought of Aristotle) which had been under pressure since Francis Bacon and Descartes, and the other was the dominant position of theology as the primary science to which other forms of investigation must bow. The former was forced to give way in the face of Newtonian physics and the latter, damaged by the new science, was gradually pushed to the margins of intellectual discourse as newer and empirically more successful disciplines came into being.

In assessing the role of the Enlightenment in the development of science, Hankins makes the following judgment: 'The creation of the new scientific disciplines was probably the most important contribution of the Enlightenment to the modernization of science.'[27] Each of the then new disciplines or sub-disciplines with which we are familiar in the modern university and which have their roots in the Enlightenment (e.g. chemistry, physics, biology, sociology, psychology, anthropology, etc.) required a method, and the model for that method was essentially that of both Bacon and Newton, that natural processes are subject to laws, that these laws can be observed and seen to be constant, and that empirical analysis of natural processes can yield practical results.

The scientific events of the eighteenth century were in many respects one great experiment, where the important element was not the actual results which were achieved, but the fact that the experiment was conducted at all. From the historical perspective it matters little whether the new conjectures on the age of the earth or the biological details of reproduction were correct, what was crucial was that the way of approaching these questions had changed, from a mainly deductive method based on the citation of authority and consistency with theological principles to a more inductive method based on empirical investigation and the formulation of laws. G.E. Lessing's comment that it is 'not the truth that a man possesses, or believes that he possesses, but the earnest effort which he puts forth to reach the truth, which constitutes the worth of a man. For it is not by the possession, but by the search after truth that he enlarges his power …'[28] epitomizes the Enlightenment attitude to investigative method. Despite the moral tone of Lessing's language, he is not moralizing about how good people should spend their time, but rather formulating a dynamic concept of truth; what Lessing is assuming is that truth may not be easily found, that it requires a search and that the possession of 'truth' may not be the greatest achievement. It is a dynamic concept of truth and of the method of investigation and as such is the antithesis of the static concept of revealed truth which characterized the religious orthodoxy of the time.

Thus, what is of greatest importance in studying the relation of science to religion in the Enlightenment is not the content of the scientific discoveries, but the horizons opened up by the scientific method itself. Despite the intellectual excitement generated by discoveries such as that of the self-regenerating polyp, few people abandoned religion because of advances in science – it was more that science offered an alternative rationale and helped form an atmosphere in which the rejection of religion was possible. That rejection began to happen more forcibly in the following century, the century of scientific positivism, but its roots were sown in the Enlightenment.

The crucial step which began the dethronement of theological truth from its high status was the belief that the progress of science in understanding the natural world could also be achieved in the analysis of human society. When that step was taken, the theological understanding of the human person was, if not explicitly abandoned, at least left conveniently to one side; but very often it was left aside for good. The concepts of creaturehood, original sin, grace, the immortal soul, Providence, miracles and other Christian doctrines no longer formed the interpretative framework within which the human being was studied and conceptualized. Instead, we became citizens, patients, minds, children of nature, products of reason and of education. In the Enlightenment the mediaeval image of the contemplation of truth gave way to realization of the Baconian image of the search for truth, and in that change of image – when humanity becomes the object of its own search for truth – is to be found the origin of the modern, secular human sciences.

So much for humanity, but what of God? From Descartes to Laplace, God's role in the great world system was eroded, and Pascal's intuition that to use God as a metaphysical prop in the cosmological theatre would prove self-defeating was borne out. Alexander Koyré has argued that the pivotal point in the fall from power of the concept of God was the victory of the Newtonian over the Leibnizian concept of divine activity: Leibniz's concern was not to make God responsible for the good or bad running of the world, Newton's was that the workings of the universe should portray the infinite power and presence of God. But where Newton saw the power of God, others saw natural processes: the pull of gravity became a property of matter alone, the clockwork universe was seen to be self-perpetuating, and space ceased to be the locus of the divine presence and became instead 'the frame of the absence of all being, consequently also of God's'.[29] As Koyré observes, by the time Laplace made his famous comment to Napoleon, it was not so much his theories which had no need of the hypothesis of God but rather the world he described therein.

The Morality of Innocence: Jean-Jacques Rousseau

As has been emphasized throughout, the Enlightenment was not a uniform movement, with a single overarching policy or strategy. There were significant differences between the leading thinkers on almost every matter of importance. The common cause of the Enlightenment lay not in what its most famous proponents agreed on but more in what they rejected: the weight of tradition, the power and influence of the church, superstition in all its forms, obscurantism in the sciences, and an overly negative vision of human potential. And, as we saw with the deists, there were also those who wished to accommodate religion to progress, purify it of all unnecessary baggage, and advance it to a clear and natural purity. This, too, can be seen as an Enlightenment ideal.

It is hardly surprising, then, that there were tensions within the Enlightenment itself and that there were significant thinkers outside its conventional boundaries whose thought in many respects ran counter to some of the Enlightenment's central ideals. In this chapter we shall look at the most significant of these thinkers, the enigmatic figure of Jean-Jacques Rousseau.

Rousseau (1712–78) was one of the most interesting individuals of the era, a man who was enormously creative and influential, yet who managed to alienate almost all his close associates through his idiosyncrasies and paranoid character. Rousseau was a Genevan Calvinist who briefly converted to Catholicism (for reasons that had little to do with personal conviction and much to do with securing for himself an income), yet who was motivated more by his own understanding of his own emotions than by any religious system of morality. His most productive literary years were spent in Paris where he struggled to make his way. He fathered five children by his lover, an illiterate servant, all five of whom were given up for adoption.

In Book II of his *Confessions* there is an intriguing anecdote from Rousseau's early life which gives an insight into the quirks of his personality, but unfortunately leaves us with as many puzzles as answers to the true character of this enigmatic man. Rousseau has been befriended by a Mme de Vercellis, and on her death he steals an old pink and silver ribbon from her house; he is discovered and immediately blames the young cook, Marion, whom he describes in glowing terms in his *Confessions* as honest, blameless and lovable. They are both dismissed and the guilty memory of the event continued to haunt Rousseau forty years later. What is remarkable, however, is not so much this deceitful act or Rousseau's remorse but his protestations in the *Confessions* that he accused Marion because of his friendship for her, as she was in his mind at the time. He adds – astonishingly – that it was not fear of punishment but his fear of shame and disgrace that caused him to lie, allied to his young age (although he was in his late twenties at the time) and the inability of the accusers to see the truth. He exonerates himself and concludes that he was little to blame, yet he continues to feel great remorse; what he is experiencing is an attempt at gross self-justification which he knows to be another deceit. Rousseau's life and writings are full of such contradictions, but this should not be taken as an *ad hominem* argument to invalidate his thought as a whole. In his case however, because of his emphasis on the sensibility of the individual human heart, it is difficult wholly to dissociate his own personal experiences (of which he made so much) from the content and impact of his writings.

So while Rousseau's writings do reflect this unique approach to ethics and while his explanations for his own behaviour were a confusing amalgam of high-sounding prose and self-justifying rationalizations, in his style of writing and in the daring of his ideas he was one of the great French writers of the eighteenth or of any other century. But Rousseau was not a philosopher in the classical sense of being a thinker who develops a systematic body of work; he was rather a writer who took on great themes: the nature of the human person, the constitution and responsibilities of society, the purpose and end of religion. Reading Rousseau is both a rewarding and infuriating experience, for the brilliance of his ideas are intermingled with the idiosyncrasies of his character. It seems that many of his contemporaries had a similar experience with Rousseau himself, for his thought was much admired yet he quarrelled with Diderot, d'Alembert, Hume and many others.

However, his thought was radically independent and he is a crucially important figure in the Enlightenment in so far as he shared some of its ideals yet rejected many others. Rousseau's works leave his legacy open to conflicting interpretations: he is often considered to be the father of Romanticism, a major influence on the development of democracy and the first modern individual; alternatively, he can just as easily be read as a proto-totalitarian or merely self-obsessed neurotic. The former interpretation continues to be the most common, and that is why Rousseau deserves consideration under the rubric of currents running counter to the Enlightenment mainstream: he does not fit neatly into the picture of the rational man of the eighteenth century, who placed his faith in progress, scientific achievement, and common reason.

In his early adulthood Rousseau made his living variously as a kept lover, a copyist of music, as secretary to the French ambassador to Venice and as an occasional writer (including writing some entries on music in the *Encyclopédie*). Living in Paris in the late 1740s he was acquainted with the philosophes, but was really on the fringe of the group and had so far achieved little of note. One hot October day in 1749 Rousseau walked the six miles from Paris to the prison at Vincennes to visit the incarcerated Diderot (imprisoned for his *Letter on the Blind*). As he walked he read a publication called the *Mercure de France* and came across notification of a competition staged by the Academy of Dijon for a prize on the topic: 'Has the revival of the arts and sciences done more to corrupt or to purify morals?' According to his own account Rousseau was overwhelmed by ideas on the topic to such an extent that he remained for half an hour transfixed to the spot, weeping with the enormity of his insights.

After this road to Damascus experience he arrived at Vincennes in a highly excited state and outlined his ideas to Diderot, who encouraged him to enter for the prize, advocating that Rousseau take up the view that the other entrants would not. It was good advice, for Rousseau's essay – *Discours sur les sciences et les arts* (*Discourse on the Sciences and the Arts*, 1750) – won the prize and gained him immediate fame. Had his essay pandered to the expectations of the time and replied to the question in the affirmative – as no doubt the greater part of the intelligentsia would have expected – then Rousseau might well have faded back forever into the obscurity from which he came; however, his answer was in the negative. In highly rhetorical language Rousseau attacked many of the so-called 'benefits' of modern civilization, the decadent luxury of the life of the city, and the pretensions of the arts and sciences to better the lot of humanity; even printing and books were to be considered more futile searching after useless knowledge.

This might appear as an astonishing thesis to win a prize at the same time as the first volume of the *Encyclopédie* was being published, but Rousseau seemed to strike a deep chord in his readers. Even if they did not fully agree with him, they found a resonance in his belief that human beings were essentially good and that it was circumstances – society, learning, artistic affectation – which made them bad and resulted in the evils of society. In this discourse Rousseau is developing the ideas which would later land him in much trouble with Catholic and Protestant authorities alike: mankind is not inherently bad, but inherently good, and evil is the product not of theological offences but of social factors which can be traced and explained, a position which is a clear rejection of the doctrine of original sin.

These ideas were developed further in his *Discours sur l'inégalité* (*Discourse on Inequality*, 1755). Here, Rousseau argued that compassion is the great natural virtue of human beings, the virtue from which all other virtues – friendship, generosity, mercy, etc. – flow. It is compassion for others which limits the destructive tendencies of excessive love of self, stimulates greater equality and thus provides for the success of the human species. For Rousseau love of self should properly give rise to compassion, and such compassion is greatest in 'a state of nature', where we do not need laws or the morals established by society. Humanity before the advent of society is marked by moral innocence and by this compassionate feeling for the well-being of others. It is not rationality which rules in the perfect state of nature, but feeling and empathy with one's fellow humans.

Modern society, however, is far from a state of nature. In a famous passage Rousseau asserts that the first person to enclose a piece of ground and say 'This is mine' was the founder of society as we know it. If those people around the first defender of private property had not been so gullible as to accept this, then so much of the evil, horrors, wars and misfortunes that have befallen humanity could have been avoided; the truth is that the earth belongs to no one and its produce belongs to everyone. In Rousseau's primordial mythology the Garden of Eden existed all right, but its perfection was not spoiled by disobedience of the divine command but by the desire of the first *bourgeois* to possess that which belonged to all, nature itself. The original sin could be found not in the desire to be like God by eating of the tree of knowledge but in the desire to be different from everyone else through the possession of real estate.

So, according to Rousseau, inequality and the other evils of society are the result of the desire for private property; this desire gives rise to inequality, already present to some extent in the differing natural abilities of persons. To preserve private property, law is required, but the real destructive result of law is the consolidation of inequality and the foundation of discrete communities, each subject to a ruler. Rousseau sees a tripartite structure of oppression operating on the basis of the possession of private property: first, property rights and their defence by the law gives rise to the separation between rich and poor; secondly, rulers are required to enforce the law and this gives rise to the rule of the powerful over the weak; and, thirdly, legitimate power gives way eventually to arbitrary power and the ruler becomes a despot. Rousseau concludes that revolt against despots is inevitable and that they have no right to complain about this as they themselves took power through the same use of force.

Such ideas were hardly geared towards endearing their author either to church or state. Rousseau further developed his anthropological/political thought in one of his most influential works, *Du contrat social* (*The Social Contract*, 1761), his attempt to answer his own question as to why if man was born free he is now everywhere in chains. Rousseau's answer is open to a range of explanations, from a defence of democracy to the advocation of totalitarianism. In *The Social Contract* he puts forward the idea of the 'general will', an enigmatic concept which is open to several interpretations. Discussion of the 'general will' belongs more in the realm of political philosophy than of religious studies, but it is important for our purposes on two counts.

First, Rousseau's political thought was interpreted as subversive of authority, whether of church or state in so far as it advocated participation of the citizens in the decision-making process (or, perhaps more accurately, that those who made the decisions should reach decisions which reflected the general will of the citizens). The all-embracing character of the general will meant that religion too must be subject to its dictate and to this end Rousseau advocated a form of natural religion. Secondly, it appears at times that Rousseau's ideal state owes a great deal to the political structure of his home town of Geneva – of which he frequently and proudly referred to himself as a citizen – thus raising the issue of the impact of Calvinist theology on European political theory. This topic is beyond the scope of the present work, but it is worth noting Rousseau's bitter disappointment when the Small Council of Geneva (the highest ruling body) condemned *Emile* and *The Social Contract*. The city-state which Rousseau had admired as a model of good government had shown itself somewhat less tolerant than he had anticipated. Rousseau was prepared to trace this intolerance back to Calvin himself: 'Calvin was undoubtedly a great man, but he was, in the end, [only] a man, and what is worse, a theologian. He had, besides, all the pride of a genius who feels his superiority and who is outraged that anyone disputes it with him.'[1]

Towards the end of *The Social Contract*, Rousseau outlines his view of the role of religion in society, what he terms the role of *civil religion*. He assumes this religion to be Christianity, and his understanding of the Christian religion determines what its role in the state is going to be. Rousseau's interpretation of Christianity is as a religion concerned solely with the other world; it is a purely spiritual religion. Rousseau's Christian, waiting for the world to come, is ultimately indifferent to the course of events here on earth: if his nation is prosperous the Christian is reluctant to share in that happiness for it may lead to undue pride in his country, and if things are going badly then it can only be the hand of God chastising his people. This is Rousseau's interpretation of the religion of the gospel, one of the two possible ways in which he sees religion in relation to society; focussing on the hereafter, and being indifferent to the needs of society, gospel religion (which Rousseau considers to be the 'natural' religion) does not contribute to the overall well-being of society for it turns the attention of its adherents to another world, the world to come. This gospel religion

unites people in the spiritual realm – even to the point of their con-
tinuity as a spiritual community after death – but it does nothing to
unite them in the civil realm here on earth.

The second way in which Rousseau presents religion as relating to
society is through what he calls 'the religion of man'. This is the established religion of the state, with prescribed dogmas and rites, which
sees all other forms of religion as foreign and threatening. The
'religion of man' operates so as to make religion subservient to the
needs of the state, so that through the beliefs and rituals of the religion
it is the state, and not God, which becomes the true object of worship.
Here the true pope is the prince, the true priest is the magistrate,
impiety is equated with breaking the law, and martyrdom is to die for
one's country. But this arrangement is not wholly advantageous, says
Rousseau, for it is founded on a deception and results in a superstitious form of religiosity which replaces true worship with empty
ceremony. Further, equating one's own religion with the state results
in intolerance of other forms of belief, which paradoxically leads to
conflict with other peoples and thereby endangers state security.

As with so many aspects of Rousseau's thought there is a tension
here between his desire for a pure and personal form of worship and
belief and his desire that religion bolster the laws, authorities and
internal structure of the state, and he can see the advantages and
dangers in both possibilities. However, these are the only two possibilities open to Rousseau, for he rejects completely the possibility that
religion would operate alongside the state as a parallel power, for he
had first-hand evidence from French Roman Catholicism of the
pitfalls this could bring for the state.

This reflects a tension inherent in Rousseau's home and model
state, Geneva, where the Calvinist form of theocratic government
existed in an at times uneasy relationship with the liberating
Protestant emphasis on the purity of the gospel and the inviolability of
the individual conscience. To put this more prosaically, Rousseau
wishes to have his bread and to eat it too: his ideal state would therefore be one in which all the citizens adhered in freedom both to a pure
form of natural religion and to the laws and authority of the state.

However, given the unlikelihood of this ever becoming a reality,
and given that in Rousseau's view it is to the advantage of the state that
each citizen has a religion which inculcates in them a sense of duty, the

ruler should take matters into his own hands and decree what the civil religion of the state should be. The beliefs of this civil religion would be less like religious dogmas and more like 'social sentiments', encouraging people to be good citizens. Anyone who would not adhere to the decreed beliefs would be banished, not because they were heterodox religious believers but because they were bad citizens! Rousseau's dogmas of civil religion turn out to be a straightforward recommendation of deism with a social twist. He advocates belief in a powerful, intelligent and good deity, eternal life (in which there will be reward for the good and punishment for the bad), plus the social contract and the laws of the state. These are his 'positive dogmas'; his one 'negative dogma' concerns tolerance and intolerance, and it sits in uneasy contradiction with his view that anyone who does not hold to the positive dogmas should be banished from the state. Rousseau believes that religious intolerance and civil intolerance are inseparable, the former usually giving rise to the latter, with priests becoming the true powers in the state. Therefore, only those forms of religion should be tolerated which themselves tolerate others. The belief that salvation consists only in membership of a particular church is admissible only when that church is the state; in other words, the only sect allowed absolute status is the sect of everyone together under the rubric of the state.

Rousseau's real target here is the Roman Catholic Church and the power which it exerted in French society in the eighteenth century. His dogma of tolerance is restricted to those who (unlike the Roman church) would not make themselves too powerful vis-à-vis the state or other religious groups. But Rousseau's intolerance of the perceived intolerance of those who did not adhere to his dogmas of civil society results in inconsistency and contradiction, for an imposed tolerance through the imposition of a sort of common denominator of belief is ultimately no tolerance at all. Rousseau would seem to have been aware of this contradiction and tried to avoid it by making the religious dogmas of the state the only dogmas of the church, so that his ideal state was a theocracy in which the theocratic ruler was not the priest or elder, but the prince or ruler. The key to this move lies in the minimalist dogmas of civil religion, but these themselves are open to objection, qualification and denial, and in the end it is difficult to see how his schema could be at all workable in practice.

The inescapable flaw in Rousseau's theory of civil religion is that he ultimately reserves the appellation 'intolerance' for the views of those who desist from his own ideal, and this is a recipe not for toleration but for oppression. It is this type of tendency in Rousseau – to advocate the imposition of an ideal in order to rid society of perceived faults – which has allowed many commentators to see in him the precursor of totalitarian systems of thought. But this dilemma faced by Rousseau – how or whether to tolerate those who do not share one's basic assumptions on tolerance and see it as a form of weakness or supplication – is one common to all theorists of toleration, and was a particularly acute problem in a period of European history in which religious wars were still fresh in the mind and religious conflict and disputes never too far away. Rousseau's problem remains our problem too as, for example, forms of Islam which do not share our society's views on toleration continue to raise theoretical and practical problems for our political, social and religious institutions.

A more simple and appealing picture of toleration than that of the theory in *The Social Contract* can be seen in Rousseau's novel *Julie, ou La Nouvelle Héloïse* (1761) where he presents us with a model relationship of tolerance, the marriage between the virtuous atheist Wolmar and the pious Julie. While neither can accept the beliefs of the other this does not prove detrimental to their relationship; Wolmar can see the personal and psychological benefits of Julie's religious beliefs, while for her it is Wolmar's goodness and the idyllic tranquillity of their home that are of ultimate importance. Rousseau was neither an atheist nor a conventional Christian, so the couple's ability to live in peace with their differences can be read as a didactic example of tolerance aimed at the warring parties of atheists and orthodox believers, whom Rousseau saw as equally mistaken in the excess of zeal which they showed for their respective positions. In the innocence of her belief Julie demonstrates to the atheists (the circle of d'Holbach which Rousseau so disliked) that it is possible to be an orthodox Christian who is fully sincere in belief yet tolerant of the views of others; in combining moral goodness and family life and a respect for the beliefs of Julie with a gentle and sceptical atheism, Wolmar shows the guardians of orthodoxy that atheism does not necessarily lead to moral corruption and an attack on religion. In the estimation of Rousseau, if the antagonists could not see that the extremes of dogmatic orthodoxy and dogmatic atheism were equally fallacious, and given that they were unlikely to be persuaded of the truth of the opposite view, they could at least attempt to see that it was possible to live in relative harmony with their differences.

It was not, however, Rousseau's political theory which was to cause the storm which raged around him for the remainder of his life but parts of his theory of education. More precisely, it was the theological content of *The Confession of Faith of the Savoyard Vicar* in Book IV of *Emile* (1762), his treatise on education, published, according to the *Confessions*, only a month or two after *The Social Contract*. In *Emile* Rousseau's rejection of the Christian doctrine of original sin comes to complete expression. Emile, the eponymous boy whom Jean-Jacques is educating, is truly a *tabula rasa*, a creature of innocence whom Rousseau pointedly places in a garden in which there are no rules, no taboos to be broken and no divine punishment to be meted out. Rousseau's aim is to show that freed from the structures, opinions and illusions of society Emile can become a wholly natural man, living in harmony with himself and with nature. Emile is to be a creature who stands outside the normal boundaries of morality and social convention; Rousseau aims to make him, to employ a Nietzschean anachronism, a creature beyond the conventional morality of good and evil.

To this end he gives Emile a single book to read, a fine paradox for one who despises *all* books and considers them a plague on childhood yet who is himself writing a book (but such paradoxes abound in Rousseau). The book is Defoe's *Robinson Crusoe*, the bible of the solitary man, creating himself without the aid or hindrance of society. The choice of book, most importantly that it is not the Hebrew/Christian Bible, is indicative of Rousseau's intention to reject Christian morality (and this from a man who claimed that he himself read the Bible every night in bed and had completed it five or six times). The morality of Emile will be one in which his desires, inclinations and needs are paramount. Rousseau's principle is that our first duty is to ourselves and not to others. He attempts to invert what he saw as the normal pattern of raising children, namely that they are taught their duties before their rights, by teaching Emile first his rights and them showing him that his rights must be balanced by the duty to respect the rights of others.

In Emile's garden – his 'island' – he learns with the aid of his tutor

Jean-Jacques how both to put himself first yet also to become conscious of the rights of others. In Book II of *Emile* Rousseau presents us with a parable through which Emile learns an important moral lesson. With the aid of his tutor Emile plants some beans; they are his property, the fruit of his own labour and he takes great delight in their growth. But arriving one day to water them, Emile discovers that his beans have been dug up. This is his first taste of injustice and he is both angry and distraught. Emile and Jean-Jacques discover that Robert the gardener has dug up the beans and they call him. When they complain about his action the gardener retorts that Emile's beans were planted over the seeds of some Maltese melons which he had planted; now Emile has both lost his beans and will not have the pleasure of eating the wonderful melons.

At Jean-Jacques' suggestion a compromise, a social contract, is reached: he and Emile will receive a part of the garden for their use and in return will give Robert the gardener half of what they produce. Thus Emile learns that his own rights and needs come first, but that they cannot override the rights of others, and that where conflict arises a compromise of rights is the best solution. In this short parable Rousseau combines his theory of rights with a lesson in morality: rights and duties coincide. It is in Emile's interest that he respects the gardener's property, for in respecting the rights of the gardener he guarantees protection of his own rights. Thus Rousseau presents us with a form of natural morality based on recognition of one's own rights, and a consideration of the rights of others resulting in the compromise of the social contract. We have here no external authority, either divine or secular, nor a social hierarchy which abrogates the rights of the weak in favour of the strong. Everyone has natural rights, and this cannot be denied even if in practice some will have more power than others (Emile, after all, must give *half* his produce to the gardener in return for a small tract of land).

Under the guidance of Jean-Jacques, Emile develops from the child of nature to become the natural man. At the end of Book III (when Emile is fifteen) he has learned all the virtues relating to himself. He is hard-working, patient and courageous; he does not fight against necessity and therefore, although he does not yet understand what death is, he is already well-prepared for it. Above all, Emile is self-sufficient, not merely in material terms through his garden, but he is morally and intellectually independent. He is without prejudice and as innocent of faults as one could expect; he has reached the threshold of adulthood without harming anyone else. Emile is not a child of God but a child of nature; he is not the pilgrim on his way to heaven, but the solitary man at home on the island; he does not bear the mark of original sin but the mark of innocence; and he is at last ready to take the great step towards adulthood and enter into society. Books IV and V are concerned with Emile's emergence into the adult world, and in particular with his discovery of his sexuality and the relation between the sexes.

On the latter topic, Rousseau has received much criticism for his – in our terms – plainly sexist view of women. Emile's companion Sophie does not receive the education offered Emile, for in Rousseau's view women were incapable of comprehending the higher forms of knowledge: 'The quest for abstract and speculative truths, principles, and axioms in the sciences, for everything that tends to generalize ideas, is not within the competence of women ... Regarding what is not immediately connected with their duties, all the reflections of women ought to be directed to the study of men or to the pleasing kinds of knowledge that have only taste as their aim; for, as regards works of genius, they are out of the reach of women.'[2]

Early feminists were quick to see that Rousseau's denigration of women's powers were in tension with the liberating ideas on education which he advocated for males and that these principles could equally be applied to young women as to young men. Mary Wollstonecraft for example, in her *A Vindication of the Rights of Women*, considers Rousseau's view that the customary and traditional pastimes of girls – dolls, sewing and the like – are a natural part of being female to be 'so puerile as not to merit a serious refutation'.[3]

It is simply another paradox of Rousseau that in his own brilliant reflections on education the role he stipulated for women was as much a product of social conditioning as the social mores and behaviour which he so despised in the wider society. This issue deserves a much more detailed treatment than we can give it here and the debate on the nature of the sexes has come a long way since Rousseau. But within the limited parameters of his view Rousseau did see the co-operation between the sexes as being mutually rewarding, and *Emile* ends on the optimistic note of Emile and Sophie becoming parents. The circle of education has been completed and Emile knows that he is well-prepared to educate his own child as he himself has been educated by Jean-Jacques.

Emile marks a significant turning-point in the Western understanding of education. Rousseau paints a picture of education not as conformity to authority, the memorizing of influential texts, the knowledge of religious truth, or as inculcation with the community's myths; instead Emile is educated through a process of *personal self-development*. He is one of the first of a type which is very common to us today: the individual who searches for truth within, who struggles to find meaning through attention to oneself. There is therefore a very modern spirituality present in Rousseau's portrayal of Emile, and it is a deeply humanistic spirituality.

However, Rousseau was no naive idealist; he was well aware that a 'state of nature' contained dangerous and violent depths, but he saw that education was a process of recognition of these dangers and the development towards maturity through recognition of one's freedom *and* attention through the use of conscience to the claims of other moral subjects. With Rousseau's *Emile* we come to see that morality cannot remain extrinsic to the person, but must be integrated into the understanding of oneself as both independent but also in relation. Therefore the moral autonomy of the individual is defended against any external authority – family, church, state or other body – which would attempt to usurp it. This does not mean, however, that Rousseau's prodigy is a moral solipsist, for he comes to recognize and appreciate the moral claims of others. Thus the enduring value of *Emile* is to be found not only in the fact that it is a storehouse of moral, psychological, social and religious insight, but primarily in Rousseau's defence of our freedom to discover the grounds of one's own moral self-awareness without relapse into sheer subjectivism, and as such it remains as a crucially important text in the history of moral education.

It is clear that Jean-Jacques does not bring Emile up as a Christian. The God in his garden is the vague presence of the 'Author' of all things, and much of Christian belief (e.g. original sin, the need for redemption, the moral imperative to put others' needs before one's own) is implicitly rejected. This prepares the way for the natural religion expounded by the vicar of Savoy. The story of the vicar of Savoy is recounted to Emile by Jean-Jacques as a thinly-disguised experience from his own youth. The vicar has lost his clerical post due to a sexual indiscretion and now finds himself working in an almshouse; he befriends the 'young expatriate' and eventually confides in him his own beliefs. In his reflection the vicar has come to reject scepticism and dogmatism equally, and yet can find no resolution of his problems in the writings of the great philosophers, whom he regards as lost in a morass of criticism and lies. He resolves therefore to follow his own 'inner light' and reject all systems. Like Descartes he must satisfy himself that he is a thinking being, but unlike Descartes, who mistrusts sensations as potential illusions, he does this by first becoming aware of his existence as one who experiences sensations and progresses from there to the conclusion that as he is capable of reflecting on these sensations he is a thinking and intelligent being.

Having established his own credentials the vicar – again like Descartes – next establishes the existence of God. He does so by a rather conventional argument from causality, concluding that the universe is moved by a will and that this will belongs to an active and thinking being, which must therefore exist; to this being he attributes also intelligence and power. These are the first two articles of faith of the vicar of Savoy. So far this is a minimal theology, for the vicar argues that reasoning about the nature of God is to be avoided on the grounds that not thinking about the deity is less insulting to it than thinking badly about it, a comment which is strongly reminiscent of Bayle's remarks on atheists.

The third article of faith of the vicar combines a rejection of materialism with a defence of human freedom. Rocks and trees do not sense or think in the way humans sense and think; sensing and thinking humans, on the other hand, produce acts which imply will, an 'immaterial substance'. That this will is directed towards the choice of what we consider to be good for ourselves does not imply lack of freedom. To the contrary, as actions are caused by the will of free beings (according to the vicar to say otherwise would be to reject the principle that there are no effects without causes) human action is caused by a free human will. This argument is lacking conviction and is open to several objections, but it is not the logic of the argument which is of significance, but the fact of the locating of the will and of freedom solely in the human person. There is no room here for freedom marked by original sin, the workings of Providence or the principle of Christian theology that doing good is a result of the action of divine grace. Unhappiness comes from the abuse of our freedom and moral evil is the result of our own choices.

And what of death? It is no longer the wages of sin and the gateway to heaven or hell, but rather a remedy of nature: 'Who would want to live always? Death is the remedy for the evils you do to yourselves; nature did not want you to suffer forever.'[4] This interpretation of freedom, life and death is much more a naturalistic than a theological one, even if freedom from all divine interference is itself a divine gift: for the vicar of Savoy God succeeds most by being absent. In a passage which by implication prefigures Nietzsche's proclamation of the death of God, the vicar celebrates God for making man like God: free, good and happy. But when the creature has the gifts of the Creator, it is tempting to speculate on the possibility that there is no further need for the Creator. Of course Rousseau was not an atheist, but the God of the vicar of Savoy is not the God of the church of which he is a priest nor is this the God of the Calvinist awaiting the divine word. This is clearly the God of deism.

But in his deism the vicar of Savoy is reluctant to speculate too much. His methodology results in a severe parsimony of beliefs. He considers the question of hell, for example, as a useless one for we have no idea whether the torments of the wicked will last for eternity or not, and it matters more to recognize hell here and now in the hearts of the wicked. Similarly with the idea of creation, which the vicar finds 'obscure and incomprehensible', accepting it only because it appears to make more sense than the proposition that everything came from nothing. He is mistrustful of the use of analogy to speak of the deity, as employed by the classical Western philosophy and theology. The vicar employs a severe *via negativa*, insisting that the less he can conceive of the deity the more He can be worshipped, concluding that the best use of reason in relation to God is for reason to destroy itself before God's greatness.

This viewpoint is indeed as paradoxical as it seems. The vicar of Savoy rejects both scepticism and reason (especially reason in the Cartesian sense of deductive rationality), yet requires some reason – albeit a minimum – to establish that the Creator exists. Unlike Pascal he cannot fall back on revelation or an intense faith commitment; his belief is subjective, intuitive and minimal. This becomes ever more clear when he addresses the question of morality. His rules for correct conduct are not drawn from philosophical principles but can be found within himself, 'written by nature with ineffaceable characters in the depth of my heart. I have only to consult myself about what I want to do. Everything I sense to be good is good; everything I sense to be bad is bad.'⁵

This, of course, is moral subjectivism and relativism writ large and Rousseau was well aware that it was so. Such subjectivism would have been perceived as alarming by the church and many of Rousseau's contemporaries, but his achievement was in perceiving clearly what most modern psychology and ethical theory has come to recognize, namely, that each individual is the ultimate arbiter of their own morality and what may appear evil to one person or to a million people may appear good to another. The vicar of Savoy tempers the evident shock of this relativism by appealing to conscience, which reminds us that doing what we consider 'good' at someone else's expense may not be truly following nature. This however, does not temper the conclusion: 'All the morality of our actions is in the judgment we ourselves make of them.'⁶ If some of Rousseau's pronouncements on the state of nature may appear primitive and wishful, he here appears thoroughly modern; there is no morality 'out there', either divinely given or rationally deduced. What goodness we do we do because compassion provokes in us a desire for the happiness of others as well as of ourselves, and conscience is this awareness which enables us to look outside ourselves to judge actions as 'good' or 'bad'. For Rousseau, it is conscience which raises humanity above the level of the beasts.

The vicar of Savoy goes on to articulate Rousseau's rejection of a strict empiricism. There are some things properly innate but they are not 'ideas' such as the existence of God or the immortality of the soul; they are 'sentiments', namely 'the love of self, the fear of pain, the horror of death, the desire of well-being'.⁷ These innate sentiments are the basis of our existence, for we are primarily sentient beings. Rousseau owes a great deal to Descartes, but again and again inverts him: we are not governed by reason, but by feeling, intuition, sentiment. God is not the ground of my reason which, circuitously, must be proven by my reason; rather God is postulated by intuition which senses the divine through nature and the 'inner voice'. Like Descartes the vicar of Savoy begins with himself, but unlike Descartes he does not then require God to guarantee him certainty of himself; he gains this certainty through his inner voice and requires no other guarantee, and in so doing epitomizes those who followed Descartes' starting-point of the self but declined to use God as a cog in the system. In this the vicar of Savoy has more in common with the twentieth-century Western religious consciousness than he does with that of his own time.

The vicar continues his heterodox profession of faith with an explicit rejection of original sin: 'Ah, let us not corrupt man! He will always be good without difficulty and always be happy without remorse!'[8] In the vicar of Savoy and in Rousseau's other writings we find one of the most explicit rejections of original sin in the eighteenth century. Human beings are essentially good; they are responsible, yes, for the evil they do, but this responsibility is purely natural and has no theological overtones of disobedience of the divine commandments. Here we are presented with an alternative anthropology and morality to that which had dominated Western Christendom since the time of Augustine in the fourth and fifth centuries. We are no longer marked by guilt and remorse; the source of our affliction is social and educational, and by changing these conditions we can change the outcome. In rejecting original sin the vicar of Savoy – and Rousseau – rejected the need for a saviour and thus denied the whole Christian dispensation. Rousseau's robust defence of the idea of the innate goodness and innocence of the human being – a somewhat tarnished idea in the twentieth century – was a significant step in the eighteenth century's attempts to formulate an alternative anthropology. What is emerging is not a monolithic or even single coherent alternative, but rather a series of critiques which undermine the integral relations of the Christian belief system, not by proving them wrong – if such a thing were possible – but by offering alternative explanations and solutions of a purely naturalistic nature which cast the traditional Christian anthropology as one alternative among others and no longer as the single locus of truth.

The vicar of Savoy is well aware of the challenge of relativism to religious truth. He concludes his profession of faith with some arguments common to eighteenth-century attacks on revealed religion. If there are so many religions, how is one to find out which of them is the true one? The answer is that only the book of nature is open and intelligible to all. Or, how are we to know that revelation is truly from God when it is mediated through fallible human beings, and why has God not spoken to each of us directly? How can non-Christians be blamed for not knowing Jesus, or non-Jews for not knowing Moses, or non-Muslims for not knowing of Muhammad if what they believe is simply an accident of where they were born? And what of miracles? They are only taken to be true because they fit with doctrine, but doctrine itself relies for its authority on miracles, a circular argument surely. The vicar concludes that the only true worship is the worship of the heart, and gives the young Rousseau a piece of Socratic advice: 'Know how to be ignorant.'[9]

Rousseau attempts to deflect criticism of the *Confession of Faith of the Savoyard Vicar* by protesting that he has included it not as a rule to be followed in religious matters, but as an example to his pupil of how one should reason not from authority or custom, but according to the light of nature alone, and go no further than the limited conclusions this method allows. This protestation lacks conviction, to say the least, and despite the many radical theories and ideas in *Emile* it was the *Confession of Faith* which caused an uproar. According to Rousseau's own account in the *Confessions*, *Emile* received a great deal of private praise from the commentators but little public approval. Rousseau was convinced that it was the best of his books but in his naivety could not see the reason for the reticence of those who praised it (like d'Alembert, for example, who wrote an effusive letter to Rousseau praising *Emile*, but with an unerring sense for self-preservation neglected to sign it). Living outside Paris, Rousseau was unaware, or chose to be unaware, of the storm that was to break over him. To the very end Rousseau refused to believe that he was in danger until his friends came with a final warning in the middle of the night of 8/9 June 1762 that he was to be arrested in the morning. Rousseau fled to Switzerland, actually passing on the road the police who were sent to detain him. It was the beginning of what was to prove a desperately unhappy and itinerant final sixteen years of his life.

Despite the misery of much of his life and the acute paranoia that made his relationships with his peers so difficult, Rousseau did not take a negative interpretation of the order of things; he was stoical towards his own frequently jejune existence and an inveterate optimist regarding the world as a whole. The basis for this optimism was his deism and the belief in Providence that this allowed. His religious optimism and the rationale for it can be found in a letter to Voltaire of 18 August 1756, in which Rousseau set out his objections to Voltaire's *The Lisbon Earthquake*, copies of which the author had sent to Rousseau, Diderot and d'Alembert (along with his *On Natural Law*).

In *The Lisbon Earthquake* Voltaire had attacked the maxim of Leibniz (also defended by the poet Alexander Pope in his *Essay on Man*) that 'whatever is, is right'. As we have seen (see Chapter 5) the events of Lisbon shook Voltaire's deistic faith in Providence and caused him to react bitterly to what he saw as the complacent optimism of Leibniz and Pope. Rousseau takes up a defence of Providence which rejects the pessimism he now sees as inherent in Voltaire's position. Consistent with his other works, Rousseau emphasizes that the evils which befall humanity are of our own doing; it was not, after all, the deity which built the tall buildings of Lisbon which fell so easily in the earthquake. Had these houses been smaller and built in the desert, very few lives would have been lost (again we see Rousseau's belief that the city, not the garden, is the true location of the fall).

If this appears cruel that is not Rousseau's intention; he wishes us to see that the action of the earthquake was not directed at the city and its inhabitants, but that the city and its inhabitants simply happened to be there when it happened. Furthermore, who is to say that sudden and untimely death was necessarily a bad thing for these people? Perhaps it was the case that very many of them were spared unnecessary suffering by this death, and the 'disaster' was therefore a relatively good thing. Rousseau refuses to be mournful about death; although we should not forget what he calls 'the delightful consciousness of existence'[10] there is no need to despise death, for to do so can lead us to undervalue life also. Apart from the rich – who are often weary of life – and the unhappy philosophers, most ordinary people are quite happy with their lot and would not wish to change it. Rousseau's point against Voltaire is that it is not valid to generalize from one's own limited experience to abstract theories about what humans in general believe.

The question to be addressed, therefore, says Rousseau, is not the meaning of the suffering of individuals – that is indisputable – but whether the universe as a whole can be considered good. By 'good' here Rousseau does not mean primarily moral goodness – that would be to return to the problem of Voltaire – but whether or not the countless individual ills and sufferings can be seen as an integral part of the 'whole'. In other words, the things that happen to us are considered by us to be 'good' or 'evil', but from the perspective of the universe (by Providence, if one wishes) they are morally neutral. Rousseau rejects equally the piety of belief which sees 'Divine Justice' operating in events which are purely natural, and the complaints of the philosophers who rail against every tiny misfortune, expecting Providence to guard even their suitcases: 'Thus let nature act as it will. Providence is always right in the opinion of the devotees, and always wrong in the opinion of the philosophers. Whereas it is very likely that in the order of human things, Providence is neither right nor wrong; because everything depends on a certain general law, that makes no exception of persons. It is probable that the particular events which happen here below, are nothing in the sight of the Creator and Governor of the universe ...'[11]

A belief in Providence based on observation of the world does not allow us to be optimistic; the only basis for such optimism in Providence is that we believe in God and then reason inductively that all is ultimately for the best. As we saw in the case of the vicar of Savoy, Rousseau is not enamoured of attempting to prove the existence of God; he accepts this as something personal to him (a 'sentimental' rather than a 'demonstrative' proof). In this he is firmly in the camp of Pascal: reason cannot achieve anything here and it appears more fruitful to believe than not to believe, so belief is – psychologically – preferable to unbelief.[12]

Notwithstanding the fact that this leap of faith appears to be begging the question with respect to the basis of optimism, a further question of importance now arises. If, as Rousseau contends, the deity operates by general laws and is little concerned with the specifics of our moral interpretation of events, then how is the deity to be distinguished from mere fate? There is no doubt that Rousseau himself believes in the existence of the deity – as the origin of the general laws by which Providence operates, as the Author of all things and as the provider of justice in the afterlife ('if he is just and powerful my soul is immortal'). His belief in the afterlife, however, is reached by induction from the attributes of the deity, and adds nothing to his argument except some wishful thinking. Thus, by preserving the deity from blame for specific events Rousseau leaves open the possibility that the deity disappears altogether in favour of the operation of general laws which generate random effects, to which the simple and the confused attribute moral purpose.

The equation of the deity with mere fate was one of the main accusations levelled at Spinoza and it is inconceivable that Rousseau was unaware of the difficulty. This is a dilemma which exercised the mind of Kant and almost every theologian since: belief in Providence is caught between the pitfall of the problem of evil on the one hand and the abyss of fate on the other. Here in Rousseau we see one of the major contributions of the Enlightenment to the demise in Western thought of the previously dominant religious interpretation of reality. Reason cannot prove the existence of God nor provide any grounds for cosmic optimism. God does not interfere in history to punish and reward, and what we perceive as 'evil' events happen due to the laws of the universe. These laws may well be attributed to God (as by Rousseau), but why should they be if they appear to work irrespective of their origin? In any case, to continue to impute some form of moral purpose to nature serves simply to push the problem back one step, something inadequately appreciated by Rousseau. Nature is morally neutral: there is no point raging against the perceived injustice of natural events. Precisely the same problem which arose in the domain of science arises in the area of morality: if the deity operates by general and not specific laws (to paraphrase Pope) then why do we need to talk of the deity at all?

Although Rousseau was part of the Enlightenment it is clear that he also stands distinctly apart from many of its dominant ideas. Rousseau was acutely aware that the Enlightenment constituted a decisive shift in human self-understanding away from a divine-centred towards a human-centred vision of reality (although it is arguable that such a shift had been well under way since the Renaissance). But while he inevitably shared part of that process (e.g. in his deism) Rousseau was not convinced of the value of the new vision.

In his attacks on cities, the trappings of modern living, the destructive influence of utilitarian education and the decadence induced by the arts and sciences, Rousseau begins to articulate two key elements in the experience of modern humanity. The first is the unity of all culture; the bewilderment which his attack on cities and the arts caused among his contemporaries is not surprising, for his insight that human society is formed from a permanently entangled network of relations frequently operating unconsciously was an idea ahead of its time. All aspects of society's structure, even those which appear most benign, contribute to the impulses and forces which control us.

The second insight is that even in the midst of apparent success and achievement we are not free, but experience ourselves as imposed upon and therefore controlled by forces operating beyond the limits of our powers to control them. Rousseau was aware that a veneer of civilization can cover relations of domination, oppression, fear and loneliness and that an indispensable part of freedom consists in the ability to lift this veneer and perceive the reality underneath. The sheer alienation of modern living – now a cliché for every modern city-dweller – was astutely perceived by Rousseau. He saw that if a utilitarian and functional form of scientific thinking replaced the religious consciousness as the dominant mode of perceiving the world and our place in it, then a great deal of what is of essential value in human life could be lost. Hence he defended that which he saw as devalued by the spirit of his time: he advocated imagination over calculation, the individual over the powers of society, the countryside over the city, freedom over utilitarian functionalism, exquisite desire over biological sex, a mystical deism over both materialistic atheism and dogmatic orthodoxy, ethical citizenship over exploitative economic and political relations.

But all of this is not to say that Rousseau advocated irrationality. To the contrary he wished to defend reason, but to recognize its limitations. It is reason which allows us to know good and evil, but reason alone is inadequate for the fulfilment of the moral life. Conscience (which raises us to the level of awareness of other moral beings) and compassion (which provokes in us the empathy with the plight and sufferings of others which we require to do the good) are equally necessary if what reason understands in the abstract is to be realized concretely in action.

Rousseau's moral teaching is subtly but deeply destructive of traditional Christian morality. His moral agent is free and gives herself the law; there is no legitimation of any other moral authority. The free moral agent is essentially good, and therefore there is no original sin. Compassion and conscience help to truncate the dangerous freedoms which this eclipse of authority engenders, and the protection of the moral agent from the potentially destructive freedom of others is consolidated in the surrender of that freedom in the social contract; paradoxically, in giving up one's freedom one receives the security which will allow one to utilize one's freedom.[13]

Thus the moral agent is an agent in relation to society and not to God, as in the old dispensation. If there is an 'original' sin it is not found in human pride or in the love of self (what Rousseau calls *amour de soi*) which is proper to human beings, but in a society in which we are forced to conform to the rules of the majority, thereby losing the possibility for true freedom and morality. Thus Rousseau offers a plausible alternative to the Christian story of the origin of human evil and the need for redemption. He achieves a radical immanentism with regard to morality; salvation comes from within the autonomous moral subject and we are the dispensers of our own saving grace. For Rousseau human nature is corrupt – in this he was in complete agreement with Pascal – but the reason for that corruption is not to be found in a theological or metaphysical interpretation of the human subject itself. If human moral corruption was for Pascal an inescapable *a priori* of our condition as children of Adam and Eve, it was for Rousseau an *a posteriori* deviation into our own most base instincts against the positive potential of our innate goodness.

In his rejection of any innate human depravity through original sin and in his emphasis (albeit rather one-sided in his dislike of the city) on the positive effects of environment on the development of the human being, Rousseau has had an immense influence on the modern Western understanding of the human subject. His vision of human innocence was instrumental in the emergence of a de-theologized anthropology on which the rationale of the human sciences depend. He and many other Enlightenment thinkers struggled to articulate a new concept of the human subject which was not fixed within the framework of the Christian vision of salvation history extending from the Garden of Eden to the final judgment.

This was not an easy step to make, not only because of the intense cultural and psychological hold which the Christian vision had even on those freethinkers who ostensibly declared themselves free of it (it is a simple matter to declare that one does not believe in original sin, it is far more difficult to shake off the accompanying belief that humanity is inherently degenerate), but also because of conflicting tendencies within the Enlightenment itself. While many thinkers were willing to abandon what they saw as the pessimism of Christianity, they found it more difficult to articulate a convincing and appealing alternative. Both Cartesian rationalism and Lockean empiricism gave rise to a tendency to view the human being as a form of sophisticated machine, a tendency for which the advances of the scientific revolution appeared to provide a rationale and which reached its apogee in the work of La Mettrie. Rousseau, however, in disparaging so many of the 'advances' of science and civilization was free to develop an anthropology which avoided the dangers of both theological pessimism and scientific reductionism. This is one of the reasons why he is often seen as a precursor of the Romantic movement and even of later existentialism; in Rousseau the individual personality seeks truth from within her own experience, uses that experience as the criterion by which truth will be judged, and constructs morality and the ethics of her relations with others through attention to the voice of conscience.

When the novel *Julie ou La Nouvelle Héloïse* was published it became an instant sensation, one of the first romantic best-sellers. In the figure of Saint-Preux, who loves Julie but finds his love unrequited, the century was introduced to the isolated individual, alone in a world that does not conform to his desires, forging his own identity and salvation for himself. It is a thoroughly modern vision which the eighteenth century was ready to receive with enthusiasm. Rousseau's psychological insights held a mirror up to the human heart, and offered a compelling alternative to the standard Enlightenment emphasis on rationality and function. It is a poignant paradox that his own tempestuous and tortured personality was able to produce a vision of the human person which was at once positive, generous and humane. It is a vision founded on compassion – the virtue of which he made so much – and it is this above all which accounts for the enduring appeal of Rousseau's work.

Belief within the Limits of Reason:
Immanuel Kant

Germany came late to the Enlightenment. In the first half of the seventeenth century its towns, economy, political structure and population had been devastated by the religious wars. In philosophy, theology and social thought the heavy hands of Lutheran orthodoxy and post-Tridentine Roman Catholicism served to stifle the type of freethinking which was beginning to appear in France, England and the Low Countries. However, when Germany did respond to the new thinking the effect was prodigious and the Enlightenment was eventually to find its philosophical apex in the thought of Kant, whose 'critical' philosophy and the reaction which it stimulated were to provide the impetus for the dominance of German thought in the nineteenth century.

The germanic intellectual environment in which Kant developed his philosophy was marked by the influence of two principal yet conflicting strains of thought, the rationalist philosophy which dominated the universities under the influence of Leibniz and his disciple Christian Wolff (1679–1754), and the religious renewal within Lutheranism known as Pietism. Both Pietism and rationalism influenced Kant; he was raised in a Pietist family and his early philosophy was heavily influenced by Wolff, while the great achievement of his later philosophy can be considered a reaction against Wolff under the influence of Hume.

The Pietism which influenced Kant was a reaction against a form of belief which had become cold, rational and detached from the concerns of the average churchgoer. By the middle of the seventeenth century the spark of renewal which had lit the Lutheran reforms was all but extinguished and what remained was an orthodoxy enclosed in a shell of Protestant scholasticism. Theology's perceived purpose was the rational defence of the doctrinal gains made during the previous turbulent century, but its arguments frequently degenerated into logical hair-splitting. The clergy, educated in an abstract theology, seemed unable to meet the spiritual demands of their flock and, with a few isolated exceptions, there was little intellectual development coming from outside the churches which could provide a challenge or stimulate a more critical and inventive theology.

The reaction against this fossilized orthodoxy was instigated primarily by Philip Jakob Spener (1635–1705) who, influenced by the vitality of some of the Reformed churches, became determined to breathe some new life into Lutheranism. While a pastor Spener had encouraged his congregation (with some success) to pray, worship and read the Bible in their own homes. In his *Pia desideria* (*Pious Desires*, 1675), a book generally regarded as the seminal text of the Pietist movement, Spener criticized what he saw as the ossification of the Lutheran church and advocated a renewal of worship, more practical and devotional sermons, reading of the Bible by the laity and, in general, a more interior and personal form of belief. To accomplish this end he established lay-dominated devotional centres to encourage more active participation of the laity in devotion and worship. Spener and his followers were viewed as dangerous enthusiasts by the academic establishment, and their piety was contrasted unfavourably with the sophisticated theology of the universities, hence the originally abusive term 'Pietists'. Despite this opposition, Spener had highlighted the necessity of a warmer, simpler form of religion aimed not simply at the comprehension of doctrine but at engaging the believer's whole life. In 1694 Spener was instrumental in the establishment of the University of Halle, which became a major centre of Pietist thought and Lutheran missionary activity.

After Spener the most influential Pietist was Count Nicholas Ludwig von Zinzendorf (1700–60), who was the godchild of Spener. As a young man Zinzendorf showed an intense interest in religion, and when some Hussite refugees from Bohemia settled on his country estate he became their leader – with the town of Herrnhut as their base – thus founding the community which became known as the Moravian church. During his theological studies at the University of Wittenberg – a centre of Lutheran orthodoxy, as might be expected –

Zinzendorf had attempted to stimulate theological discussion with the Pietists at the University of Halle, but to no avail. His irenic approach to theology never left him, however, and his form of Pietism was characterized by a deep mistrust of theological systems and needless denominational differences. He advocated an interior religion of the heart (with the emphasis on the spiritual renewal of the individual believer) which would cut across conventional religious and national boundaries. Zinzendorf and other Pietist leaders emphasized the role of emotion and feeling in religion. With its emphasis on the experiential and the personal aspects of religious faith, Pietism stands over and against the Enlightenment tendency to reduce religion to the minimum of rational beliefs and against the propensity of Lutheran orthodoxy to defend belief through recourse to rational theology. But it nevertheless shared certain characteristics with its age, such as the emphasis on the moral commitment demanded of the individual and a mistrust of ecclesiastical power.

While Pietism occasionally gave rise to forms of emotionalism there were also some more lasting influences. The Wesley brothers in England were greatly influenced by Pietism, as was the development of Protestantism in America (where Zinzendorf himself visited several Moravian communities). Also, of course, Kant's philosophy shows distinct marks of his Pietist upbringing: e.g. his mistrust of organized religion and emphasis on moral duty, faith and the responsibility of the individual.[1] The Pietist stress on emotion and personal conviction and engagement with what one believed also served as a background influence on the development of German Romanticism.

The dominant rational theology of orthodox Lutheranism, against which Pietism reacted, is best represented in the thought of Christian Wolff, undoubtedly the most important German thinker between Leibniz and Kant. In 1707, with the help of Leibniz, Wolff was appointed to the University of Halle. He remained there until 1723 when, in a bitter dispute with the Pietists he was removed from his post by the King of Prussia, Frederick William I (the father of Frederick the Great) and, under threat of death, given forty-eight hours to leave Prussian territory. The occasion of Wolff's banishment from Prussia was the somewhat surprising one of a lecture in which he defended Chinese philosophy as of practical, ethical utility, thereby upsetting his Pietist colleagues.[2] (Wolff spent his exile in Marburg, and returned to Halle when Frederick the Great ascended the throne in 1740.)

The Pietists' wider objection to Wolff was that his theology highlighted the rational nature of doctrine as reflecting the mind of God, and he employed a rigorous theological method (quite like the methodology of Roman Catholic Scholasticism) which utilized complex divisions and subdivisions. The aim of this methodology was to show that if metaphysical philosophy employed a strictly rational method and began from sound principles then it could make the same claim to intellectual respectability as mathematics and the sciences based on mathematical reasoning.[3] Wolff, therefore, tended to disparage experience as a path to knowledge of God and this put him in direct conflict with one of the central beliefs of the Pietists, as well as leaving him open to the charge of being a follower of Spinoza, akin to being called an atheist in the intellectual climate of the time. His brand of popular Leibnizian rationalism dominated German intellectual life in the early to middle part of the eighteenth century, for his methodology was applicable across the disciplines, a fact reflected in the broad range of Wolff's own writings. Indeed Wolff's rationalism provided a model of reason which the early leaders of the German *Aufklärung* saw as potentially applicable to all spheres of life from religion to morality, education and politics. However, Wolffian rationalism was continually challenged by philosophers more sympathetic to the Pietist emphasis on knowledge gained from experience and their critique of the inability of reason to give us knowledge independent of experience provided the empiricist-rationalist dichotomy, to which Kant was to devote so much of his energy.[4]

Kant studied Wolffian theology at the University of Königsberg and was to call Wolff 'the greatest of all dogmatic philosophers'. However, the limitations of philosophical and theological rationalism were made evident to Kant when he encountered the scepticism of Hume who, as he famously remarked, woke him from his 'dogmatic slumbers';[5] Peter Gay's witticism that it was Wolff who had sent Kant to sleep in the first place is apt,[6] for by the middle of the eighteenth century the empiricism of Locke and Hume had raised challenges for rationalism of which many Wolffians in Germany were unaware and for which they were quite unprepared.

Kant's life and the structure of his intellectual journey is easily described, for he led a highly disciplined existence and never travelled very far beyond the environs of his native city; however, the popular image of Kant as a bore by whom the good citizens of Königsberg would set their watches as he took his daily walk underestimates both his character and the role which he played in the intellectual disputes of his day. The famous philosopher was born the son of a poor harness-maker, and without the help of the local pietist minister might never have received the education which was to bring forth such brilliance. He spent six years at the University of Königsberg – a small institution in a small provincial city – before taking various obscure jobs as a private tutor to wealthy families. In 1755 he took his Master of Arts degree and began to lecture at the University; for the next forty-one years (as Professor of logic and metaphysics from 1770), until retiring in 1796, he taught in a wide range of subject areas, including physics, mathematics and geography, as well as philosophy.

Kant inherited a concern with the problems of metaphysics from the dominant Leibniz-Wolff philosophy. His early work is marked by a concern with science and its relation to metaphysics, and with regard to metaphysics proper his work was concerned mainly with problems stemming from Descartes, Leibniz and Wolff. Kant was, however, a doggedly independent thinker and he became less and less satisfied not only with the answers produced by traditional metaphysics and logic but with the conceptual presuppositions and framework within which these answers were formed. Despite his reservations about many of the claims of traditional metaphysics, such as the 'proofs' for the existence of God, in his early work (up to about 1770) Kant was still trying to resolve the problems of metaphysics from within the framework of metaphysical thinking itself. His brilliant insight, which was to be the foundation for his nature, 'critical' philosophy, was that before speculative reason could be employed to analyse many of the traditional questions posed by philosophy – the existence of God, the possibility and limits of human freedom, the grounds of knowledge, the basis of morality, etc. – reason had to turn on itself and provide an analysis of the range of its own power. Reason, in other words cannot be taken for granted, and the limits of its power must be clearly delineated.

This is the meaning in Kantian philosophy of the terms 'critical' or 'critique'; a critique of reason is when reason analyses first of all itself and only then the matters to which it has been traditionally applied. In Kant's judgment traditional metaphysics lacked this necessary 'critical' first step, and thus was guilty of failing to delineate the parameters of reason. Although Kant was himself moving towards a critical philosophical method, it was the scepticism of Hume which provided him with the question for which his critical philosophy was designed to provide an answer. Kant's journey through the ruins of classical epistemology begins therefore not in Königsberg but rather in Edinburgh. Hume's critique of rationalism, while initially ignored or condemned by his contemporaries, became in the hands of Kant a weapon of critique of immense importance not only for theology and metaphysics, but also for the very Enlightenment optimism which aspired to the transparency of God, nature and mind under the clear light of reason.

Hume's theory on the origin of religion is a correlate of the critique of rationalist epistemology which lies at the heart of his philosophy. In his major work, *A Treatise of Human Nature* (1739–40), he laid down the epistemology which was to influence Kant so much. He was unconvinced by John Locke's view that while reason as such did not give us probable knowledge, experience could. For Hume experience is composed of a series of fragmented impressions working on the senses, and knowledge of the operations of cause and effect which appear to be at work in the world is not given to us *a priori* but rather comes to us from the way in which such impressions are copied into the mind. In other words, our ideas are arrangements in the mind of impressions of facts which occur in the world we inhabit, but which allow us no insight into the way things actually are. In contrast to the example of mathematics, where we can establish the certainty of a relation simply by use of the mind (e.g. that $2 + 2 = 4$ is intelligible even if we do not have four apples on the table in front of us to demonstrate its intelligibility), the world of the senses allows no access to reality itself but only to the perception formed in the mind and expressed as an idea.

What concerned Hume about this disjunction between ideas and facts (or as he describes it in the *Treatise*, between knowledge and probability[7]) was that it left the subject stranded as a mere amalgam of piecemeal items of experiences and impressions, with no underlying foundation on which knowledge of the self or of the world could be established. How then can we ever make any assertion about the way things are or ever trust our judgment again when we encounter a set of circumstances similar to what we have perceived before?

Hume's response to this problem took the form of an analysis of causality. When we see a certain effect we assume what we take to be its cause, and we posit some power in the cause which induced the effect. However, we have no way of knowing this power; all we in reality know is a series of impressions which follow one another in sequence and which have no necessary connection. Our knowledge that a particular effect has a certain identifiable cause is based not on any insight into the nature of that relation but rather to the repetition of the impressions we experience in several similar series of events. Thus, we are reduced to the gathering of impressions which will allow us to make a probable judgment that a particular action will result in a particular consequence. We are thereby able to anticipate certain events, but this anticipation does not allow us to surmise a necessary connection between the observed effect and its cause. There is no way of establishing *a priori* causality; the most we can attain is the probability of repeated experience.

Hume's sceptical conclusion[8] was a blow both to accepted common sense and to the confidence in the knowledge of the universal laws of science assumed by Newtonian physics. Its consequences for religious knowledge are evident. If ideas are the amalgamation of bitty, broken impressions, then the workings of the mind can extend no further than this assemblage of experiences. Hume's epistemology provided Kant with two fundamental criteria which were to govern his own theory of knowledge: first, that knowledge is not produced from 'within' the subject alone (the way of strict idealism) and, secondly, that while the impressions of reality on the mind are necessary for knowledge, they are not themselves constitutive of it. In order to gain knowledge we have to come into contact with the external phenomena, but also organize these phenomena rationally in the mind. But disturbed as he was by Hume's pessimistic conclusions as to the possibility of gaining knowledge at all, Kant sought a way to ground reason, i.e. to establish the basis of our knowledge of causality even though it cannot be discovered directly from the flux of direct experience. This move was necessary if the (for Kant) inviolable foundations of

Newtonian physics, namely that nature admits of necessary and universal laws which can be and are known by the rational subject, were to be preserved philosophically,

In his *Critique of Pure Reason* Kant began his analysis of this problem by means of a question: are synthetic[9] *a priori* judgments possible? By this he meant: can reason hold to something which is universal and necessary but which is not dependent upon experience? His answer was that synthetic *a priori* judgments are possible in the areas of physics and mathematics.[10] This much granted, the crucial question now becomes: how did pure reason attain to this knowledge? Kant's answer to this question entails his 'Copernican revolution' in the structure of human knowing: the universality and necessity required for true knowledge do not come from the structure of the world, which we only know in the flux of phenomena anyway, but rather from the *structure of human cognition itself*. This radical reversal of cognition, the 'turn to the subject', entails the location in the subject of the very conditions which make knowledge possible. These fundamental conditions, which lay down the rules for the structure of understanding, are called by Kant the *categories* (quantity, quality, relation, modality, and their subdivisions).

Kant's radical turn to the subject in order to ground knowledge resulted in a severe separation of subject and object, a separation which had profound implications for his philosophy of religion. To simplify Kant's complex argument here, we can say that he reasoned that it was quite natural that the appearance to the subject of the things of the world should appear to us under the conditions of our own cognitive structure; however, this entailed that we know things *only* under these conditions and therefore have no access to these things as they are 'in themselves'.

Kant thus constructed a dualism between the subject and the object on the basis of a pessimistic epistemological phenomenalism: we know only the phenomena, and what things are like 'in themselves' is not within the scope of our knowledge. This world of phenomena is the realm of scientific investigation, governed by the laws of Newtonian physics and free of metaphysical speculation. But lest we subjects are reduced wholly to the status of phenomena, Kant argues for the corresponding pole of the duality, a 'noumenal' world of the inner reality of things as they truly are. It is at this point that the limits of pure reason, become apparent; our deepest grounds are impenetrable to our reason, we cannot know what grounds our experience any more than we can know the essence of a tree or a dog 'in themselves'. Hume's scepticism has been overcome, but at a price.

Kant proceeded to apply his reasoning theologically, specifically to the rational theology of Christian Wolff, his eminent predecessor as the foremost German philosopher. Wolff's rationality had effectively replaced revelation as the foundation of faith and knowledge, putting in its place a theology which could capture the essentials of Christian faith out of its observation of the world and the use of speculative reason. Revelation was needed only to point out those things which reason had not yet managed to reach, but which were certainly within its power. Thus, when Kant attacked the commonly held view of the power of speculative reason it is not at all surprising that he was accused of undermining the foundations of religious faith.

Wolff had attempted to develop a speculative theology of the self (rational psychology), of the world (rational cosmology) and of God (rational theology). Kant dismantled each of these in turn by means of a rigorous analysis of the structure of the arguments. Rational psychology fails because pure reason does not have the power to experience whatever it is which underlies the self, and which is a *condition* of all experience (that is to say, the subject is not transparent to itself, being part of the phenomena which it perceives). Rational cosmology does not succeed because equally viable arguments may be proposed to assert and deny that the world has a beginning, that a supreme being exists, etc. (These are what Kant calls the *antinomies*, where an assertion can be neither proved nor disproved.) In his rejection of rational theology Kant essentially rests his case on the incapacity of pure reason to go beyond the bounds of its own limited sphere of operations into the realm of metaphysical certainty.

The heart of Kant's attack on rational theology is a devastating critique of the traditional 'proofs' for the existence of God. In the *Critique of Pure Reason* (1781, second edition 1787), Kant writes as follows on the 'goal' of proving God's existence: 'All the paths leading to this goal begin either from determinate experience and the specific constitution of the world of sense as thereby known, and ascend from it, in accordance with laws of causality, to the supreme cause outside the world; or they start from experience which is purely indeterminate, that is, from experience of existence in general; or finally they abstract from all experience, and argue completely *a priori*, from mere concepts, to the existence of a supreme cause. The first proof is the *physico-theological*, the second the *cosmological*, the third the *ontological*. There are, and there can be, no others.'[11]

Kant's critique of these arguments begins with a rejection of the third argument listed, the ontological argument, as he believes that the other two arguments are dependent upon it; therefore, if the ontological argument can be shown to be in error the physico-theological and cosmological arguments will fall as a consequence. The so-called 'ontological argument' was first formulated by Anselm of Canterbury in the eleventh century, and later refined by Descartes and Leibniz. Kant's major objection to the ontological argument can be summed up in one famous sentence from the *Critique of Pure Reason*: '"Being" [i.e. existence] is obviously not a real predicate; that is, it is not a concept of something which could be added to the concept of a thing.'[12]

Kant's criticism here is simple yet devastating. It is perhaps best understood through the example of a triangle which Kant himself uses. In his Fifth Meditation Descartes had asserted that we can no more think of God without existence than we can think of a triangle without three angles or a mountain without a valley. Kant responds by agreeing that as a triangle has by definition three angles it would be logically contradictory for us to deny this.

There is no logical contradiction, however, in denying the triangle together with its three angles (note that Kant is not saying that triangles do not exist, merely that if I reject the concept of the triangle I am not involved in a logical contradiction, as I would be if I accepted the idea of a triangle yet denied that it had three angles). Now the same holds true for the concepts 'God' and 'existence' as holds for the triangle and its three angles. We can without contradiction reject the statement 'God exists', for in doing so we reject existence, omnipotence, omniscience and all the other so-called 'attributes' of God.

Kant asserts that we cannot pretend to be talking about the *possibility* of something existing, and yet try to smuggle in the concept of existence as part of the definition of the very thing which we are simply discussing as possible. Claiming that something 'exists' can add nothing to it in reality even though it may add something to its concept, that is, we cannot move from the concept of something to the reality of something when it is the reality that is in question in the first place, a point made equally well by Aquinas.

Being the clear thinker that he is, Kant becomes (for him) almost irate at this 'idle and fruitless' thinking that confuses the logical with the real. In two homespun examples he says that adding the idea of existence to a concept which we have not proved is like a merchant who adds a few noughts to his cash account and thinks himself richer: or similarly, to paraphrase him, if I think I have a hundred real dollars in my wallet and find on opening it that this is actually the case, I do not therefore add *more* to my hundred dollars simply because I really have the money rather than just *thinking* I have it. In short, to say that God necessarily 'exists' proves nothing about whether there is or is not such a being.[13]

Kant goes on to argue that the physico-theological proof (sometimes called the 'teleological' proof, meaning that the world and the things in it appear to be designed for particular purposes, hence pointing to a Designer) requires the cosmological proof (the argument that if anything at all exists, then a necessary being – the originator of all that exists – must also exist). But the cosmological proof itself rests on the concept of the necessary existence of a highest reality (God); that is, it rests on the ontological proof which Kant claims to have already shown to be fallacious.[14] Kant's argument here has generally been taken as convincing, but it is not without its flaws.[15] However, irrespective of these possible flaws, Kant's attack on the classical proofs for God's existence has been extremely influential, for they have lost most of their conviction in the time since his critique.

When Kant makes his famous assertion, in the Preface to the second edition of the *Critique of Pure Reason* (1787), that he had 'to deny *knowledge* in order to make room for *faith*',[16] he is referring to the fact that he denied knowledge in the religious sphere. The term 'knowledge', says Kant, cannot be applied to the noumenal realm of the objects of religious belief because such belief can ever be only subjectively true, and 'knowledge' is that which can be held to be true both subjectively and objectively.[17] But pure reason cannot extend to objective certainty of the noumenal realm, hence religious belief is not knowledge. 'Faith' is therefore the term given to the subjective certainty of religious belief. But this faith is not irrational, it is not to be equated with what Kant calls 'opinion' (a 'mere play of the imagination'). It rather falls somewhere between 'opinion' and 'knowledge'.

So, despite his critique of rational theology, Kant did wish to preserve religious belief. In *The Critique of Practical Reason* (1788) and *Religion Within the Limits of Reason Alone* (1793) he developed his own thinking on arguments for the existence of God, and other related religious questions. As Kant believed that resolution of the question of the existence of God was something that lay beyond the power of pure, speculative reason, he approached the matter from the 'practical' perspective of morality. According to Kant, we only act rationally in attempting to achieve some end or result if we actually believe that the end can be reached, and that the things which we do to achieve that end can actually help us to attain it.

It must be emphasized that Kant wished to protect religious belief from the twin encroachments of epistemological scepticism and a scientific methodology which could be read as reductionist. But his dualism of the noumenal and phenomenal spheres split the world and human knowing in two to such an extent that what 'knowledge' of the divine we have, whether it be through faith or the moral law, can only be a pale reflection of the more secure knowledge of the phenomena available to the senses. Thus when Kant, in the *Second Critique* says that certain knowledge of God would destroy us and reduce human experience to a divine puppet show, we see that the 'knowledge' which he has in mind is that of empirical science. To be fair to Kant, of course, we must point out that he believed he had placed religious belief on a surer footing, although the weaknesses of Kant's own arguments for the existence of God and immortality show that not to be the case. The historical difficulty for theology after Kant has been that what was a distinction for him became all too easily a value judgment in the hands of the opponents of religion. This scenario is familiar to us again in the twentieth century, with the attempt of logical positivism to reduce all non-verifiable statements to a second-class status.

Having set the limits to theoretical knowledge, Kant turned his attention to ethics. In his *Groundwork of the Metaphysics of Morals* (1785) and *Critique of Practical Reason* (as well as in his later *Metaphysics of Morals* (1797)) he developed an original and highly influential ethical theory. Kant's starting point for ethics is the fundamental assumption of the autonomy of the human subject; his famous injunction *sapere aude!* ('dare to use your own reason!') applies not only in the realm of theoretical reason but in practical reason, or ethics, also. As the human person is autonomous in matters of ethics, no external authority (state, church, culture, natural law, family etc.) can set the moral law for the individual without the individual losing that which is most precious, her freedom.

The Enlightenment concept of the full autonomy of the moral subject and the concomitant principle that we create the moral law for ourselves were developed originally by Rousseau, and it was most likely Kant's reading of Rousseau which set him the challenge of explaining how we could be free of external moral constraint, yet live under a moral law of our own making. How can there be something which deserves the name of a 'law', yet can be set by each autonomous individual for themselves? Is not this a recipe for total moral relativism, with each autonomous person setting the 'law' for themselves and changing it at a whim to suit their own needs, desires and circumstances? To avoid such potential anarchy Kant had to be able to show that the moral law was indeed a law common to all autonomous moral subjects, but that it was at the same time not heteronomous (i.e. imposed from without). If morality, therefore, is not something which can be imposed from without, and if moral anarchy and relativism are to be avoided, the moral law must come from somewhere. But where is that 'somewhere'? This search for the grounds of the moral law are fundamental to Kant's understanding of morality, but of religion also, for it is his theory of ethics which will also serve as the foundation for his rational faith.

Kant draws on his noumenal/phenomenal distinction to argue that while we are not free in the phenomenal world (i.e. we are part of nature and therefore subject to the laws of nature), we can consider ourselves to be free in the noumenal sphere. But how can we say such a thing, as it is fundamental to Kant's epistemology that we have no theoretical knowledge of the noumenal? Kant's answer is that freedom can be inferred from the very fact that, as Körner puts it, 'it is the plain outcome of ordinary moral experience that we apprehend the moral law and our subjection to it'.[18] As the moral law is autonomous, our moral decisions require freedom, but as we can never have knowledge of freedom we can only ever infer it on the basis of our 'practical reason', that is, on the basis of our moral experience. Freedom remains a noumenal concept, even though we must make our moral decisions in the everyday world of phenomena. Thus we can see that in Kant's ethics the possibility of human moral freedom depends on the noumenal/phenomenal distinction, and if the noumenal is rejected then freedom collapses into the determinism of the social, political, cultural, intellectual, genetic and other forces which determine us in the phenomenal sphere. For Kant, even if the noumenal/ phenomenal distinction appears to result in a dichotomy at the heart of reality and the human person, that dichotomy is preferable to the loss of that which makes us most distinctly what we are, our freedom as rational creatures.

Kant's insistence on the autonomy of the moral agent makes his theory of ethics quite different from many other theories with which we might be familiar. Unlike Christian ethics, Kant dismisses the idea that ethical behaviour might be conformity of my will to the will of God; that would be to impose someone else's law on myself. Neither does he believe that what is good can be determined in advance of the moral agent so that she adapts her behaviour to suit it, as, for example, when we seek out the common good of humanity; nor is the idea of the greatest happiness of the greatest number, as formulated in utilitarian theories, an adequate criterion, for what leads to happiness varies from person to person, and therefore cannot be the basis for the universal morality which Kant is seeking. For Kant we cannot look to our experiences for fundamental ethical guidelines (even to the combined experiences of a community or a majority of people) because experience, as we know from Kant's epistemology, is no reliable guide in itself. What Kant seeks therefore is a principle which is *a priori* (independent of the senses and experience) universal, and which is fitting for all rational beings.

Kant has such a principle which he thinks can form the basis of ethics; he calls it the *categorical imperative*. For Kant, the categorical (i.e. absolute, unconditional) imperative is to be distinguished from the type of imperative which he saw as characterizing ethical theories before his own, that is, the *hypothetical* imperative. Hypothetical imperatives say that if you want to achieve goal *A* you must do action *B* (or *C* or *D*, etc.). Kant did not believe that an ethics whose imperatives depended on the relation of means to ends could be considered as a binding ethic, for the choice of goal was wholly conditional on the agent's desires, and the 'imperative' involved was simply finding the most suitable means to one's goals. For Kant, however, if the moral law is to be a law, as opposed to a judicious matching of means to ends, then it must be absolute, and not contingent upon the end one wishes to attain.

In the *Groundwork to the Metaphysics of Morals* Kant defines the categorical imperative as follows: 'Act only on the maxim through which you can at the same time will that it become a universal law' (he also formulates it like this: 'Act as if the maxim of your action were to become through your will a universal law of nature'). In other words, a maxim here is a basic rule which a person sets out to live by; such a rule will commit a person to actions that would put the rule into effect. Maxims may be very simple or somewhat more complex: a simple maxim would be of the sort, 'never tell lies'; a more complex maxim might be something like, 'always defend the interests of my country unless this maxim conflicts with other maxims which I consider more essential'. It should be clear that maxims may be moral or not moral; a maxim such as 'always steal from those weaker than I am' is clearly not moral, but it is a maxim nonetheless. In Kant's view the categorical imperative acts as an infallible test to distinguish moral from non-moral maxims, through the requirement that we ask ourselves whether or not we can will that the maxim be universalized (that is, could we will it that everyone does what I advocate in my maxim).

In the *Groundwork* Kant gives several examples of the categorical imperative in action. His most famous (and least contentious) example is of someone who is short of money and borrows from someone else with the promise of paying them back. The impecunious borrower, however, has no intention of ever repaying the loan; thus his maxim is always to break promises if it is to his advantage. But, Kant points out, if we try to make this into a universal law it will not work, for if everyone were to make promises with the intention of breaking them then there would be no longer any point in making promises, and the person hoping to benefit by the maxim would find that no one would lend money if it would never be repaid. Therefore the maxim, 'always break promises if it is to my advantage', results in a contradiction when it is universalized, and thus cannot be considered part of the moral law. As the test of any maxim is that it can be willed as universal by any rational being, the moral law is one – that is, we will not find that the moral law varies from time to time, culture to culture, or person to person.

Testing maxims by means of the categorical imperative would be an excellent method of distinguishing the moral person from the immoral person if everyone stated very clearly what their maxims are. But people do not do this, not only because they may be immoral, but because it is impractical. In practice we would find it very difficult to tell if someone was acting out of duty or prudence or simply habit or peer-pressure: if, for example, one of the accountants auditing the family firm has the opportunity to easily siphon off several thousand pounds to his own account, but does not do so, how can we tell whether that was due to moral principles, fear of being caught, habits of honesty inculcated from an early age, or a code of professional conduct? In most such situations I cannot tell the motivation of the other person. Even with regard to our own maxims, we are often not clearly aware of what our maxims are, as they become habitual and instinctive. But when we do become aware of our maxims and find that they pass the test of the categorical imperative, we are, says Kant, acting out of *duty*, and this for him is the highest form of moral action. Duty is not something imposed on us from without; it is rather our own awareness of the moral law which we are prepared to follow. We may occasionally do what is right out of fear, or luck, or because it is the law, but we only act morally when we recognize the universal moral law as a duty which we impose on ourselves and upon which we then act.

When we become aware of the moral law as duty, says Kant, we realize that duty more often than not conflicts with our desires; but our desires cannot be taken as the basis for morality because they are so fickle. Nor should we look for our own best ends, i.e. that which will be most beneficial to us or secure our happiness; in one of his more stern moments, Kant even goes so far as to say that doing our duty has got nothing to do with enjoying life. So even when we do what is easiest, most convenient, or we think will make us happy, when we follow our desires instead of the call of duty, the moral law imposes itself on us in the form of our awareness that doing what we desire is not always what we actually *ought* to do.

Kant offers another formulation of the categorical imperative, which he considers to be univocal with his previous formulations, and which he thinks will make it clearer why we should follow the moral law rather than our own desires: 'Act in such a way that you always treat humanity, whether in your own person or the person of another, never simply as a means, but always at the same time as an end.' Treating other rational beings as ends in themselves – not simply as a means to my own private ends – entails that the other person may never be used simply to further my own desires, a clear rejection by Kant of the well-known principle of Machiavelli (such a maxim would anyway fail the test of the categorical imperative, for I could not rationally will it that all human beings be only a means to my ends, as this would be inconsistent with my own view of myself as an end). Further, this principle entails that we must acknowledge the freedom of others to decide on their own ends, so long as those ends are themselves ethical.

It is clear that Kant's ethics is not an ethics for the isolated individual, who can set the moral law in whatever way she wishes; the moral law is common to all rational beings, hence when rational beings act in accordance with it they are all acting towards a set of common goals. This set of common goals is what Kant, in a phrase with clear religious overtones, calls a 'kingdom of ends'. We exist as moral beings in a society with other moral beings and if we acknowledge the primacy of the moral law we will discover that we are in fact working towards similar ends; even if the specific ends which we value differ from each other they can all be respected if they conform to the moral law. Kant's ethic here is an ethic of respect, which values the freedom of others, yet which combines the freedom of the moral agent with their responsibility to the moral law.

There is, however, more to the moral law than an autonomous agent testing her maxims by means of the categorical imperative. The moral law, according to Kant in the *Critique of Practical Reason*, has a *telos*, a final end at which moral action is directed. This end is what Kant calls the highest good (*summum bonum*). The highest good must combine happiness and virtue, but the problem remains as to how these two components are related. Is it as the ancient Epicureans had it, that virtue consists in awareness of one's maxims as leading to happiness; or, perhaps, it is as the Stoics held, that awareness of one's virtue is to be happy? Kant considered both these possibilities and rejected them. For him, happiness and virtue are heterogeneous concepts (that is, one can be happy without being virtuous and – in this world at least – one can be virtuous without being happy).

But if happiness does not produce virtue and virtue does not produce happiness, then how is the highest good possible of attainment at all? Kant is enough of a realist about life to see that virtue does not produce happiness (there are many good, but unhappy people around); but, he goes on to say that he can fully discount the possibility of virtue leading to happiness 'only if I assume existence in this world to be the only mode of existence of a rational being'.[19]

Here Kant is raising the possibility of an afterlife; his reasoning is that if we are required by the moral law to be morally perfect, and if such perfection is unattainable in this world, then we can as least consider the possibility of another world where such perfection could be fulfilled. Kant goes on to develop the possibility of the afterlife through the concept of holiness (holiness being when a person's will obeys the moral law perfectly). But in order to make the necessary effort to aim to achieve holiness the will must believe the goal of holiness capable of attainment, and it must *be* capable of attainment, otherwise the moral law would be demanding that which was impossible. But as we already know, perfect holiness is impossible in this life; hence the moral law tells us that the highest good is 'practically possible only on the supposition of the immortality of the soul'.[20] That is to say, happiness in proportion to virtue can only be attained in the afterlife.

This is not to be understood as a moral argument of the wishful-thinking type, that the good must be rewarded and the evil punished; it is rather a consequence of the nature of the moral law. The immortality of the soul, says Kant, is something which we can 'postulate' (that is, we can reasonably assume it without ever knowing it for certain) of the moral law on the grounds that the absolute requirement which it makes of us must be attainable. Attaining the happiness proportional to virtue entails that we make a 'practical' assumption of an afterlife.

Further, if the highest good gives us happiness in proportion to virtue, then happiness is subordinate to virtue, but is also a necessary consequence of it, because for the highest good to be attainable virtue must be the *cause* of happiness. But why should we think that this state of affairs will ever come about; who could possibly ever dish out the exact amount of happiness to go with the right amount of virtue which each of us has attained? It is unsurprising that Kant's solution to this problem is to posit the existence of God, for only God could be the cause which puts into effect the proportion of happiness to virtue required by the concept of the highest good. Now Kant is very quick to say that this is a purely *subjective* belief and that we are not bound to believe in God for this reason. This might seem a strange protestation, as he has just gone to great pains to argue that God and immortality are 'postulates' of practical reason, but it is not so strange when we recall two things: first, that all of this is theory which belongs in the realm of noumena and is therefore not something which we could be ever required to believe as a duty, and secondly, that for Kant the moral law is autonomous in that we do not first of all need to believe in the existence of God to understand it as absolute.

The key to understanding Kant's moral theory of religion is that morality is not based on religion, but rather that religion follows as a practical consequence of the absolute demands made on us by the moral law. Thus when Kant says that 'Religion is the recognition of all duties as divine commands'[21] he is not saying that I must believe in God in order to act ethically. He is rather saying that if we wish to be religious we should comprehend the moral law *as if* it were given by God, even though the moral law imposes itself on me as an absolute requirement irrespective of whether or not I believe in God.

Nevertheless, Kant does believe that morality can lead us to such belief, as we have just shown. But we can never be compelled to such belief, as this would destroy our autonomy as moral agents. Kant thus considers that he has firmly established the grounds for a 'rational faith', meaning that it is a faith which has its source in pure reason (applied theoretically and practically). But if we think that such a rational faith is the means to our happiness we are mistaken. Kant warns us that morality is simply the absolute condition (*conditio sine qua non*) of happiness but it tells us nothing of how we can achieve it. The moral law gives us no such advice or guarantees.

This theory of religion has come in for much criticism, most of which has centred on the 'postulates' of autonomy (or freedom), immortality and God. For Kant the 'postulates' belong in the noumenal realm, and as such are not directly accessible to us as rational, finite beings living in the realm of phenomena, but they are nevertheless necessary if we are to conceive of the possibility of the highest good as the end of all morality. But even if we agree with Kant on this much, what remains problematic is how we can say anything about how the postulates function in bringing about what Kant claims for them. How, for example, does immortality enable moral perfection? As we can say nothing about what form an afterlife would take, how can we even begin to understand what the immortality of an individual soul might be like? How could this soul go about reaching the moral perfection which is impossible for the finite creatures that we are? Does not morality require a world, a context of choices, and other rational beings without whom our moral choices would appear to be empty? How, in sum, can moral growth be achieved other than in the finite world which we know? Is not Kant's notion of immortality, therefore, an empty concept?

Despite this and other similar difficulties with the precise content of concepts such as the highest good, immortality and God, Kant's account of the link between morality and religion must not be dismissed too easily. Kant's greatness is that he saw a real problem in why people should aim for the highest moral standards if those standards cannot be reached (i.e. why would the moral law make an absolute demand upon us if we could never fulfil that demand?). His theory is an attempt to solve a very practical dilemma of the moral life and should be read as such, rather than as a rather backhand attempt to prove the existence of God when the classical attempts to do so had been so effectively undermined by Kant's own critique.

There is a rather cruel story, invented by the German writer Heinrich Heine, that Kant's account of moral religion was designed to restore the faith of his old butler Lampe, who was reputedly so upset by the implications of Kant's first *Critique*. The story is cruel because it misses the point of the profound difficulty Kant had in accounting for how the absolute demands of the moral law could be met. There is a kernel of truth in it, however, in so far as Kant believed that he was describing how morality and religious faith actually operate and should operate in the minds of many people, as a simple yet always *categorical* requirement which we had a genuine hope of fulfilling, even if not always in this life. What hope, indeed, would we have if we thought that our moral disposition and actions had no ultimate worth? Kant's doctrine of morality is not a gnosticism, available only to a privileged few with the intellectual resources or the strength of character to meet the demands of the moral law; it is a morality that any rational person can follow.

It is plain, then, that Kant did not see moral agents as isolated individuals standing apart from the great mass of humanity. The categorical imperative demands that we treat other people as ends in themselves, so we cannot be ethical in isolation. Thus, in following the moral law each moral agent is of necessity involved in reciprocal relations with other moral agents who do not view each other merely as means to private ends. Therefore, according to Kant, the moral law impels us towards the formation of a moral community.

In *Religion Within the Limits of Reason Alone*, Kant formulated his understanding of what such a community would be like. It is, first, to be distinguished from the political community. The political community that is the state operates by means of coercion, but no such coercion is possible in morality because it would contravene the autonomy of the moral subject. Further, the moral community (or, as Kant calls it, the 'ethical commonwealth') extends beyond the boundaries of each particular political community to embrace the whole of humanity; the moral law recognizes no political limits. If the highest good is promoted among human beings, it must be promoted as a *social* good, not merely as something which is good for a large number of individuals.

Also, promotion of the highest good is something which is a duty for the human race as such, and not simply for its individual members, and as a whole the human race works towards the creation of what Kant calls 'a universal republic based on laws of virtue'.[22] Kant rejects the possibility, advocated by Rousseau, that in such a community the people create the law for themselves, because such a law, even if it is created by the people, is always *external* and coercive, and not *internal* and autonomous as the moral law requires. This means that achieving this end of a 'universal republic' is something which we cannot be certain is within our own power; hence, Kant argues, its achievement – required by the moral law – presupposes the existence of 'a higher moral Being', God.

If we now recall that for Kant 'Religion is the recognition of all duties as divine commands', we can see that he is attempting here to

establish how God might be related to the 'ethical commonwealth' and
not only to the individual moral agent. What comes first is the demand
of the moral law, which we then view – for reasons which Kant has
presented in the second *Critique* – as divine commands (this means
that anything which might appear as a 'divine command', but which
is opposed to a demand of duty, should be rejected). The demands of
duty themselves, therefore, should be seen as divine commands, and
God – as both law-giver and final arbiter of each one's moral worth –
should be seen as the ultimate ruler of the moral community. Hence,
concludes Kant, 'an ethical community can be thought of only as a
people under divine commands, i.e as a *people of God*'.[23]

The definition of the 'ethical commonwealth' as 'a people of God'
has clear connotations of the Christian doctrine of the church, and
may appear to many readers of Kant as a somewhat disappointing conclusion given his claim to have established the autonomy of morality.
But Kant has a very particular view of the distinction between the
'people of God' as the ideal of an ethical commonwealth and those
churches and religious communities which are so marked by human
limitation and failure; as Kant puts it: 'How indeed can one expect
something perfectly straight to be framed out of such crooked wood?'[24]
Kant is prepared to go so far as so call the 'people of God' (as he has
defined it) a 'church', but it is a church with particular characteristics:
it is *universal*, that is, it has no sectarian divisions; it is purely *moral*,
that is, it is motivated by nothing other than the moral law; it is
guided by the principle of *freedom*, that is, reciprocal freedom as in
a republic, avoiding the extremes of both hierarchical rule and individualism; it is, finally, unlike any empirical organization in that its
constitution is the moral law established *a priori*, thus avoiding the
arbitrary changes which mark so many human institutions. Kant sums
up this church of moral faith as 'a voluntary, universal, and enduring
union of hearts'.[25]

How, then, are the already existing human communities called
'churches' (Kant calls their faith 'ecclesiastical faith' as distinct from
his understanding of a pure 'religious faith'[26]) to be understood in
relation to this ideal church based on moral faith? Is Kant advocating
that a new church be started and the existing ones closed down due
to their inadequacy? These churches are, from Kant's perspective,
inadequate because they are founded upon competing claims of

particular revelations occurring in history, and can thus never be truly universal. Kant, however, is not a naive idealist who thinks that a new church based solely on moral faith would be any better than the existing institutions, for human nature being what it is this church would soon succumb to the faults of any human institution. Kant does not see it as God's concern to tell us what *form* the ideal church should take – that is our responsibility; hence we can continue to work within the existing institutions (and forming new ones if necessary) to make them more like the universal ethical community which is the ideal church. The existing 'ecclesiastical faiths' can therefore form the foundation – or, as Kant says, the 'vehicle' – for that universal community of people under the moral law as given by God which forms the true church.

Kant's uncompromising insistence on observance of the moral law as the only true religion, leads him to a severe judgment on the practices and structures of 'ecclesiastical faiths'. Christianity, properly understood, is a rational religion, which requires no additional beliefs beyond those available to reason itself. Kant regards worship as mere superstition, in that it can add nothing to one's adherence to the moral law, and merely serves to humiliate the worshipper in his attempts to placate the deity as he might some potentate. Indeed he regards all religious activities such as pilgrimages, sacrifices, penances, offerings, etc. as mere superstitions which can deflect our attention from the one thing that truly matters, living by the moral law. Such activities are 'illusions' in so far as they foolishly attempt to work on God in order to bring about something which is of our own desiring. The clergy-laity distinction he regards as 'humiliating', and calls the clericalism which rules the ecclesiastical faiths a form of 'spiritual despotism'. For Kant 'true enlightenment' lies in knowing the distinction between the 'pseudo-service' of ecclesiastical religion (with its hierarchies, doctrines, services and prayers) and the true religion which is the service of God through adherence to the moral law.[27]

Kant's vision of a 'true religion' may seem unnaturally cold and lacking in an appreciation of how ethical behaviour is intricately bound up with cultural and symbolic expression, of how human structures and organizations provide the matrix within which our moral lives take shape, and of how even apparently debased human systems and communities can be the *loci* of the highest ethical conduct. But

despite this austere tone, Kant did not think that we could have a form
of free-floating rational community, independent of the everyday
realities of what human beings actually do and how they organize
themselves; his aim was simply to hold a mirror up to our actual
practices in the fullest awareness of what was actually demanded of us
by the moral law. There is no doubt that in his critique of religious
thought and practice, in his demand that we take responsibility for our
own moral lives, in his advocacy of toleration and rejection of all
sectarian differences, he formulated a vision of the human person
before God that still stands as one of the greatest achievements of
Enlightenment thought.

The rigour of Kant's philosophy and the emphasis which he placed
on the correct use of reason should not be misconstrued as an indication of the dominance of rationalism in German thought in the second
half of the eighteenth century. Kant's great achievement, we must
recall, was to delineate the limits of reason, and provide a sharp criticism of the rationalism which had preceded him. In his critique of
reason he succeeded in simultaneously weakening the claims of reason
and placing it on a more secure footing. But not all his contemporaries
shared his estimation that the correct understanding and use of reason
was the most important intellectual task of the time. There were those
in Germany for whom the abstract, analytical and universalist thought
of the philosophes and their German counterparts was a poor substitute for the 'deeper' emotional, psychological, artistic, cultural,
ethnic, religious and national elements which actually go to form
human individuals and societies. The reality of the cultural matrix in
which we live could not be susceptible to one dominant explanatory
model, into which all variety of culture and experience was expected
to fit. Thus, Germany saw the development of new models of the
human person and society: an emphasis was placed on the intuitive (as
distinct from the rational) power of the individual mind, more attention was devoted to the power of imagination, to the folklore of the
common people, to the inspiration of the creative talent, to religious
and cultural traditions which may not have amounted to much at the
court of critical reason, but which nevertheless played a major role in
the way in which individuals and communities interpreted their
experience of the world in which they lived.

One of the seminal figures in this gradual revolt against reason was

Johann Georg Hamann (1730–88), who was born in Konigsberg and was both a friend and a critic of Kant. Hamann was influenced by the sceptical tradition of Socrates, Francis Bacon and David Hume and came to mistrust the confidence in reason which he saw in the dominant intellectual circles. Unlike many sceptics of the time, however, he did not settle for recourse to the empirical or for common sense solutions to the dilemmas of reason. Hamann instead had recourse to a mystical form of religious belief which eschewed any attempt to explain Christianity rationally. 'Proofs' are useless: 'Our own existence, and the existence of all things outside us, must be *believed*, and cannot be determined in any other way.'[28] For Hamann, reality must be grasped as a whole and this cannot happen if reason attempts to break it down into artificial component parts. Religious belief, too, cannot be justified on rational grounds and can only be grasped mystically. The human person is more than the rational; we are imaginative, passionate, bodily and sexual beings. The 'achievements' of the Enlightenment – e.g. the rationalization of religion, scientific discoveries, the increased specialization of the human and natural sciences – are unnatural abstractions, simply futile attempts to control a reality which lies beyond the control of a faculty as weak as human reason.

Hamann influenced the two thinkers who are most often associated with the anti-Enlightenment trend in German thought in the late eighteenth century, namely Johann Gottfried von Herder (1744–1803) and Johann Wolfgang von Goethe (1749–1832). Through his emphasis on aspects of the human person other than the rational, Hamann helped spark the *Sturm und Drang* (storm and stress) movement of the 1770s, a cultural and artistic movement which explicitly rejected reason in favour of imagination and artistic intuition. Hamann's insight that thought and language are intimately bound together influenced Herder's work on the importance of the traditions of a language carried on in its folk traditions (such as its songs) and this in turn was instrumental in the emergence of a strong German literary tradition and in the Romantic movement's concern with the sensual nature of language.

The *Sturm und Drang* movement introduced into the German intellectual environment the notion of *Empfindsamkeit* (feeling), in which attention is given to a subject – a person, nature, a work of art, a piece of music, even an entire culture – not through rational analysis, but through a sympathetic appreciation of the qualities of the subject itself. *Empfindsamkeit* offers an epistemology which is less concerned with theoretical knowledge of the world and more with the impact which the world makes on the one who is experiencing it; thus, we do not stand over and against the world as its masters and dissectors, but we are rather actively participating in its very processes. In attempting to reduce such a world to the component of its own analysis, reason is merely chasing its own tail.

The death of Kant in 1804 marks a decisive turning-point in the history of European thought. What distinguishes the era of Louis XIV, Reubens, Poussin, Bernini and Monteverdi from the era of Napoleon, Darwin, Wagner, Nietzsche and Marx is the emergence of reason as a scalpel to be applied to all areas of life, the arts, the human person, the structure of society, nature and, of course, religion. Nothing can any longer be merely accepted, it must be explained and justified. Even where the scalpel of reason was too sharp for some (such as the mystique of nature found in many of the Romantics of the early nineteenth century) there were only attempts to temper reason in its application to realms which were considered better left unassailed, while other areas of life – religion being one notable example – continued to be prime targets. The intellectual foundations of the widespread secularization of Western society which occurred in the nineteenth and twentieth centuries were laid between Descartes and Kant.

Conclusion

At a distance of two hundred and fifty years since the high point of the Enlightenment it is possible to look back and paint a bright picture of the era in broad interpretative strokes about which there is a great deal of agreement among scholars: the emphasis on the universality of reason; the shaking off of 'external' authorities; the belief in the universality of human nature and a brave attempt to focus on what unites, rather than divides us; a rejection of 'prejudice' in all its forms; an emphasis on toleration and the search for simplicity in religion; a general belief in progress and the rejection of all that appeared to hinder it. This is Enlightenment as Kant saw it: the emergence of humanity from the darkness and dependency of its self-imposed infancy to the brightness and freedom of adulthood.

But it is also possible to see another side of the Enlightenment: a concept of reason which appears to mirror a particular ideal of detached, male, rationality; a failure to realize in practice the high ideals of equality and toleration; a naive belief that advances in science and technology could solve many onerous human problems; a devaluing of the emotional, affective and self-expressive dimensions of the human person; a simplistic understanding of religion which failed to take account of the importance of tradition, ritual and due authority and which unfairly misrepresented the views and practices of the Jesuits and others; a caricature of the past which portrayed it – the mediaeval period in particular – as stagnant and hidebound by authority.

The Enlightenment is undoubtedly open to both interpretations, and this fact alone alerts us to the perils involved in using the term 'Enlightenment' at all, for when one looks back at the period it is extremely difficult to distinguish any clear and unified train of thought which one could point to as defining precisely what constituted

'Enlightenment'. Is the Enlightenment to be taken as encompassing eighteenth-century thought and culture as a whole or is it better to restrict its scope to a few leading thinkers who explicitly identified themselves with a new way of thinking? If one wishes to understand the era should one look first to the equanimity of the atheist David Hume as he lay dying, undisturbed by any concerns about divine judgment or an afterlife and say that in his life one sees at last the model of the free and rational human being? Or should one look to the brave new world of the United States, founded with a loud declaration of Enlightenment ideals but built on the economic foundations of slavery, and point to the dark side of Enlightenment, the repressed horrors which no amount of enlightened rhetoric can mask?

This dilemma of interpretation is complicated by the fact that in several respects the Enlightenment contained within itself its own antithesis. For example, as Kant was writing the philosophy which is regarded as the apex of the Enlightenment, Goethe was producing the literature which would help activate a romantic counter-current; and, as the thought of Rousseau illustrates, at the heart of the Enlightenment were thinkers who rejected several of its most cherished ideas; in religious thought, too, the case of Pascal shows that even before the 'Enlightenment' proper and its attendant deism there was present a critique of the futility of attempting to establish religious faith on the basis of reason.

These difficulties are, perhaps, in the end intractable and rather than try to define what belongs to the Enlightenment and what does not it is more profitable to regard the Enlightenment not as a programme of thought or as simply an interesting historical period, but rather as a particular cultural space within which there emerged new ideas, new developments, even new scientific disciplines, and which has shaped for better or for worse the world in which we live today.

In terms of religious thought the most significant legacy by far of this cultural space – this possibility for the formation of new discourses – is a predominantly secular culture. Christian anthropology no longer sets the agenda for our understanding of our own nature, but must compete with a range of world-views from scientific materialism to the pseudo-mystical 'new age' philosophy. In most Western countries the churches have little or no political power left. Even among believing Christians morality is generally considered to be a matter for the individual and not for the church authorities to work out and pass on as doctrine. In the sciences, the religious world-view – if not rejected out of hand – has become redundant to the methodology of scientific enquiry. Theology now considers biblical criticism essential to an understanding of the Christian message, rather than as a threat to revelation. In education the state has usurped the power and influence which the church once held as its own. In the promulgation of ideas a secular intelligentsia and a widespread public media have made the control of thought an impossibility, and rendered the very concept of intellectual authority problematic. All of these factors have their roots in the Enlightenment.

But is there not another side to this picture also? Has not religion persisted despite the enormous attraction of a purely secular alternative? Do we not see in many of the positive achievements of modern secular culture deep echoes of the values of the Jewish and Christian traditions, with their respect for human dignity and justice and an emphasis on the importance of each individual person? Have not science and technology contributed to our enslavement to a rationalized culture, as well as to our undoubted liberation from many of the limitations of the past? Have not the horrific wars of this century shown us once again the fearful potential for evil in the human heart? Is it not true that the human need for cultural, political and scientific fulfilment must be complemented by some form of spiritual fulfilment also? And, is not the case that, rather than the elimination of religion from our societies, what is preferable is the presence of a critical and constructive form of religious expression which respects the achievements of secular culture but is capable of holding that culture to account also?

It is now quite common to hear intellectuals blame the Enlightenment for many of the difficulties with which modern society has been faced. The most famous and important critique of the Enlightenment in this century came with the publication in 1947 of Theodor Adorno's (1903–69) and Max Horkheimer's (1895–1973) *Dialectic of Enlightenment*, which argued that the Enlightenment notion of reason as objective and abstract, when isolated from any critique of its own ideological underpinning, results in a non-critical concept of reason which equates rationality with mere technological efficiency. Conceived in this way, reason becomes simply a method, empty of ethical reflection, interested only in rationalization and implementation; such a concept of reason, said Horkheimer and Adorno, leads not to freedom and emancipation but to the slavery and horrors of the Nazi gas-chambers.

In the philosophy of ethics, too, the Enlightenment vision appears less than healthy. The recent influential work of Alasdair MacIntyre (1929-) has presented us with a pessimistic picture of the heritage of the Enlightenment ideal of the autonomous ethical agent. In *After Virtue* (1981) MacIntyre argued that the Enlightenment's attempt to develop a universal ethical framework in which the individual would construct her own moral values free of the encroachment of society, religion or tradition was bound to fail, and has resulted only in a form of individualistic emotivism which both reflects and contributes to the dissolution of traditional communities and social bonds. MacIntyre advocates that we return to an understanding of ethics as located in the practices of particular communities and traditions, and suggests the Aristotelian virtues as one viable ethical tradition which could offer us a way out of the maze of moral relativism in which Western culture finds itself.

Theology has also, in recent years, seen an attack on the dominant trends which developed in response to the challenge of the Enlightenment. The so-called 'father of modern theology', Friedrich Schleiermacher (1768–1834), in responding to the epistemology of Kant, constructed a theology which placed the emphasis on the religious experience of the believer and played down the cognitive claims of religious belief. The resultant 'liberal theology' which developed under the influence of Schleiermacher's thought – especially when allied to the influence of inter-religious dialogue in this century – placed the accent on the unity of all religious experience and the common factors which bound the religions together, while also attempting to give a rational justification for religious belief in general.

Some theologians, dissatisfied with the attempts of liberal theology to respond to the Enlightenment critique of religion through a defence of the rationality of religious belief, and its emphasis on what was perceived as a rather amorphous concept of 'religious' experience, began to speak of a 'post-liberal theology' which would reassert the particularity of the Christian message. In 1984 George Lindbeck's *The*

Nature of Doctrine argued that liberal theology had failed Christianity and, drawing on some aspects of the philosophy of Wittgenstein as a source, advocated a 'cultural-linguistic' concept of religion which perceived the religions as discrete cultural systems which must be interpreted in terms of their own internal self-understanding, and not in terms of some false concept of universality or common purpose. This approach had the advantage of simply side-stepping the Enlightenment's epistemological challenge to religious belief by isolating it within its own meaning-system and frame of reference. 'Post-liberal theology', while of course indebted to much from the Enlightenment, is essentially therefore a rejection of the theological version of the Enlightenment's emphasis on the universality of human meaning-making. Our cultural and religious systems, it says, are not reducible to the common denominator of universal human nature and are not susceptible to the form of critique which the Enlightenment threw at religion.

I have chosen these examples from political philosophy, ethics and theology to illustrate very briefly how the ideals of simplicity, universality and commonality of purpose can give rise to unforeseen and, at times, unfortunate consequences (one could of course add to these numerous other examples, in particular from 'postmodern' theorists who reject all forms of universality, objectivity or abstraction as ideologically suspect and potentially oppressive, preferring instead to play in the world of ever-turbulent and shifting patterns of signs which surround us). But if we understand one thing above all about the Enlightenment, it is that it is precisely as Horkeimer and Adorno warned us, a dialectic, a very sharp two-edged sword.

After the Enlightenment we cannot turn back the hands of time and pretend that its vision, ideals, achievements and errors never happened. We are destined to live with the legacy of Enlightenment reason in its many forms. But reason can never rest content with its own self-interpretation; when it does so it has become an ideology. This means that we must be ever vigilant about the language and ideas which we employ, but it also means that we can never pin down an ultimate meaning, a final definition of what Enlightenment was or is – in the end we can have no one story of Enlightenment, no one final interpretation.

There is an etching by the Spanish artist Goya (1746–1828) – done sometime in the period 1793–96 – which shows a man (a draughtsman or a writer) asleep at his desk, his head cradled in his arms and his legs crossed. Above his head bats, owls and other indeterminate but threatening creatures of the night swarm and screech alarmingly, while behind him his cat looks around in alarm. On the side of the desk the words are written: *El sueño de la razon produce monstruous* (this could be rendered as either 'the dream of reason produces monsters' or 'the sleep of reason produces monsters'). Goya, a man whose paintings captured much of the violence of his times, was acutely aware of the depths to which the human spirit could sink and especially of the consequences of uncritical political or religious commitments. When reason, reflection and critical awareness are absent the monsters of injustice, oppression and intolerance raise their heads.

As someone who travelled widely in Europe yet whose identity was closely bound to the Spanish culture to which he always returned, Goya lived the tensions between the new cosmopolitan culture of the Enlightenment and the traditional political and religious world of his homeland. This tension is not unlike the experience of anyone who continues to be interested in the question of religion today; we too live in an in-between world of the religious tradition on the one hand and the critical demands of post-Enlightenment modernity on the other. One could, of course, avoid this tension by no longer taking seriously the claims of the religious tradition or by retreating to the opposite pole and immersing oneself safely in religious authoritarianism. But both alternatives involve the sleep of reason, for neither religion nor modernity is going to disappear; if we are to avoid the recurrence of monsters in our midst we can only do so by remaining awake to the dangers of violence, intolerance, hatred and oppression which always threaten us and in which religious belief is all too often complicitous. If we do so, we could perhaps venture to say that in the sphere of religion we do not – to paraphrase Kant – live in an enlightened age, but rather one of ongoing enlightenment.

Notes

Chapter 1   Changing Ideals

1 Although philosophe is a French word, it is used commonly enough in English not to merit italicization.
2 Ernst Cassirer, *The Philosophy of the Enlightenment*, Princeton University Press 1951, p. 13.
3 Norman Hampson, *The Enlightenment:An Evaluation of Its Assumptions, Attitudes and Values*, Pelican Books 1968, p. 106.
4 See Werner G. Jeanrond, *Theological Hermeneutics: Development and Significance*, SCM Press and Crossroad 1994, pp. 39–43. Also Hans Frei, *The Eclipse of Biblical Narrative: A Study in Eighteeth and Nineteenth Century Hermeneutics*, Yale University Press 1974.
5 Keith Thomas, *Religion and the Decline of Magic*, Weidenfeld and Nicolson 1971, p. 521.
6 On the origins and decline of the witchcraft craze in Europe see also H. R. Trevor-Roper, *The European Witch-Craze of the Sixteenth and Seventeenth Centuries*, Penguin Books 1969.
7 Phyllis Mack, Introduction to *Women and the Enlightenment*, Margaret Hunt, Margaret Jacob, Phyllis Mack and Ruth Perry (eds), The Haworth Press 1984, p. 6.
8 See Genevieve Lloyd, *The Man of Reason: 'Male' and 'Female' in Western Philosophy*, Methuen 1984, pp. 58–64.
9 Roy Porter, *English Society in the Eighteenth Century*, The Penguin Social History of Britain (gen. ed J. H. Plumb), Penguin Books 1990, p. 266.

Chapter 2   Enlightenment, Power and Context

1 Michael Buckley, *At the Origins of Modern Atheism*, Yale University Press 1987, p. 37 agreeing with the views of Peter Gay.
2 Peter Gay, *The Enlightenment: An Interpretation*, Vol. 1, *The Rise of Modern Paganism*, Weidenfeld and Nicolson 1966, p. 338.
3 See John McManners, *Death and the Enlightenment: Changing Attitudes to*

Death among Christians and Unbelievers in Eighteenth-Century France, Clarendon Press and Oxford University Press 1981, pp. 440–444 and passim.

4 Roy Porter, 'The Enlightenment in England', in Roy Porter and Mikulas Teich (eds), *The Enlightenment in National Context*, Cambridge University Press 1981, p. 5.

5 See Roy Porter, *English Society in the Eighteenth Century*, pp. 168–176.

6 See James K. Cameron, 'The Church in Scotland from the Reformation to the Disruption', in Sheridan Gilley and W. J. Shiels (eds), *A History of Religion in Britain: Practice and Belief from Pre-Roman Times to the Present*, Blackwell 1994, pp. 129–150. The importance of the Scottish Enlightenment to the Enlightenment as a whole is much greater than our examination of religious thought would indicate. For a detailed treatment see A. Chitnis, *The Scottish Enlightenment: A Social History*, Croom Helm 1976 and Nicholas Phillipson, 'The Scottish Enlightenment' in Porter and Teich (eds), *The Enlightenment in National Context*, pp. 19–40. On the relevance of David Hume's philosophy for religious thought see Chapters 6 and 9.

7 Quoted in S. K. Padover, *The Revolutionary Emperor*, Jonathan Cape 1934, p. 224.

8 Edmund Burke, *Reflections on the Revolution in France* (1790), Penguin Books 1968, pp. 181–82.

9 The incident is recounted in J. R. Pole, 'Enlightenment and the Politics of American Nature' in Porter and Teich (eds), *The Enlightenment in National Context*, p. 206.

10 J. R. Pole, 'Enlightenment and the Politics of American Nature', p. 199.

11 Henry F. May, *The Enlightenment in America*, Oxford University Press 1976, p. xiv.

Chapter 3   God and the Clarity of Reason: René Descartes

1 J. G. Cottingham, R. Stoothoff, D. Murdoch (eds), *The Philosophical Writings of Descartes* (Vols 1 and 2), Cambridge University Press 1985, Vol. 1, p. 120.

2 This question is considered in more detail by Peter Markie, 'The Cogito and its importance' in John Cottingham (ed.), *The Cambridge Companion to Descartes*, Cambridge University Press 1992, pp. 140–173.

3 Cottingham et al. (eds), *The Philosophical Writings of Descartes*, Vol. 2, p. 19.

4 These arguments are also to be found in condensed form in Part IV of *The Discourse*.

5 Paul Edwards (ed.), *The Encyclopedia of Philosophy*, Vol. 2, Macmillan and The Free Press/Collier-Macmillan 1967, pp. 348–49.

6 Cottingham et al. (eds) *The Philosophical Writings of Descartes*, Vol. 2, p. 54.

7 The term 'dualism' can be used to refer to any form of radical separation of two realities (e.g. in theology: God-world, sin-grace, sinner-saved). Dualism has a long history in Western thought, and is usually traced to Plato's theory that the world we experience is only a shadow of the 'real' world of ideal Forms.

8 Lloyd, *The Man of Reason: 'Male' and 'Female' in Western Philosophy*, p. 50.

9 Quoted in John Cottingham (ed.), *A Descartes Dictionary*, Blackwell 1993, p. 163.

10 Voltaire, *Letters Concerning the English Nation* (1733), ed. Nicholas Cronk, Oxford University Press 1994, Letter XIV, p. 64.

Chapter 4   Burning Faith: Blaise Pascal

1 Pascal in Richard H. Popkin (ed.), *Pascal: Selections*, Macmillan 1989, pp. 69–70.

2 Pascal in Popkin (ed.), *Pascal Selections*, p. 111.

3 The exact way in which the notes should be arranged has long been an issue of dispute among Pascal scholars. Here I follow the arrangement of A. J. Krailsheimer, whose translation of the *Pensées* is available in the *Penguin Classics* paperback series (Penguin Books 1966). The numbers refer not to pages but to the number of the relevant fragment in the Krailsheimer edition.

4 The conversation was published as *Conversation with M. de Saci*, and can be found in Popkin (ed.) *Pascal Selections*, pp. 79–89.

5 Voltaire, *Letters Concerning the English Nation*, Letter XXV, p. 123.

Chapter 5   The Distant God of Deism

1 Ernst Cassirer, *The Philosophy of the Enlightenment*, p. 13.

2 Cassirer, *The Philosophy of the Enlightenment*, p. 13.

3 Spinoza, *Ethics*, Part II, prop. VII, J. M. Dent 1910 (Everyman Edition), pp. 41–42.

4 Spinoza, *Ethics*, Part II, prop. XI, p. 46.

5 Spinoza, *Ethics*, Part I, prop. XIV, p. 11.

6 See Herbert of Cherbury, *De Veritate*, in Ninian Smart, *Historical Selections in the Philosophy of Religion*, SCM Press 1962, pp. 85–104.

7 Herbert in Smart, *Historical Selections in the Philosophy of Religion*, p. 89.

8 John Locke, *An Essay Concerning Human Understanding* (1690) Book II, XXIII, 33.

9 Gay, *The Enlightenment: An Interpretation*, Vol. 1, p. 327.

10 Alexander Pope, *Essay on Man*, III/IV.

11 Butler, *The Analogy of Religion, Natural and Revealed* (1736), Introduction.

12 Thomas Paine, *The Age of Reason* (1794), in *The Thomas Paine Reader*, Michael Foot and Isaac Kramnick (eds), Penguin Books 1987, p. 401.

13 Paine, *The Age of Reason*, p. 400.

14 Paine, *The Age of Reason*, p. 419.

15 Paine, *The Age of Reason*, p. 421.

16 Samuel S.B. Taylor, 'The Enlightenment in Switzerland', in Porter and Teich (eds), *The Enlightenment in National Context*, pp. 72–89.

17 Taylor, 'The Enlightenment in Switzerland', pp. 73–74.

18 Taylor, 'The Enlightenment in Switzerland', pp. 88.

19 Taylor, 'The Enlightenment in Switzerland', p. 80.

Chapter 6   From Scepticism to Atheism

1 Bayle quoted in Elizabeth Labrousse, *Bayle*, translated by Denys Potts, Oxford University Press 1983, p. 83.

2 Buckley, *At The Origins of Modern Atheism*, p. 196.

3 Buckley, *At The Origins of Modern Atheism*, p. 196.

4 Cassirer, *The Philosophy of the Enlightenment*, p. 141.

5 Cassirer, *The Philosophy of the Enlightenment*, p. 147.

6 Arthur M. Wilson, *Diderot*, Oxford University Press 1972, p. 247.

7 D'Alembert, *Preliminary Discourse to the Encyclopedia*, in Simon Eliot and Beverley Stern (eds), *The Age of Enlightenment: An Anthology of Eighteenth-Century Texts*, 2 Vols, Open University Press 1979, Vol. 2, p. 131.

8 The incident is recounted in Wilson, *Diderot*, pp. 155–160.

9 Diderot, *Letter on the Blind*, in Jonathan Kemp (ed.), *Diderot: Interpreter of Nature, Selected Writings*, Lawrence and Wishart 1936, p. 27.

10 Diderot, *Letter on the Blind*, p. 29.

11 Buckley, *At The Origins of Modern Atheism*, p. 222.

12 Quoted in Wilson, *Diderot*, p. 444.

13 Quoted in Gay, *The Enlightenment: An Interpretation*, Vol. 1, p. 399.

14 David Hume, 'Of Miracles', *An Inquiry Concerning Human Understanding* (1748) Section X, in Patrick Sherry (ed.), *Philosophers on Religion: An Historical Reader*, Geoffrey Chapman 1987, p. 97.

15 Hume, 'Of Miracles', in Sherry (ed.), *Philosophers on Religion*, p. 99.

16 David Hume, *Dialogues Concerning Natural Religion* (1779), edited with introduction and notes by Martin Bell, Penguin Books 1990, p. 87.

17 Hume, *Dialogues Concerning Natural Religion*, p. 97.

18 Hume, *Dialogues Concerning Natural Religion*, p. 45.

19 Hume, *Dialogues Concerning Natural Religion*, p. 53.

20 See Isser Woloch, *Eighteenth-Century Europe: Tradition and Progress, 1715–1789*, W. W. Norton 1982, pp. 291–95.

Chapter 7   New Light or Old?: Science and Religion

1 Richard S. Westfall in John W. Yolton et al. (eds), *The Blackwell Companion to the Enlightenment*, Blackwell 1991, p. 367.

2 Leibniz, quoted in Carl B. Boyer, *A History of Mathematics* (second edition, revised by Uta C. Merzbach), John Wiley and Sons 1991, p. 391.

3 Introduction to John Fauvel et al. (eds), *Let Newton Be!: A New Perspective on His Life and Works*, Open University Press 1988, p. 7.

4 Newton, *Principia*, in Leonard Cowie (ed.), *Eighteenth-Century Europe: Documents and Debates*, John Wroughton (gen. ed), Macmillan 1989, p. 30.

5 John Henry, 'Newton, Matter and Magic', in Fauvel et al. (eds), *Let Newton Be!*, p. 141.

6 See Ian G. Barbour, *Religion in an Age of Science*, SCM Press 1990, pp. 218–20.

7 Voltaire, *Letters Concerning the English Nation*, Letter XIV, p. 64.

8 John Hedley Brooke, *Science and Religion: Some Historical Perspectives*, Cambridge University Press 1991, p. 137.

9 See Arthur Koestler, *The Sleepwalkers: A History of Man's Changing Vision of the Universe*, Penguin Books 1959, p. 536.

10 Leibniz in H. G. Alexander (ed.), *The Leibniz-Clarke Correspondence*, Manchester University Press 1956, p. 12.

11 See Henry 'Newton, Matter and Magic', pp. 132–133, for an illustration and further explanation.

12 John W. Yolton, *Thinking Matter: Materialism in Eighteenth-Century Britain*, Blackwell 1984, pp. 92–93.

13 Newton, quoted in Alexander Koyré, *From the Closed World to the Infinite Universe*, John Hopkins University Press 1968, pp. 227–228.

14 Barbour, *Religion in an Age of Science*, p. 4.

15 See Yolton *Thinking Matter*, pp. 107–126.

16 Thomas L. Hankins, *Science and the Enlightenment, Cambridge History of Science Series*, G. Basalla and W. Coleman (eds), Cambridge University Press 1985, p. 129.

17 Hampson, *The Enlightenment: An Evaluation of Its Assumptions, Attitudes and Values*, p. 127.

18 See Hankins, *Science and the Enlightenment*, pp. 131–133; and Brooke, *Science and Religion: Some Historical Perspectives*, p. 173.

19 See Hankins, *Science and the Enlightenment*, p. 127.

20 Horace Walpole in W. S. Lewis (ed.), *The Yale Edition of Horace Walpole's Correspondence*, Yale University Press and Oxford University Press 1961, Vol. 30, p. 208.

21 See Hankins, *Science and the Enlightenment*, p. 170.

22 See Brooke, *Science and Religion: Some Historical Perspectives*, p. 180 and M. S. Anderson, *Europe in the Eighteenth Century*, Longman 1976, pp. 346–47.

23 G.L. Leclerc, Comte de Buffon, *Histoire, naturelle, générale et particulière, avec la description du cabinet du roi*, translated by John Lyon, in Eliot and Stern (eds), *The Age of Enlightenment: An Anthology of Eighteenth-Century Texts*, Vol. 2, p. 165.

24 Hampson, *The Enlightenment: An Evaluation of Its Assumptions, Attitudes and Values*, p. 220. The figure of 70,000 years was published in Buffon's *Epoques de la nature* (1778).

25 Jeanrond, *Theological Hermeneutics: Development and Significance*, p. 36.

26 Marquis de Condorcet, *Sketch for a Historical Picture of the Progress of the Human Mind*, in A. J. Ayer and Jane O'Grady (eds), *A Dictionary of Philosophical Quotations*, Blackwell 1992, p. 96.

27 Hankins, *Science and the Enlightenment*, p. 11.

28 G. E. Lessing, quoted in in Ayer and O'Grady (eds), *A Dictionary of Philosophical Quotations*, p. 251.

29 Koyré, *From the Closed Word to the Infinite Universe*, p. 275.

Chapter 8   The Morality of Innocence: Jean-Jacques Rousseau

1 Rousseau, quoted in John Hope Mason, *The Indispensable Rousseau*, Quartet Books 1979, p. 243.

2 Jean-Jacques Rousseau, *Emile or On Education* (1762), translated with introduction and notes by Allan Bloom, Penguin Books 1979, p. 386.

3 Mary Wollstonecraft, *A Vindication of the Rights of Women* (1792), in *Political Writings*, edited with an introduction by Janet Todd, Oxford University Press 1994, p. 109.

4 Rousseau, *Emile*, p. 281.

5 Rousseau, *Emile*, p. 286.

6 Rousseau, *Emile*, p. 287.

7 Rousseau, *Emile*, p. 290.

8 Rousseau, *Emile*, p. 293.

9 Rousseau, *Emile*, p. 313.

10 Jean-Jacques Rousseau, *Letter to Voltaire*, in Eliot and Stern (eds), *The Age of Enlightenment: An Anthology of Eighteenth-Century Texts*, Vol. 1, p. 100.

11 Rousseau, *On Providence*, in Eliot and Stern (eds), *The Age of Enlightenment: An Anthology of Eighteenth-Century Texts*, Vol. 1, p. 103.

12 It was precisely this sort of understanding of religious belief (i.e. as psychologically useful and desirable) which Freudianism took as the weak point of religion (as illusions which could well be delusions) and attacked so vehemently.

13 For a recent critique of the hidden ideological dimension of this move see Terry Eagletor, *The Ideology of the Aesthetic*, Blackwell 1990, pp. 24–26.

Chapter 9   *Belief within the Limits of Reason: Immanuel Kant*

1 On Kant's concept of belief in a personal God as one of 'trust' (a concept which shows the influence of pietism), and how this differs from deism, see Allen W. Wood, *Kant's Moral Religion*, Cornell University Press 1970, pp. 160–174.

2 Hans Küng, *Does God Exist?*, SCM Press and Doubleday 1984, p. 593.

3 See Frederick C. Beiser, 'Kant's Intellectual Development' in Paul Guyer (ed.), *The Cambridge Companion to Kant*, Cambridge University Press 1992, pp. 26–61.

4 Beiser, 'Kant's Intellectual Development', p. 30.

5 The remark is to be found in the Preface to Kant's *Prologemena to Any Future Metaphysics That Shall Come Forth as Scientific* (1783). Bieser, 'Kant's Intellectual Development', pp. 54–55, argues that the importance of Hume struck Kant fully in about 1772, although he had been aware of Hume's scepticism since 1759.

6 Gay, *The Enlightenment: An Interpretation*, Vol. 1, p. 329.

7 See Hume, *A Treatise Concerning Human Nature*, Book I, Part III, Sections I and II.

8 Hume's scepticism should not be understood as total Pyrrhonism, completely inimical to reason. He was also sceptical about scepticism, for like Kant after him he was concerned to define the power of reason as well as its limits. See Norman Kemp Smith, *The Philosophy of David Hume: A Critical Study of its Origins and Central Doctrines*, Macmillan and St Martin's Press 1966, pp. 446–449.

9 That is, judgments, and also propositions, in which the predicate adds something to the subject, as opposed to simple analytic, tautologous, judg-

ments (e.g. 'All men are men').

10 An analysis of Kant's argument is not our concern here; however, it is easily demonstrated that synthetic *a priori* judgments are possible in mathematics: the answer to the multiplication of 23, 445 by 6,784 is not immediately present to consciousness without calculation, and is hence a synthetic proposition (i.e. the predicate *adds* to the subject). But mathematics holds necessarily and universally independently of our calculations; therefore synthetic *a priori* judgments are possible.

11 Immanuel Kant, *Critique of Pure Reason*, second edition, translated Norman Kemp Smith, Macmillan and St Martin's Press 1933, pp. 499–500.

12 Kant, *Critique of Pure Reason*, p. 504.

13 Kant's critique of the ontological argument is often considered to be decisive, but the argument continues to have its defenders. See, for example, Norman Malcolm's critique of Kant in John Hick (ed.), *The Existence of God*, Macmillan 1964, pp. 47–70.

14 See Kant, *Critique of Pure Reason*, pp. 507–514.

15 See Allen W. Wood, 'Rational theology, moral faith, and religion' in Guyer (ed.), *The Cambridge Companion to Kant*, pp. 394–416.

16 Kant, *Critique of Pure Reason*, p. 29.

17 Kant, *Critique of Pure Reason*, p. 646.

18 S. Körner, *Kant*, Penguin Books 1955, p. 153.

19 Immanuel Kant, *Critique of Practical Reason*, translated with an introduction by Lewis White Beck, The Liberal Arts Press 1956, p. 118.

20 Kant, *Critique of Practical Reason*, p. 126.

21 Kant, *Critique of Practical Reason*, p. 134. In his *Religion Within the Limits of Reason Alone* (translated with introduction and notes by Theodore M. Greene and Hoyt H. Hudson, Harper Torchbooks 1960), Kant qualifies this to emphasize that the moral law is not given objectively as a divine command: 'Religion is (subjectively regarded) the recognition of all duties as divine commands', p. 142.

22 Kant, *Religion*, p. 89.

23 Kant, *Religion*, p. 91.

24 Kant, *Religion*, p. 92.

25 See Kant, *Religion*, p. 93.

26 See Kant, *Lectures on Philosophical Theology*, translated by Allen W. Wood and Gertrude M. Clark, Cornell University Press 1978, p. 62.

27 Kant, *Religion*, p. 167.

28 Hamann, quoted in Isaiah Berlin, *The Age of Enlightenment*, Penguin Books 1956, p. 270. Berlin emphasizes Hamann's role as the precursor of some modern philosophies of language.

Select Bibliography

Anthologies and Primary Sources

Alexander, H. G. (ed.), *The Leibniz-Clarke Correspondence*, Manchester University Press 1956.

Ayer, A. J. and O'Grady, Jane (eds), *A Dictionary of Philosophical Quotations*, Blackwell 1992.

Berlin, Isaiah, *The Age of Enlightenment*, Penguin Books 1956.

Burke, Edmund, *Reflections on the Revolution in France*, Conor Cruise O'Brien (ed.), Penguin Books 1968.

Butler, Bishop Joseph, *The Analogy of Religion, Natural and Revealed* (1736).

Cottingham, J. G., Stoothoff, R. and Murdoch, D. (eds), *The Philosophical Writings of Descartes* (Vols 1 and 2), Cambridge University Press 1985.

Cowie, Leonard (ed.), *Eighteenth-Century Europe, Documents and Debates*, Macmillan 1989.

Diderot, Denis, *Rameau's Nephew/d'Alembert's Dream*, translated with introductions by Leonard Tancock, Penguin Books 1966.

Eliot, Simon, and Stern, Beverley (eds), *The Age of Enlightenment: An Anthology of Eighteenth-Century Texts*, 2 Vols, Open University Press 1979.

Gay, Peter, *Deism: An Anthology*, Princeton University Press 1968.

Hume, David, *An Inquiry Concerning Human Understanding* (1748).

Hume, David, *Dialogues Concerning Natural Religion* (1779), Martin Bell (ed.), Penguin Books 1990.

Kant, Immanual, *Religion Within the Limits of Reason Alone*, translated with introduction and notes by Theodore M. Greene and Hoyt H. Hudson, Harper Torchbooks 1960.

Kant, Immanuel, *Critique of Practical Reason*, translated with an introduction by Lewis White Beck, The Liberal Arts Press 1956.

Kant, Immanuel, *Critique of Pure Reason*, second edition, translated by Norman Kemp Smith, Macmillan and St Martin's Press 1933.

Kant, Immanuel, *Lectures on Philosophical Theology*, translated by Allen W. Wood and Gertrude M. Clark, Cornell University Press 1978.

Kemp, Jonathan (ed.), *Diderot: Interpreter of Nature, Selected Writings*,

Lawrence and Wishart 1936.

Lewis, W. S. (ed.), *The Yale Edition of Horace Walpole's Correspondence*, Yale University Press and Oxford University Press 1961.

Locke, John, *An Essay Concerning Human Understanding* (1690).

Mason, John Hope, *The Indispensable Rousseau*, Quartet Books 1979.

Paine, Thomas, *The Age of Reason* (1979), in *The Thomas Paine Reader*, Michael Foot and Isaac Kramnick (eds), Penguin Books 1987.

Pascal, Blaise, *Pensées*, translated A. J. Krailsheimer, Penguin Books 1966.

Popkin, Richard H. (ed.), *Pascal: Selections*, Macmillan 1989.

Redman, Ben Ray (ed.), *The Portable Voltaire*, Penguin Books 1977.

Rousseau, Jean-Jacques, *The Confessions*, translated with and introduction by J. M. Cohen, Penguin Books 1953.

Rousseau, Jean-Jacques, *Emile* or *On Education*, translated with introduction and notes by Allan Bloom, Penguin Books 1979.

Sherry, Patrick (ed.), *Philosophers on Religion: An Historical Reader*, Geoffrey Chapman 1987.

Smart, Ninian, *Historical Selections in the Philosophy of Religion*, SCM Press 1962.

Sullivan, Robert E., *John Toland and The Deist Controversy: A Study in Adaptations*, Harvard University Press 1982.

Voltaire, *Letters Concerning the English Nation*, Nicholas Cronk (ed.), Oxford University Press 1994.

Other Works

Adorno, Theodor and Horkheimer, Max, *Dialectic of Enlightenment*, translated J. Cumming, Verso 1986.

Anderson, M. S., *Europe in the Eighteenth Century*, Longman 1976.

Barbour, Ian G., *Religion in an Age of Science*, SCM Press 1990.

Becker, Karl, *The Heavenly City of the Eighteenth-Century Philosophers*, Yale University Press 1932.

Berlin, Isaiah, *Against the Current: Essays in the History of Ideas*, Henry Hardy (ed.) with introduction by Roger Hausheer, Clarendon Press 1991.

Black, Jeremy, *The British Abroad: The Grand Tour in the Eighteenth Century*, St Martin's Press 1992.

Boyer, Carl B., *A History of Mathematics* (second edition, revised by Uta C. Merzbach), John Wiley and Sons 1991.

Brooke, John Hedley, *Science and Religion: Some Historical Perspectives*, Cambridge University Press 1991.

Buckley, Michael, *At the Origins of Modern Atheism*, Yale University Press 1987.

Cassirer, Ernst, *The Philosophy of the Enlightenment*, Princeton University Press 1951.

Chappell, Vere (ed.), *The Cambridge Companion to Locke*, Cambridge University Press 1994.

Chitnis, Anand, *The Scottish Enlightenment: A Social History*, Croom Helm 1976.

Crocker, Lester G., *An Age of Crisis: Man and World in Eighteenth-Century France*, John Hopkins University Press 1959.

Doyle, William, *The Old European Order, 1660–1800*, Oxford University Press 1978.

Eagleton, Terry, *The Ideology of the Aesthetic*, Blackwell 1990.

Edwards, Paul (ed.), *The Encyclopedia of Philosophy*, 4 Vols, Macmillan and The Free Press/Collier-Macmillan 1967.

Fauvel, John et al. (eds), *Let Newton Be!: A New Perspective on His Life and Works*, Open University Press 1988.

Frei, Hans, *The Eclipse of Biblical Narrative: A Study in Eighteenth and Nineteenth Century Hermeneutics*, Yale University Press 1974.

Gay, Peter, *The Enlightenment: An Interpretation*, Vol. 1, *The Rise of Modern Paganism*, Weidenfeld and Nicolson 1966.

Gilley, Sheridan and Shiels, W. J. (eds), *A History of Religion in Britain: Practice and Belief from Pre-Roman Times to the Present*, Blackwell 1994.

Guyer, Paul (ed.), *The Cambridge Companion to Kant*, Cambridge University Press 1992.

Hampshire, Stuart, *Spinoza*, Penguin Books 1951.

Hampson, Norman, *The Enlightenment: An Evaluation of Its Assumptions, Attitudes and Values*, Pelican Books 1968.

Hankins, Thomas L., *Science and the Enlightenment, Cambridge History of Science Series*, G. Basalla and W. Coleman (eds), Cambridge University Press 1985.

Hazard, Paul, *European Thought in the Eighteenth Century: From Montesquieu to Lessing*, Meridian 1963.

Hazard, Paul, *The European Mind, 1680–1715*, Meridian 1963.

Hufton, Olwen, *Europe, 1730–1789: Privilege and Protest*, Harvester Press 1980.

Hunt, Margaret; Jacob, Margaret; Mack, Phyllis and Perry, Ruth (eds), *Women and the Enlightenment*, The Haworth Press 1984.

Jeanrond, Werner G., *Theological Hermeneutics: Development and Significance*, SCM Press and Crossroad 1994.

Kemp Smith, Norman, *The Philosophy of David Hume: A Critical Study of its Origins and Central Doctrines*, Macmillan and St Martin's Press 1966.

Koestler, Arthur, *The Sleepwalkers: A History of Man's Changing Vision of the*

Universe, Penguin Books 1959.

Koyré, Alexander, *From the Closed World to the Infinite Universe*, John Hopkins University Press 1968.

Küng, Hans, *Does God Exist?*, SCM Press and Doubleday 1984.

Labrousse, Elizabeth, *Bayle*, translated by Denys Potts, Oxford University Press 1983.

Lloyd, Genevieve, *The Man of Reason: 'Male' and 'Female' in Western Philosophy*, Methuen 1984.

May, Henry F., *The Enlightenment in America*, Oxford University Press 1976.

McManners, John, *Death and the Enlightenment: Changing Attitudes to Death among Christians and Unbelievers in Eighteenth-Century France*, Clarendon Press and Oxford University Press 1981.

Oppenheim, Walter, *Europe and the Enlightened Despots*, Hodder and Stoughton 1990.

Outram, Dorinda, *The Enlightenment*, Cambridge University Press 1995.

Padover, S. K., *The Revolutionary Emperor*, Jonathan Cape 1934.

Palmer, R. R., *Catholics and Unbelievers in Eighteenth-Century France*, Princeton University Press 1939.

Porter, Roy, and Teich, Mikulas (eds), *The Enlightenment in National Context*, Cambridge University Press 1981.

Porter, Roy, *English Society in the Eighteenth Century*, Penguin Books 1990.

Porter, Roy, *The Enlightenment*, Macmillan 1990.

Scott, H. M. (ed.), *Enlightened Absolutism: Reform and Reformers in Later Eighteenth-Century Europe*, Macmillan 1990.

Shennan, J. H., *Liberty and Order in Early Modern Europe: The Subject and the State, 1650–1800*, Longman 1986.

Spinoza, *Ethics* (1677), J. M. Dent (Everyman Edition), 1910.

Thomas, Keith, *Religion and the Decline of Magic*, Weidenfeld and Nicolson 1971.

Trevor-Roper, H. R., *The European Witch-Craze of the Sixteenth and Seventeenth Centuries*, Penguin Books 1969.

Wade, Ira O., *The Intellectual Origins of the French Enlightenment*, Princeton University Press 1971.

Willey, Basil, *The Eighteenth-Century Background*, Ark Paperbacks 1986.

Wilson, Arthur M., *Diderot*, Oxford University Press 1972.

Wollstonecraft, Mary, *A Vindication of the Rights of Women* (1792), in *Political Writings*, edited with an introduction by Janet Todd, Oxford University Press 1994.

Woloch, Isser, *Eighteenth-Century Europe: Tradition and Progress, 1715–1789*, W. W. Norton 1982.

Wood, Allen W., *Kant's Moral Religion*, Cornell University Press 1970.

Yolton, John W., et al. (eds), *The Blackwell Companion to the Enlightenment*, Blackwell 1991.

Yolton, John W., *Thinking Matter: Materialism in Eighteenth-Century Britain*, Blackwell 1984.

Index